Rugby L Bravehe

The History of Scottish Rugby League

By Gavin Willacy

The Scottish Development XIII that played against the North East at
Meadowbank in 1994 (Photo courtesy: Scottish RL)

LONDON LEAGUE PUBLICATIONS Ltd.

Rugby League Bravehearts
The History of Scottish Rugby League

Cover photos: Front: Alan Tait (photo: David Williams), Dave Valentine (photo: Courtesy Robert Gate). Back: 1995 Scotland team versus Ireland at Dublin (photo: David Williams), Graeme Thompson (photo: Courtesy Graeme Thompson), Glasgow Schools at Old Trafford 1997 (photo: Courtesy Graeme Thompson).

The views expressed in this book are those of the individuals concerned, and are not necessarily those of the Scottish Rugby League or London League Publications Ltd.

First published in Great Britain in June 2002 by:
London League Publications Ltd. P.O. Box 10441, London E14 0SB

ISBN: 1-903659-05-1

Cover design by:	Stephen McCarthy Graphic Design 46, Clarence Road London N15 5BB
Layout:	Peter Lush
Printed and bound by:	Catford Print Centre, PO Box 563, Catford, London SE6 4PY

For Dave Valentine and his legacy

Foreword: Alan Tait

I never thought I would see the day when I played for Scotland at Rugby League, let alone captain the side. But it was a great honour for me to lead the team out in the Emerging Nations World Cup in 1995, and a tribute to those who helped establish the game in Scotland over many years.

John Risman rang me and asked if I wanted to play in that World Cup. I'd already turned down England and retired from international Rugby League. But to make my comeback for my country was too good an opportunity to miss. Mind you, when I saw the sort of players we had arriving from all corners of Britain - a dentist, someone from the RAF, a load of students - I was panicking! I thought we'd bitten off more than we could chew. But they showed us respect and earned it back. They put their bodies on the line for their country. You could not fault them.

We had three bloody hard games in a week and, as one of the three permitted professionals, I was expected to play in all three! We beat the US and Russia - both of whom didn't take a backward step – and then gave the Cook Islands a real run for their money. It was a tough week, but I really enjoyed it. We were all there for the love of the game and it was superb. I got quite emotional before kick-off, with our piper playing the anthem.

By the end, we had such a good squad we were all playing for the jersey - the lads who were left out were desperate to play. But we all had a good *craic* afterwards! It didn't matter where the lads were from: I speak with an English accent, unfortunately, but accents mean nothing as long as you are passionate enough and give it everything.

My Dad (former Workington player Alan Sr.) would certainly have loved to have pulled on the Scotland jersey. They had enough Scots down there in the sixties and early seventies to have had a team but he never got that chance.

In 1996, we played on home territory for the first time, and beat Ireland at Firhill. That was my first game of rugby in Scotland since I'd left Kelso for Widnes eight years earlier. Next time I played in Scotland it was Rugby Union: I was talking to Scottish Union clubs straight after that game, before Rob Andrew snapped me up for Newcastle.

I was a bit disappointed in the 2000 World Cup, when a lot of Australians appeared from nowhere to play for Scotland. Rugby League scouts always used to be looking in the Borders for players - I remember them coming round our house - but they seem to concentrate on their own back yards now, where they have a superb record in bringing young players through the academy system.

However, I'm glad Scotland Rugby League are giving youngsters a chance now because that is the future. There are a lot of gifted young Scottish rugby players and the more chances they have to represent our country, the better.

Edinburgh, April 2002

Acknowledgements and thanks

I would like to thank John Risman, Graeme Thompson, Kevin Rudd, Mark Dingwall, Mark Senter, Clive Mason, Kate Cochrane, Mal Reid and all the Scotland players, SRL and club officials and supporters whose time has helped me give Scottish Rugby League a historical record.

Many thanks also to Peter Lush, Dave Farrar, Michael O'Hare and Tony Collins for their help in producing the book; to David Williams, Robert Gate, Mike Haddon, Graeme Thompson, Ian Wilson, the Oldham Rugby League Heritage Trust and Michael Turner for providing photos; the Rugby Football League and Super League for permission to reproduce publicity leaflets.

Thanks to Geoffrey (Tailor) Highland Crafts Ltd, Kiltmakers of 57/59 High Street, Royal Mile, Edinburgh EH1 1SR for permission to use the SRL tartan. They can be contacted on 0131-557-0256.

Most of all I would like to thank my wife, Jo, for her endless patience and support.

Gavin Willacy

About the author

Gavin Willacy was born and bred in St Albans to Lancastrian parents who'd spent their early married years in Pontefract and encouraged their son to take an interest in Rugby League despite the lack of local action. During three years at Salford University he could occasionally be seen at The Willows, but more often waiting for Swinton Lions to clear off the all-weather pitch so he could start football training! Watching the 1990 Kangaroos pull up outside his window for a workout on the university fields was an added bonus though. A Preston North End FC devotee, it was not until lodging with a mate who had Sky TV that his love of League was re-ignited. He is now a regular at London Broncos and has become Press Officer for St Albans Centurions.

A freelance sportswriter, despite the Scottish name, he has no Scottish affinity, but is fascinated by international Rugby League.

Preface

As a working class lad from Barrow who went to grammar school and played Rugby Union until I went to college in Cardiff, I knew how it felt to take up the Rugby League from scratch. I wanted to emulate my childhood hero, Willie Horne, and although I turned professional with Barrow, I was never going to make it and when I got a bad arm injury, I concentrated on my true vocation: teaching PE.

I ended up doing a PhD and lecturing at Aberdeen University in the mid-sixties. I ran their Rugby Union team and became coach of Scotland Students Union side around 1973. By 1987, I felt Rugby Union was going stale and it was good timing when David Oxley at the RFL and Martyn Sadler asked me about getting a Scotland Rugby League team together for the Student World Cup. Oxley knew what I was doing up here because he'd seen a big piece *The Guardian* had done on me, all about the ridiculous conflict between League and Union.

I had enemies in the Union camp, but the students were always on my side, so it was no surprise to me that most of my first XV at Aberdeen took up League. I preached team unity, cohesion and hard work and the lads responded. The first year we just had two or three Sunday sessions, teaching them the basics, like the play the ball: an introduction to the sport. Soon we were going on pre-season trips to France, having training camps and playing amateur clubs in Cumbria.

The progress the lads made was amazing. They'd return to their Union clubs and be bursting through tackles, creaming people and confident with the ball in hand. The clubs would ask: 'What the bloody hell's happened to you?'! All of this was done on the back of a six or eight week season squeezed between Easter and their final exams. Their Union team-mates saw what League could do for your game and wanted to play, too.

When I joined the RFL my remit included recruiting for, and coaching, Scotland Students. When I started, the Volvo I got had 46,000 miles on the clock. Eighteen months later it had 156,000 – amazing. It was very interesting, though. I'd go to Union clubs and talk about this strange sport of Rugby League that they'd probably seen on television.

I knew the players' social backgrounds and was aware that there was nowhere for them to play once they'd left university. They weren't going to go and play amateur League in some horrible, windswept public park when they could play Union, change in a pleasant clubhouse and play golf with the chaps on a Sunday. So I was trying to get them to understand that League was good for them, that they would benefit from it. I wanted to change that cloth cap image: these were the future world leaders, the teachers, the doctors, the solicitors. If I could get them to realise what a bloody good game League is, when the name Rugby League came up they'd say, "That's okay, that is" and want to get involved, as sponsors, administrators or whatever.

I was trying to put rugby into perspective, to use my academic background and contacts to make playing Rugby League a pleasurable experience. That much of what is happening in Scotland now is the same as back then - summer rugby, foreign tours, training camps, team bonding – suggests that I succeeded. I certainly enjoyed it.

Dr Malcolm Reid - Founder of Scottish Rugby League. Alicante, May 2002

Patrons:
We would like to thank the following for their support:
Andy Borthwick Newcastle RLFC
Neil Hendry Ellon RFC. 2002: BT Cellnet Bowl Winners; National League Division 4 Winners
Glen Howitt glh@Vitol.com
Ian Johnston Youth Sport Development Officer Worthing Borough Council
Kevin Rudd Scottish Students Coach Rudd_Kevin@hotmail.com
Ken Edwards www.stalbanscenturions.com
Graeme Thompson RFL Player Development Officer
Ross van der Hoek ex-Scottish Student & Canadian internationalist. Always Believe and Achieve Your Dreams!!!
Caro Wild RFL Regional Development Manager London & South East

Scottish Rugby League: www.scotlandrugbyleague.org.uk
Email: info@scotlandrugbyleague.org.uk

RFL Scotland Development Officer: Mark Senter
Community Recreation, Glasgow City Council, 20, Trongate, Glasgow G1 5ES
Tel: 0141-287-3906. Mobile: 07764-627252. Email: mark.senter@cls.glasgow.gov.uk

Contents

Gavin Willacy interviewing Scottish Students coach Kevin Rudd at
England students versus Queensland Students, December 2001
(Photo: Peter Lush)

Interested in Rugby League?

London League Publications are a specialist sports and hobbies
publisher. To order our free book-list, write to us at the address below.
Our Rugby League magazine, *Our Game*, is of interest to anyone who
follows the game, or is interested in sports history. To order a copy of
the latest issue, send a cheque for £2.00 to the address below.
(Cheques to London League Publications Ltd, no credit card orders).

London League Publications Ltd, PO Box 10441, London E14 0SB.

1. Scotland join 'The Greatest Game'

Scotland Rugby League's motto 'No conceit in victory, no despair in defeat' could well have been coined for Rugby League in general or, in particular, the sport's attempts to spread the greatest game to the world.

For every minor success story in that mission, there are a handful of failures, a series of mini burst bubbles as League's attempts at expansion flourish in the hands of dedicated volunteers only to wither once their energy levels are exhausted and the hurdles placed before them become too large.

It must seem ludicrous to outsiders that despite being just a couple of hours' drive away from the heartlands, Rugby League is seen as a foreign sport in Scotland, one that is trying to get a foothold in the nation's sporting psyche.

However, attempts to establish Rugby League in Scotland are, by the game's somewhat idiosyncratic standards, going well. Over a decade after former Barrow player Dr Mal Reid first introduced Rugby League to his Union players at Aberdeen University, a very steady increase in playing numbers and teams has seen Scotland's League-playing base widen and its' foundations solidify.

The emphasis has moved more than once - initially only played by students, Scotland then had a few doses of full-time professional League with the Super League roadshows and a star-studded national team, before financial cutbacks underlined the need for the amateur game to grow and become the SRL's priority in the 21st century.

When Scotland launched its own Rugby League Conference in the summer of 1997, just six clubs existed, each with just one often-cobbled-together team. At the same time, the Scottish Rugby Union had nearly 200 clubs, in ten divisions, each with several teams, thus making the game available to players of all standards. Union is the country's second team sport to football, a nation-wide pastime enjoyed by thousands, albeit - outside of the Borders region - concentrated almost entirely around the middle and upper classes.

And yet like much of southern England, there is an enormous potential audience and player pool for League in Scotland, a legion of sportsmen who would be interested in rugby if it weren't for the snob element, the rah-rah brigade which epitomises 'kick-and-clap'.

Although League's best chances of becoming established in Scotland were either side of the world wars when a stream of Scots came south to turn professional, there are still opportunities for a fast, tough, highly-skilled and non-sectarian alternative to Rugby Union and football.

Unfortunately, Rugby League faces a real battle to gain acknowledgement in the Scottish media, let alone appropriate coverage. When Scotland coach Shaun McRae said after the World Cup, "to take the game back to the M62 corridor, it will eventually become extinct, there will be a gradual process of dying out", BBC Scotland's website headline was 'Rugby League faces slow death' (my quote marks, not their's).

And on the morning of the first Ashes test in November 2001, a game in which a (albeit not actually Scottish) Scotland international, Richard Horne, was the shock selection for Great Britain against the world champions, the only mention of Rugby League in the *Scottish Mail on Sunday* was a line about Halifax's financial problems.

To them, the big match did not exist, ignoring the news value of Horne's selection. Instead, they ran four pages on Scotland's triumph over Tonga in a Union friendly. It was not a surprise that beneath the half-page picture of Jim McLaren scoring a try there was no mention of his Rugby League upbringing in Australia nor his Scotland Rugby League honours.

The day after Great Britain's amazing triumph over the Australians, the *Daily Record* had a small wire report hidden away in the middle of the paper, with no mention of Horne's role in the victory.

The pro-Union bias in the British media is unquestionable, particularly from the BBC and broadsheet papers, staffed by former public schoolboys who grew up playing Union. It is as bad in Scotland as it is in England. But is it justified?

The week after the thrill of beating Tonga, the SRU's 'Kilted Kiwis' made it 24 games against the All Blacks without a win, leaving them eighth in the world rankings, behind Australia, New Zealand, South Africa, England, France, Ireland and Wales. Take out the Springboks and you have the Rugby League world rankings. Scotland RU have won just 43% of their 500 test matches and yet no-one dismissed them as make-weights, not to be taken seriously. The corporate money keeps flooding in and Murrayfield is usually packed for internationals.

The general feeling in League circles is that it can have no impact in Scotland, that Union is too big there. 'They have one rugby, why want another?' And that is probably at least partially correct. In the foreseeable future, Scotland will never have a Rugby League team that will pack Murrayfield. They will never have a league of full-time professional clubs. Every village in Scotland will not have a Rugby League team.

What is a more realistic aim for Rugby League in Scotland is to continue growing at grass roots level, for more schools to play and thus provide more players for an increasing number of amateur clubs, who should have closer links with universities. Rugby League can make summer rugby to available to Union players and increase it's core of League-dedicated players. And by taking showcase professional games to Scotland, like the Challenge Cup Final, the Scots can see at first hand what all the fuss is about.

Mal Reid sprinkled the seed among the students for that dream to grow in the 1980s, John Risman, as coach to the student side watered it and George Fairbairn, as national team manager, made sure it did not go to waste. These are just three of the men responsible for the 'Sassenach' sport of Rugby League existing in Scotland and giving the nation of Dave Valentine, Roy M. Kinnear and John Wilson among many others, something of which they could justifiably be proud.

Spreading the word: Scotland versus Ireland 1998 at Kilmarnock - Scotland's first home amateur international (Photo: Courtesy Scottish RL)

Part 1: Early days

Lomond Valley Raiders - 1997 Scottish Champions
(Photo: Courtesy Scottish RL)

2. Early international matches in Scotland

England 17 Australia 17
3 February 1909. Celtic Park, Glasgow. Attendance: 3,000

A year after they originally planned to take the game to Scotland, the Northern Union pulled off a bit of a coup. The Rugby Football Union were in dispute with the Scottish Rugby Union (SRU) because the English had allowed the inaugural All Blacks to be paid a three shillings 'daily allowance' on their visit to these shores. The SRU believed that this broke rugby union's strict laws on amateurism. Consequently, the Calcutta Cup game planned for January 1909 had been cancelled.

The NU moved in to fill the gap, although staging a one-off event in new territory had little impact, as we discovered over the next century. Only 3,000 turned up to see the Australians on a February Wednesday afternoon at one of Scotland's major football grounds. Awful weather did not help but this was a disappointing crowd given that it was half-day for many and the receipts of £116 suggests entry was cheap.

The game itself was remarkable for two things: the Kangaroos' comeback, scoring three tries in the last 10 minutes to snatch a draw, and the role played by Dally Messenger, who went on to become a legend down under, the 'Dally M Award' for the season's best player being named after him. He kicked the last conversion to level the scores.

It would have been an exciting finish in any code, and the game had a favourable review from one Scottish newspaper which said: "It appears to us rather as attenuated Rugby football with the more cumbersome features eliminated." Most of us would agree with that a century on. The report continued: "Consequently it is similar yet dissimilar to the older game. Where the resemblance to soccer comes in we fail to see."

The writer continued: "The Northern Game is however replete with nerves and exciting movements, many of which were executed with considerable skill and finesse. Heeling out is elevated to a fine science and this more than anything accounts for the sparkle which every now and then fires the imagination."

Despite the thrill-a-minute entertainment and superior skill level on show, the same impressed writer concluded: "The prospects of Scotland being converted to the Northern Union game are about as remote as the conversion of the Jews to Christianity." His comments reflected the strength of Union in the middle class, and the domination of football among the working class.

This classic did not, however, count as a test match because it was England, rather than the Northern Union test side, against the tourists' midweek side. Only five of the England team - Lomas, Jukes, Mann, Longworth and Smith - were in the Northern Union (i.e. Great Britain) side which won the third test 12 days later at Villa Park, 6-5.

Ten of the Australian test side at Villa played in Glasgow and, amazingly, all but Walsh and O'Malley played the day after the Celtic Park clash, when the tourists stopped off at Carlisle on the way back south to play Cumberland at Devonshire Park. It was no wonder the county side turned over the exhausted tourists, 11-2.

Ten of the England side on display in Glasgow reconvened to beat the over-worked Australians 14-7 in a hastily arranged 'representative match' at Goodison Park, Liverpool on Wednesday 3 March. It was staged to raise funds for the tourists at the end of the lengthy tour, but snow ruined the game and kept the crowd down to 4,500. Another game was probably not well received by the Kangaroos' players at that stage of their tour.

England: Gifford; Miller, Lomas, Dickenson, Batten; Jolley, Lally; Jukes, Higson, Mann, Smith, Longworth, Robinson.
Australia: Bolewski; Morton, Messenger, Heidke, Devereux; Anlezark, Holloway; Walsh, Burdon, O'Malley, Graves, Pearce, Courtney.
Scorers:
England: Tries: Miller (2), Longworth tries; Goals: Lomas (4).
Australia: Tries: Morton, Walsh, Pearce; Goals: Messenger (4).
Referee: E. H. Smirk

Northern Union 11 Australia 11
16 December 1911. Tynecastle, Edinburgh. Attendance: 6,000

The first and only official test in Scotland is notable for Harold Wagstaff, the 'Prince of Centres', scoring his only two tries for Great Britain in an 11-11 draw. He was playing against an Australian side which actually included one New Zealander, forward A. R. H. Francis.

8

On a cold December day, the turnout of around 6,000, in the days when travelling from the north of England to the Scottish capital was a day's journey and to be avoided when possible, would now be considered impressive. Unfortunately, in those days with few counter-attractions and massive sporting attendances, it was thought disappointing.

The Northern Union's aim was "to place their special game in challenge with that favoured by the Scottish schools and aristocracy of the capital". The *Yorkshire Post* claimed that "there is no antipathy to the Northern Union as such in Scotland". However, 90 years later, although the RFL have not yet managed to establish the game in Scotland, not for the want of trying by a lot of dedicated people.

One of the problems with taking a 'foreign game' to the Scottish people was that they could not keep track of the score. With no scoreboard at Tynecastle, it was reported that: "the mode of scoring... seemed to puzzle many, and at the close there was some doubt, as one could hear, whether the match was lost or drawn".

A similar problem arose in 1998, when Tony Smith scored a drop goal for the Lions against New Zealand at Watford in the last second of the game. The scoreboard credited him with two points and thus a 24-23 win for Great Britain. Those in the know had to inform locals new to the game that the match had actually been drawn.

The Northern Union side had taken the lead after only three minutes when Harold Wagstaff, who made his Huddersfield debut at 15 and first played for England against the Australians at 17, took advantage when Billy Farnsworth dropped a kick, but Alf Wood's conversion failed and two minutes later Farnsworth made amends when he dribbled down the left, feeding speed merchant Dan Frawley for the equalising try.

The NU pack was soon on top and forced an error which Batten intercepted, passing to Huddersfield's Davies who created a try for skipper Lomas. The Kangaroos were rocking and when full-back Hallett misjudged a kick to touch, Wagstaff nipped in to stroll under the posts - Wood converted.

With the Northern Union in control, the game turned after 50 minutes when they were reduced to 12 men, Wood going off injured. The Kangaroos took advantage in the forwards, Craig dribbling through and skipper McKivat picking up to score. When Francis converted, the gap was just three points.

Russell went on the overlap to score the equalising try with 10 minutes left, but not only did the NU hang on for a draw, they almost won it - and kept the series alive - when Batten almost crept over and then Jenkinson missed the opportunity to put Wagstaff in for his hat-trick.

Having lost the series two years earlier partly due to injuries, the Australians had clinched this one thanks to the same ill fortune falling on the home side.

This was the last test to be played in Scotland for 90 years... and counting.

Northern Union: Wood, Jenkinson, Wagstaff, Lomas (c), Batten, Davies, Smith, Ramsdale, Winstanley, Gronow, Clark, Woods, Harrison.
Australia: Hallett; Russell, Farnsworth, Gilbert, Frawley, Farnsworth, McKivat (c), Francis, McCue, Cann, Courtney, Noble, Craig.
Scorers:
NU: Tries: Wagstaff (2), Lomas; Goal: Wood.
Australia: Tries: Russell, Frawley, McKivat; Goal: Francis.
Referee: F. Renton

3. Representative matches: Scots, Great Britain and 'Other Nationalities'

While there was no actual senior Scotland team in existence until 1995, Scottish Rugby League players were regular members of Other Nationalities, and some also played for Great Britain.

Roy Kinnear was the first Scot to play for Great Britain, winning a solitary cap against Australia in 1929. William Welsh toured France in 1937 on behalf of a Rugby League XIII, and Bob Robson played for English Rugby League team against France in 1945-6, although these matches were not classed as full test matches.

Dave Valentine made his Great Britain debut in 1948, and won 15 caps, including captaining the World Cup winning team in 1954. David Rose played in that tournament, but was never capped again. In 1951, Leeds's Drew Turnbull won his solitary cap for Great Britain against New Zealand.

In the 1960s, Charlie Renilson made seven Great Britain appearances, plus one as a substitute, and Robert Valentine, Dave's younger brother, played against Australia in 1967. In more recent times, George Fairbairn won 17 Great Britain caps in the 1970s and 1980s, and a further 15 for England. Alan Tait played 10 times for Great Britain, with a further four substitute appearances between 1989 and 1993. Hugh Waddell, who played for Scotland in Dublin in 1995, had played five times for Great Britain and once for England.

However, the 'Other Nationalities' all-star team of 'foreigners' based in English Rugby League offered more opportunities for Scots to play international Rugby League. It first played against England before the Antipodean sides toured the northern hemisphere, and continued to do so in the 1920s, providing additional international opposition.

In 1935, following the development of the game in France, a European Championship was born. In 1949, Other Nationalities - how typical of Rugby League to undersell what should have been known as 'The World All Stars' or some such marketable name - were invited to join and competed against England, Wales and France until the championship was suspended in 1956. It was reborn in 1969, but the Other Nationalities team were not invited to compete.

Ironically, in the same way as Scotland were criticised in 2000, Other Nationalities (ON) were dismissed by some journalists and supporters (most notably in Wales) as 'cosmetic' and not a genuine international side. While this was true, they were certainly a superb rugby team packed with fantastic players. When they gelled, they could beat the best the other European countries had to offer.

There were rarely enough first generation Scots playing professional Rugby League to form their own team, but with some recruits from north of the border, coupled with second and third generation Scots, a stand-alone Scotland team could have competed in the European Championship after the Second World War.

Instead, illustrious Scottish professionals like Roy Kinnear, Dave Valentine and George Wilson won caps alongside Irishmen, resident Australians and Kiwis, South Africans and anyone else who did not fit the tiny clutch of national teams available.

Their record was impressive, especially as they were granted just three 'home' matches - versus France at Hull in 1951, versus Wales at Warrington in 1953 and the final match, versus France at Leigh in 1955 - when the opposition did not have the crowd behind them. In retrospect, it is a shame and perhaps surprising that no Other Nationalities games were taken to Scotland, especially when Dave Valentine and company were in the side.

In 1974, in an attempt to revive the County Championship, an Other Nationalities team competed for a couple of seasons. There was not much interest, with most attendances being below 2,000.

Challenge matches versus England

5 April 1904 at Central Park, Wigan.
Won 9-3. Attendance: 6,000
A poor game played 12-a-side, although England started with 11 due to a late arrival. Jim Moffatt and George Frater were Scotland's representatives.

ON: Smith, Llewellyn, Harris, Lewis, D. Thomas (Salford), Davies, Brady, Rhapps, Moffatt, Frater, D. Thomas (Oldham), Buckler.
Scorers: Tries: Harris, D. Thomas (Salford), D. Thomas (Oldham).

2 January 1905 at Bradford Park Avenue.
Lost 11-26. Attendance: 6,000
Despite leading 11-0 at half-time, a side with 12 Welshmen, 2 Scots - Laidlaw and Scott - and one Irishman conceded six second-half tries, four to Wigan winger James Leytham.
ON: Gunn. Freear, P. Thomas, Llewellyn, Dechan, Hopkins, S. James, Laidlaw, Osborne, D. Thomas, D. Rees (Bradford), D. Rees (Salford), G. Thomas, Scott, Buckler.
Scorers: Tries: P. Thomas, Llewellyn, Dechan; Goal: Gunn

1 January 1906 at Central Park, Wigan.
Drew 3-3. Attendance: 8,000
Andrew Hogg and Anthony Little were Scotland's representative in this new year's day draw.
ON: Gunn, Jowett, Jones, Llewellyn, Hogg, S. James, W. James, D. Rees (Salford), Watkins, Shugars, Francis, Little, Thomas, Davies, Osborne.
Scorer: Try: W. James

15 October 1924 at Headingley, Leeds.
Won 23-17. Attendance: 3,000
Five tries to each side, with Sullivan's goals giving ON a narrow victory. Halifax's Scottish forward Jock Beattie scored one of ON's tries.
ON: Sullivan, van Heerden, Parker, Jones, Evans, Gerram, Hurcombe, van Royeen, Gronow, Brown, Thompson, Beattie, Baker.
Scorers: Van Heerden 2, Jones, Thompson, Beattie; Goals: Sullivan 4.

Other Nationalities vs England 7 April 1930. The Scots are Roy Kinnear (right, back row and Jimmy Gill (right, front row). (Photo courtesy Robert Gate)

13

4 February 1926 at Recreation Ground, Whitehaven.
Lost 11-37. Attendance: 7,000

Having trailed 16-0, ON, featuring Scots Andrew Murdison and George Swan, got back to 19-11 before fading.

ON: Sullivan, Evans, Murdiston, Booysen, Ring, Fowler, Hurcombe, Hodder, Sage, Swan, Thompson, Edwards, Rees.

Scorers: Tries: Evans, Murdison, Booysen. Goal: Sullivan.

20 March 1929 at Headingley, Leeds.
Lost 20-27. Attendance: 5,000

Scot Roy Kinnear marked his debut for Other Nationalities with two tries, but could not save his team from a seven point defeat.

ON: Sullivan, Andrews, Kinnear, O'Rourke, Mills, Moores, Rees, Thompson, White, Jenkins, Mason, Stephens, Watkins.

Scorers: Tries: Kinnear 2, Andrews, Jenkins; Goals: Sullivan 4.

7 April 1930 at Thrum Hall, Halifax. Won 35-19.
Attendance: 2,300

Inspired by Sullivan, a Kiwi-based ON side strolled to victory, despite Warrington centre Dingsdale scoring a hat-trick for England. Kinnear and Gill were Scotland's representatives, Kinnear scoring a try.

ON: Sullivan, Mills, Kinnear, Gill, Brown, Davies, Williams, Thompson, White, Hutt, Mason, Hall, Watkins.

Scorers: Tries: Brown 3, Davies 2, Mills, Kinnear, Mason, Hall; Goals: Sullivan 4.

1 October 1930 at Knowsley Road, St Helens
Lost 18-31. Attendance: 10,000

Two tries from Wigan's Kiwi winger Lou Brown could not save ON from a 13 point defeat. Roy Kinnear was Scotland's representative.

ON: Sullivan, Hardgrave, Kinnear, O'Rourke, Brown, Thomas, Rees, Hutt, White, Williams, Mason, Meredith, Kilpatrick.

Scorers: Tries: Brown 2, Hutt, White; Goals: Sullivan 3.

30 March 1933 at Lonsdale Park, Workington.
Lost 27-34. Attendance:11,000

Confusion over an obstruction try scored by St Helens' Kiwi winger Hardgrave led to some in the Thursday afternoon crowd to think the final score was 34-30. Jimmie Douglas was Scotland's representative.

ON: Sullivan, Harris, Moores, Shankland, Hardgrave, Busch, Jenkins, Thompson, White, Mason, Douglas, Thomas, Armbruster.

Scorers: Tries: Harris 2, Hardgrave, Busch, Armbruster; Goals: Sullivan 6.

European Championships and other post-war matches

1949-50

19 September 1949 versus England at Borough Park, Workington.
Won 13-7. Attendance:17,576

Other Nationalities dominated Borough Park's first international with Scottish full-back Wilson scoring the first try supporting a break by Valentine.

ON: Wilson, Bevan, Paskins, Bartlett, Cooper, Devery, Jackson, McMaster, Kearney, Pansegrouw, Bath, Mudge, Valentine.

Scorers: Tries: Bevan 2, Wilson; Goals: Devery, Bath.

22 October 1949 versus Wales at The Park, Abertillery.
Won 6-5. Attendance: 2,000

Driving, freezing rain and lightning not only kept the crowd to a minimum, but prompted both skippers to ask the ref Charles Appleton to abandon the game. He refused and Other Nationalities, featuring Dave Valentine at loose forward, snatched a dire game by a point.

ON: Hunter, Bevan, Paskins, Devery, Cooper, Mountford, Jackson, McMaster, Kearney, Bath, Clues, Payne, Valentine.

Scorers: Tries: Bevan, Cooper.

10 January 1950 versus France at Stade Velodrome, Marseille.
Lost 3-8. Attendance: 22,580

There was little shame in this narrow defeat, which enabled England to clinch the title by beating Wales. A year later France, inspired by the legendary Puig-Aubert, won a test series 2-1 in Australia.

ON: Hunter, Bartlett, Paskins, Devery, Nordgren, Mountford, Jackson, McMaster, Kearney, Daly, Clues, Robson, Valentine.

Scorers: Try: Bartlett.

1950-51

10 December 1950 versus France at Stade Municipal, Bordeaux.
Lost 3-16. Attendance: 28,000

Brian Bevan got the only points for an ON side with Dave Valentine at loose forward, in front of the biggest crowd to ever see them play.

ON: Cook, Bevan, Bartlettt, Clark, Cooper, Mountford, Jackson, McMaster, Bath, Daly, Clues, Mudge, Valentine.

Scorers: Try: Bevan.

31 March 1951 versus Wales at St Helen's, Swansea.
Won 27-21. Attendance: 5,000
Described as 'a delightful game' of 'tactical brilliance' in newspaper reports, ON won a classic in which Salford's Bob Robson was drafted into the pack and did well on a pitch packed with star performers.

ON: Cook, Bevan, Allan, Paskins, Cooper, Henderson, Proctor, Mudge, Kearney, Daly, Clues, Robson, Valentine.

Scorers: Tries: Bevan, Allan, Paskins, Cooper, Henderson, Proctor, Clues; Goals: Cook 3.

11 April 1951 versus England at Central Park, Wigan.
Won 35-10. Attendance: 16,860
A vintage performance by Brian Bevan clinched this European championship game for Dave Valentine's ON side with a hat-trick, including a classic 75-yard interception try.

ON: Hunter, Bevan, Allan, Devery, Cooper, Mountford, Jackson, Daly, McKinney, Mudge, Bath, Robson, Valentine.

Scorers: Tries: Bevan 3, Daly, Mudge; Goals: Devery 5, Bath 2.

1951-52

3 November 1951 versus France at The Boulevard, Hull.
Won 17-14. Attendance: 18,000
ON won a brutal game thanks to a Lionel Cooper hat-trick of tries. Edouard Poncinet was dismissed ten minutes from time after knocking out three of ON's ten Australians.

ON: Hunter, Bevan, Paskins, Devery, Cooper, Henderson, Kelly, McMaster, McKinney, Mudge, Clues, Burke, Valentine.

Scorers: Tries: Cooper 3; Goals: Devery 4.

1 December 1951 versus Wales at The Park, Abertillery.
Won 22-11. Attendance: 3,386
Dave Valentine dominated the forward battle as ON seized control from the very first minute when superstar Brian Bevan scored a trademark try with a scorching long distance break. Despite the crowd being reported as nearer 10,000 than the official figure, it was Wales' last home match in this era.

ON: Hunter, Bevan, Paskins, Devery, Cooper, Henderson, Kelly, Burke, McKinney, Mudge, Clues, Bath, Valentine.

Scorers: Tries: Bevan 2, Devery 2, Paskins, Cooper; Goals: Devery, Bath.

16

3 January 1952, Stamford Bridge, London
Friendly: British Empire X111 26 New Zealand 22
Attendance: 6,800

An afternoon crowd saw a promotional game which was added to the programme of the Kiwis tour of Europe. The Empire side had too much flair for the tourists, Lionel Cooper earning the plaudits with a hat trick.

Empire XIII: Cunliffe; Bevan, Allen, Ward, Cooper; Broome, Pepperell; Barton, McKinney, Prescott, Bath, Clues, Valentine.
Scorers: Tries: Cooper 3, Bevan, Allan, Valentine; Goals: Ward 4.

23 April 1952 versus England at Central Park, Wigan.
Lost 18-31. Attendance: 19,785

Barrow's legendary stand-off Willie Horne put on a superb display for the English against the likes of Bevan and Bath (Warrington), Cooper and Valentine (Huddersfield) and Clues (Leeds).

ON: Hunter, Bevan, Paskins, Allan, Cooper, Verrenkamp, Kelly, McMaster, McKinney, Bath, Clues, Mudge, Valentine.
Scorers: Tries: Bevan 2, Allan 2; Goals: Bath 3.

1952-53

18 October 1952 versus England at Fartown, Huddersfield.
Won 31-12. Attendance: 20,459

ON bounced back from an 11-5 deficit to win with Bevan scoring four tries. Peter Henderson (two) and Lionel Cooper also scored tries, two of the five Huddersfield players in the side playing on their home ground.

ON: Hunter, Bevan, Paskins, Devery, Cooper, Henderson, Kelly, Daly, McKinney, Mudge, Bath, Clues, Valentine.
Scorers: Tries: Bevan 4, Henderson 2, Cooper; Goals: Devery 3, Bath 2.

23 November 1952 versus France at Stade Velodrome, Marseille.
Won 29-10. Attendance: 17,611

A rare nightmare display by French legend Puig Albert helped ON score five second-half tries to complete a comfortable win.

ON: Hunter, Bevan, Lynch, Devery, Cooper, Henderson, Kelly, Daly, McKinney, Mudge, Clues, Bath, Valentine.
Scorers: Tries: Bevan 2, Devery, Cooper, Henderson, Kelly, Valentine; Goals: Bath 4.

15 April 1953 versus Wales at Wilderspool, Warrington.
Lost 16-18. Attendance: 8,449
Other Nationalities went on to win the European title despite giving away a 16-7 lead against the Welsh.
ON: Phillips, Bevan, Allan, Devery, Cooper, Mountford, Black, Daly, Ellean, Mudge, Bath, Clues, Valentine.
Scorers: Tries: Cooper, Black, Clues, Valentine. Goals: Bath 2.

1953-54

7 October 1953 versus Wales at Odsal, Bradford.
Won 30-5. Attendance: 14,646
The first floodlit European Championship match was one of Wales' last in this period. With no European Championship in 1954 due to the World Cup, Wales disbanded as an international team until 1968.
ON: Phillips, Bevan, Paskins, Devery, Cooper, Robinson, Dawson, Wilson, Ellean, Mudge, Clues, Mossop, Valentine.
Scorers: Tries: Bevan 2, Cooper, Robinson; Goals: Phillips 5.

18 October 1953 versus France at Stade Municipal, Bordeaux.
Won 15-10. Attendance: 12,490
Two Brian Bevan tries saw the Other Nationalities side clinch a fine win.
ON: Phillips, Bevan, Paskins, Lynch, Cooper, Robinson, Black, Wilson, Ellean, Mudge, Clues, Mossop, Valentine.
Scorers: Tries: Bevan 2, Robinson; Goals: Phillips 3.

28 November 1953 versus England at Central Park, Wigan.
Lost 22-30. Attendance: 19,072
Four tries from Swinton's Peter Norburn clinched the European crown for England.
ON: Phillips, Bevan, Paskins, Devery, Cooper, Robinson, Dawson, Wilson, Ellean, Mudge, Clues, Mossop, Valentine.
Scorers: Tries: Bevan 2, Cooper, Robinson; Goals: Phillips 5.

French Rugby League 20th Anniversary match
3 January 1954. France 19 Combined Nations 15 at Lyons
Dave Valentine was Scotland's representative in this friendly match. The Combined Nations side included players from the USA and Italy.
Combined Nations: Ward, Lampshire, Sellers, Mclellan, Cooper, Banks, Helme, Phillips, Richardson, McKinney, McNally, Vigna, Valentine.
Scorers: Tries: Banks, McKinney, Vigna; Goals: Ward 3.

1954-55

17 November 1954. Rugby League XIII versus Australasians
Dave Valentine played in this floodlit post World Cup match at Odsal. The Australians won 25-13.

1955-56

12 September 1955 versus England at Central Park, Wigan.
Won 33-16. Attendance: 18,232
With no national team to play for, several Welsh stars joined Other Nationalities, making them an awesome side. They put on a magnificent display with a hat-trick of tries by new local hero Billy Boston (who was, incredibly, never capped by Wales at League or Union), two tries for Brian Bevan – his ninth in four internationals at Wigan - and one try and six goals for another Welshman, Lewis Jones of Leeds.
ON: Moses; Bevan, Lynch, Jones, Boston; Price, Banks; Thorley, McKinney, Kelly, Bath, Clues, Valentine.
Scorers: Tries: Boston 3, Bevan 2, Bath; Goals: Jones 6.

18 August 1965, Crystal Palace, London.
Friendly: Commonwealth XIII 7 New Zealand 15
Attendance: 1,200
This promotional game drew a paltry crowd and saw the Kiwis clinch a win in the last 10 minutes. Charlie Renilson was Scotland's representative.
Commonwealth XIII: James; Jones, Hagan, Wood, Lake; Broatch, Hepworth; Dolton, Drui, Ravitale, Fogerty, Hicks, Renilson; Substitutes: Schultz, Orchard.
Scorers: Try: Ravitale; Goals: James 2.

County Championship

14 September 1974 versus Lancashire at Salford
Lost 13-14. Attendance: 1,750
Rob Valentine, then in the twilight of his career with Keighley, came on as a substitute for ON in this narrow defeat. He was Scotland's sole representative in the side's debut in the County Championship.
ON: Wallace, Fielding, Willicombe, Wilson, Bevan, Wilkins, Diabra, Butler, Jarvis, Gray, Gallacher, Mantle, Coslett. Sub: Valentine.
Scorers: Tries: Wilson, Gray, Fielding; Goals: Coslett 2.

25 November 1975 versus Lancashire at St Helens
Lost 7-36. Attendance: 1,500
Scots John Hegarty, and Alan Tait (senior), who came on as a substitute, played for ON in a heavy defeat to a strong Lancashire side.
ON: Wallace, Bardens, Willicombe, Hegarty, Vigo, Moncreiff, Sheppard, Gibbs, Parry, Watts, Rowe, Coulman, Knighton. Subs: Tait, Pomering.
Scorers: Tries: Barends 2; Drop-goal: Wallace.

The record

Other Nationalities' record was excellent. They matched England almost point for point and win for win, beat Wales four out of five attempts and lost only twice to the French in six meetings. It was no surprise that the Celts (and Antipodeans) would raise themselves against the English but to preside over the Welsh at a time when they had a star-studded, settled side was equally impressive. The County Championship matches did little to revive a tournament that was already being subsumed by club competitions, and on occasion attendances fell below 1,000, despite some impressive playing talent being on display.

Roy Kinnear playing for Wigan in the 1929 Challenge Cup Final. He made three appearances for Other Nationalities. (Photo: Courtesy Robert Gate)

4. War brings Scots into the fold

Probably the first Scotland team to play at a major Rugby League venue were, fittingly considering how League eventually took root in Scotland, a group of student Rugby Union players. And it was only thanks to the Second World War that this happened.

During the First World War, in 1916 the RFU had decreed that in the forces, Northern Union players could play with Rugby Union players in *bona fide* Naval and Military teams, and made it clear that this only applied during the war. The ruling did not apply to munitions workers, and was immediately revoked at the end of the war.

In the Second World War, following the precedent of their move in the First World War, the RFU again lifted their ban and allowed servicemen from a League background to play with and against Unionites almost from the start - 12 November 1939 - of the War. The Welsh Rugby Union, in the cause of national unity, reluctantly followed suit, but the Scottish RU did not agree with the move, and objected to the playing of the two Union versus League matches under Union rules in 1943 and 1944.

The distinction between the codes was blurred under the auspices of the Northern Command Sports Board - the Armed Forces administration of sporting activities - and the Privates, Corporals and Gunners of Rugby League's working class servicemen played alongside and against the Captains, Majors and other officers from Rugby Union backgrounds.

Indeed, in January 1943, a Union team played a Combined Services League team at Leeds' Headingley ground and, a year later, at Bradford's Odsal, both under 15-a-side rules. Not surprisingly, the far more athletic and skilful League players triumphed 18-11 and 15-10.

It was at this time that Scotland were at last represented on League territory, albeit in a Union sevens competition. It is not known whether the Scots competed at previous events but they were certainly among eight mixed-code teams invited to an annual Rugby Sevens tournament at Headingley on Saturday 15 April 1944.

Although Sevens is obviously something of a hybrid game, matches were played under Union rules, which should have suited the Union teams, but instead, the team representing the RFL won the Golden

Trophy (all proceeds to Northern Command Sports Board Welfare Funds), and not for the first time, apparently.

Two Scottish teams were present: Northern Command Scottish (the Scottish members of the armed forces based in northern England) and Scottish STC (Universities). They were up against Northern Universities, the RAF, Universities Athletic Union (UAU), The Rugby League, Northern Command English and Northern Command Welsh. It was a right royal mixture of personnel gathered on the turf of one of League's prime clubs. The Northern Command English had local lads Sergeant/Instructor A.M. Guest of Castleford and Pte S. Newbound of Hunslet playing alongside Lt P.R.H. Hastings of Oxford and England.

The RAF included Welsh internationals C. H. Evans (Leeds - Rugby League) and Sgt Walters (Cardiff - Rugby Union) together with Dixon, Rees and Roper of Leeds, Boyer of Oldham and Halifax's Brereton. The Welsh had R.L. Francis of Barrow, R. Lloyd of Castleford and Bradford Northern legend Trevor Foster.

The Rugby League's side was: D. Jenkins (Leeds and Wales), K. Brookes (Wakefield Trinity), J. Lewthwaite (Barrow), R. Rylance (Wakefield), C. Murphy (Leeds and Wales), L. Clarke (Hull KR), and E. Jones (Leeds).

The difference between the cross-pollenization of Welsh rugby and the isolation of Scottish players is clear in the Scottish teams at such an event. While the Welsh included a mixture of League and Union players, the Scots were all Union men, almost certainly under the direction of the SRU. For the record, here are the teams which represented Scotland at Headingley at the 1944 Sevens.

Northern Command Scottish VII *(red, white and black jerseys)*
Pte H.K. Carruthers (Galashiels), Capt McGregor (Rosslyn Park), Pte Crozier (Hawick), Cpl R. Cowe (Melrose and Scotland), CSM M. Burrell (Melrose and Scottish Services), Pte A. Crawford (Melrose and Scottish Services), Capt R. M. L. Anderson (Aberdeen University).

Scottish S.T.C. (Universities) VII *(dark blue jerseys)*
Cadet E. Douglas (Edinburgh), Cadet J. Innes (Edinburgh), Cadet D. Provan (St Andrews), Cadet J. Stewart (Glasgow), Cadet R. Lind (St Andrews), Cadet K. Jack (Glasgow), Cadet W. Wilson (Edinburgh).

It is interesting to see that the Scottish teams should be composed of players from Aberdeen University, where in the 1980s, the game began in Scotland; Edinburgh University, which produced several players for the early Scotland Student XIIIs; and the borders (Melrose and Galashiels), which provided the majority of professionals from north of the border. If both Scottish sides had reached the final, every player on a major Rugby League pitch would have been Scottish - a certain first!

The great rugby divide was immediately reintroduced in peacetime, and was the first business of the RFU after VE day. Although the Yorkshire RFU president said before the match at Headingley in 1943 that: "there could be no line of demarcation between men in uniform", no-one was surprised when the codes remained enemies after the war. John Wilson, the RFL's Scottish secretary, said he did not think League and Union would ever play under one banner. Tony McCarthy wrote in his book *War Games*: "the demeaning, sad and sometimes absurd saga (Union's apartheid) continued". Rugby League was not recognised by the Armed Forces until 1994, and only then after pressure from the Rugby League Parliamentary Group and BARLA.

There were two unsuccessful attempts by a Glaswegian consortium to gain a place in the Rugby Football League after the war, although these were both connected with greyhound racing stadiums. In February 1949, an application for Glasgow Black Eagles to play out of Steppes Stadium in the city was refused. They tried again four years later, this time intending to be based at White City Stadium, but were still turned away.

Sevens rugby gave further opportunities for Scotland and Rugby League to mix. In May 1963, a Rugby League VII consisting of Leeds players and Whitehaven's Scots Brian Shillinglaw and Alex Cassie were scheduled to play in the Jedburgh Gala, although it is unclear whether they actually did. In the summer of 1963, Whitehaven won a Sevens tournament in Kelso. Their team included Gary Close, Ken Evans, Alan Burns, Dave Hazeldon, Tom Pullin and Peter Kenny. In the Halifax Sevens on 24 April 1964, a Scotland team competed for the first time. The eight man squad was: Ron Cowan, Drew Broatch (both Leeds), Ally Ford, Rob Valentine (both Huddersfield), Brian Shillinglaw, Glenn Turnball (both Workington), Charlie Renilson and Hugh Duffy (both Halifax).

From a Photo by J. & E. Flamo, 16, Prince Albert Street.

Two Scottish Oldham Rugby League heroes. Left: George Frater. Below: Jim Moffatt. On the back of Moffatt's photo, he wrote about his career: "The season before I joined Oldham, in the seven a side sports at the end of the season, Melrose got second place, but we had to go into the final game with five men. Frater, Jim Telfer and I were the three forwards 1896. In my third match for Oldham I was appointed Leader of the Forwards. Lancashire Senior Competitions won by Oldham 1897-8 Northern Union 1897-8 Cup ties won by Oldham against Hunslet 1898 - 1899 Lancashire Senior competition won by Oldham 1900 - 1901. Lancashire and Yorkshire met at Rochdale for the County Championship won by Lancashire 1900-1901. Yorkshire Senior Competition won by Leeds 1901-2.

Won my Yorkshire county cap.

First time six forwards were tried out 1903. First time Other Nationalities game was played, we beat England at Wigan.

Six forwards Frater, Laidlaw and I were three

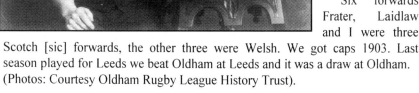

Scotch [sic] forwards, the other three were Welsh. We got caps 1903. Last season played for Leeds we beat Oldham at Leeds and it was a draw at Oldham. (Photos: Courtesy Oldham Rugby League History Trust).

24

Part 2: Students show the way

The 2001 Student Europa Cup Squad (Photo: Kevin Rudd)

5. Scottish Students: The game's roots

As with Rugby League itself, if it was not for Rugby Union, Rugby League would not exist in Scotland. For the roots of Rugby League north of the border lie at Aberdeen University, where a former Rugby League professional-turned-lecturer, Dr Malcolm Reid, was coaching the Union team.

League had been played in British universities only since the late 1960s. Although the first student League match was played in Sydney in front of a 60,000 crowd in 1920, in a hangover from post-war Britain, where working class kids were not encouraged to go into higher education, it was not until the era of the Beatles, flower power and Colin Dixon that the 13-a-side game got a look-in among academia.

Former Great Britain international Cec Thompson helped launch a League club when he was a mature student at Leeds University in 1968. Leeds played Liverpool at Widnes in Britain's first ever inter varsity match: it was "as if a class barrier had been broken down" suggests Thompson.

Great Britain Students played their first international in 1973, Oxford (founded 1977) played Cambridge (founded 1980) in the first Varsity RL match at Fulham in 1981, and Wales debuted in 1984. But Scotland remained untouched. Not for long, though.

In 1987, David Oxley at the RFL approached Reid, a lecturer at Aberdeen, and asked if he thought he could get a Scotland side together for the 1989 Student World Cup in York. Reid was confident he could, given what League had to offer Union players in terms of balls skills, tackling technique and adventure.

The fact that he was coach of Scottish Students Rugby Union team was not a major problem. Since a furore in the mid-1970s when England's Union Students reacted to a defeat by Scotland by publicising Reid's past as a former journeyman professional at Barrow, Widnes and Blackpool - "they thought I had horns growing out of my head" he jokes now - Reid had eased his way around the ludicrous restrictions placed on him by Union's authorities.

"Mal Reid had been sowing the seeds for some time," explained history graduate Dominic Hubbard, better known as Liberal peer Lord

Addington. "I played for Scotland Students Union team, and he kept asking us if we'd be interested in trying League."

By the end of the year, a recruitment campaign based on a few posters and off-the-cuff comments had seen Reid raise a side, formed mainly of Scottish Union-playing students who fancied trying their hand at the more expansive game.

"About 80 or 90 per cent of that first Scotland Students side was from Aberdeen University," explained Addington, who qualified through a Scottish mother and later played for London Scottish RFC. "It was Mal's project - he'd been building up to it for quite a while.

"As an ex-professional, he was only allowed to coach Union because he was employed to coach sport by the university. We played about half-a-dozen games against teams like Lancaster University and teams around the Barrow-in-Furness area where Mal was from, before our first international."

Even though it represents the country, the students team is not entirely Scottish. It is open to Scots, those with Scottish parents or grandparents, or those studying at Scottish institutions. For example, the 1992 World Cup squad included Irishmen Mike Kerr and Paul Gowdy, who were studying at Edinburgh and Dundee Universities respectively.

The first game

Scottish Students' first match was a few days before Christmas 1987, when they traipsed down to play against Lancaster University, coached by Reid's brother. "We'd trained for about six weeks," recalls Reid. "I had about three lads from Stirling and one from Dundee and the rest were from Aberdeen. Once we'd settled down we won quite convincingly and the next day we played a combined Lancaster College / University team and won that as well."

Three months later, Scotland Students made their international debut, against Wales, who were coached by Clive Griffiths, as a curtain-raiser to a St Helens versus Castleford Challenge Cup tie at Knowsley Road. It was an historic, if not exactly highly-technical, encounter.

"We won, but only because we converted our tries," recalls Lord Addington, whose brother Mike Hubbard (see chapter 11) was in the Scottish side at the 1989 Student World Cup. "There's a video of the game with me wandering around - I got a bang on my leg early on and could hardly walk. But we knuckled down and stripped them of possession a lot. Not strictly legal but we got away with it.

I played prop in both codes and soon realised that if you pushed in a Rugby League scrum it caused havoc. Most teams just have a rest in the scrums. We won the scrums against the head several times, even though it was frowned upon. We'd send the scrum-half round to pounce on the loose ball."

A decade later, the notion of complete novices like Addington - now sports spokesman for the Liberal Lords and a member of the All-Party Parliamentary Rugby League Group - playing for Scotland seems folly. But getting a team out on the pitch, let alone one organised enough to take part in a World Cup, was a major achievement by Reid and one which all Scottish Rugby League fans should be eternally grateful.

1989 Student World Cup

The second World Cup tournament - New Zealand had hosted and won the first, in 1986 - was played throughout English Rugby League's heartlands, although all the teams stayed and trained at York University.

The day before the tournament, sponsors NatWest held a launch at which the Dutch team turned up in clogs and the Scots in the now obligatory kilts. Organiser Bev Risman rather romantically called it "a sea of colour and glamour". From then on, Scotland RL teams attended almost all official functions in the national dress.

Despite losing all three group games, Scotland were by no means embarrassed. Indeed, their 36-22 loss to eventual champions Australia was an extraordinary result for a team which had only been in existence a few months and which was full of players who had only taken up the code the previous year. "We had a real mish-mash of people," says Scotland boss Reid, who had left Aberdeen University to work at the RFL. "We took part rather than competed."

In the final, Australia beat England 10-5 despite being under the cosh from the home side for most of the game, watched by an incredible 10,000 crowd in bright sunshine at Wigan's Central Park.

1992 Pepsi Student World Cup

After the experiences in 1989, Reid decided that if Scotland were going to take part in another World Cup, they would "do it properly". Training camps and tours followed and, despite losing warm-up matches to England (15-31 at Wycliffe College) and France (12-24 at Limoux), the narrow defeats gave Scotland heart for the task ahead in Australia: three games in five days against three southern hemisphere sides.

The opener against Papua New Guinea - the only country where Rugby League is the national sport - should have been a baptism of fire for Scotland. Instead, they romped to victory, winning 42-14.

That put Scotland in fine spirits for the biggest job of all, against the Australians on their home turf just three days later. There was no shame in the 38-10 defeat against the world champions, coached by former Cronulla and Parramatta player John McMartin and skippered by Marty Moore. The Aussies went on to beat Tonga in the final, but the 32-14 scoreline shows that Scotland's 56-12 hammering by the Tongans in the final group game was no disgrace, although just one day's rest after the Australia match didn't help Scotland's cause. Tonga included half-back Willie Wolfgramm, who played in the 1995 senior World Cup before joining Swinton Lions.

Scotland had scraped into the last eight but had to play another of the world's top Rugby League nations - the 1986 student champs New Zealand. Yet again, Scotland did themselves proud with a battling performance before being squeezed out, 24-18, in the last 10 minutes: a fantastic effort in their fourth match in eight days.

Scotland overcame that disappointment to beat Ireland and Western Samoa in the Plate competition. That gave them a reunion with the 'auld enemy' in the final: England. "We had it won by half-time," says Reid. "We murdered them." History had been made.

The team's only experienced Rugby League player, Craig Errington, who went on to join Swinton, was voted man-of-the-match and was selected in the Team of the Tournament. Full-back Nick Mardon, later of London Broncos, pushed him mighty close on both fronts.

However, most of these ever-improving players had nowhere to play once they graduated. Open age Rugby League was almost non-existent in Scotland and it was another three years until a senior international team was formed. Assistant manager Vaughan Yates, who had played at full-back in the 1989 event, was a case in point. The Edinburgh University graduate became a graphic designer, one of many former Scottish Students lost to the game in that era.

A change of management

Staff reductions at the RFL saw Mal Reid quit his role as Scotland boss, leaving Student Rugby League Director Bev Risman to replace Reid with Risman's younger brother, John, the former Welsh international and Fulham full-back.

John Risman gathered together a team he could trust and rely upon: former Workington Town coach Keith Davies, who had been working with Cameron Bell at Carlisle, and physio Vic Semple, the strapper at Derwent Park. All three knew each other well and lived around the Cockermouth area of Cumbria.

"I basically inherited the squad that had played in the 1992 World Cup and had to prepare them for a Home Nations tournament in 1993," recalled John. "We had more than 40 students at a trial day at Moray House in Edinburgh. We'd rely on word of mouth around the student scene. If we had one lad from a university, we'd tell him to go back and ask his mates if anyone else fancied it. Once we got hold of anyone any good at a trial, I wouldn't let them go.

The Scots brought personalities with them, lads like Billy Gamba, Nick Mardon and Iain Stanger. But we built the squad around a very, very social atmosphere so players wanted to play for us."

That's not to say Scotland Students was a drinking club with some rugby thrown in. Far from it. Risman had better things to do than that.

1994-95: The French tour

After narrowly avoiding humiliation in the 1994 Home Nations tournament in Aberavon, Risman started preparations for the 1996 World Cup. A tour of France was considered a great success, Risman describing it seven years on as the best he has been on with any student side. Both games - against an Aquitaine regional side and a France Students side including five full internationals - were lost but Risman was pleased with a 'creditable performance... with passion and pride at the heart of it'.

The trip could be considered the turning point in Scottish Rugby League. The players had been bewitched by the intoxicating, partisan nature experience of representing Scotland.

"The lads got wrapped up in it all," Risman explained. "We had the bagpipes and all that, and it created such an impression that those lads were hooked. They wanted to play for Scotland."

So much so that many of that squad were to be capped at full level the following year, during which Scotland put a in a far more competitive showing in the student Home Nations tournament in Warrington, despite losing to eventual champions England and runners-up Wales.

1996 Halifax Student World Cup

The bulk of Scotland's squad from 1996 were the players who represented the country in the first two senior internationals, both against Ireland, either side of the tournament. Kevin Rudd was one exception - as a Yorkshireman living in Scotland, studying at Edinburgh University, he was not yet eligible for the senior side.

Scotland warmed-up for the tournament with a win over England at Durham, a result that built up even more tension for the clash between the 'auld enemies' in the World Cup itself.

"They were really upset by that," reminisces an amused Risman. "Their captain and coach came off crying. They swore they'd take revenge on us in the World Cup... but they didn't."

After thrashing Japan in their group opener at Wilderspool, Scotland repeated the victory over England, winning 10-4 in a real battle on a miserable night (especially for the English) at Gateshead. However, five games in less than two weeks took its toll as Scotland lost to France, South Africa and Russia to finish eighth. They even had to borrow a South African player to make up the numbers for their final match.

But the tradition of the Student World Cup was developing rapidly, with all the teams staying at Warrington Institute and the closing banquet at Salford providing superb memories – especially for the Scots who bonded with the Russians after their play-off.

"The Student World Cup is a great occasion," wrote Graeme Thompson for the Student Rugby League Alumni website. "There is good rugby, pride in representing your country, the new friends you make and 200 student rugby players descending on Mr Smiths nightclub. Twelve student squads gathered in Warrington for two and a half weeks sounds like a recipe for disaster, and it certainly brought some memorable moments, such as the USA's night of shaving their heads marine-style and running around the campus; the Kiwis practising their 'haka' and the Russians their vodka drinking."

1997-98: All change

Thompson, by then Scotland's Rugby League development officer, took over the team for the 1997 Home Nations and, assisted by former full international Andy Knight, selected a squad containing 12 Scottish-based students and only six exiles. This altered the balance of the squad compared to previous regimes but many of the new born-and-bred Scots such as Michael Loakman, Craig Cooper, Wesley Henry, Nicky McLeod, Sam Clarke and Matthew Geraghty were missing from the squad 18 months later, their lack of League experience costing them dear.

Scotland lost to Ireland at West of Scotland RFC and Wales in Cheltenham, but after thrashing Ireland in a friendly in Belfast, hopes were high for the new-look European Championship in 1998. However, despite a lengthy preparation programme, Scotland were still beaten by Wales and Ireland before the now inevitable close game with England, which they also lost. Before France's visit to Glasgow, Thompson left to join London Broncos, handing over the coaching reigns to hooker Kevin Rudd. He could not stop the losing streak despite an impressive second-half comeback and a powerful display by prop Ash Carroll which won him man-of-the-match in the *Rugby Leaguer*. Scotland were left with the wooden spoon and England's 8-4 defeat by France saw Wales snatch the European crown.

1999 *The Independent* Student World Cup

Under Rudd and Risman, Scotland prepared for the latest international tournament more extensively than before. They lost a friendly to Wales, 33-22 in blistering heat at Pontyclunn RFC, and spent a week in training camp at Cockermouth YHA before playing British Police in September.

But despite all that, and having several players with professional experience including Workington Town trio Chris Houston (signed from West of Scotland RFC), Craig Fisher and former Manly Sea Eagle Andrew Lambert, Scotland flopped when the tournament began. They failed to beat the South African Rhinos in their opening game in Glasgow, poor kicking denying them a win which they had counted on, and defeat by England sent them into the Plate competition.

All the teams gathered in Hull for the latter stages, which were marked by a street parade by every nation, including the kilted Scots of course. The Scotland lads also did their bit for the community, coaching kids at William Gee School.

Scotland recovered well from their early disappointments, thrashing Japan 70-0 and seeing off a stubborn Canada side in the final to allow a delighted Ash Carroll to lift the World Plate. The World Cup itself was won for second time by New Zealand, who beat England 46-16 in the final at The Boulevard.

That left Scotland joint sixth in an all-time Student World Cup table: only Australia (22), New Zealand (18), France (11), Wales (10) and England (9) have won more games than Scotland's six. Their 17 matches puts them behind the same five nations in games played, showing what a force Scotland have become at that level.

And the experience had been a wonderful one for all involved. You only have to see some of the testimonials written by Scotland's players to appreciate that: Tommy McGhee (Edinburgh Reivers RU): "The best two weeks of my rugby career;" Stu Connell: "The best bunch of rugby boys ever;" and Ash Bellamy: "What a bunch of great guys – best rugby memories ever."

2000-01: Stepping up a level

After a mixed '*Manchester Evening News* Championship of Great Britain & Ireland' in 2000 in which they lost to England at Leigh, beat Wales at Chorley, but lost to the Irish at Castleton, Scotland stepped up their preparations for the 2002 Student World Cup.

With a comprehensive and intense programme which most top club sides would consider challenging - using St Helens's and Wigan Warriors' training facilities during the Home Nations had given the squad a taste of the big time - the 2001-02 season was a watershed one for Scotland Students. They won three out of four games on tour in southern France before the real action began with the trip to the former Soviet state of Tartarstan in early September for the Europa Cup.

The squad flew to Moscow and then travelled by overnight train to deepest Kazan, stepping into the unknown with real hopes of a medal having come on in leaps and bounds from the side that was once seen to be just making up the numbers.

Having paraded in their kilts in front of an incredible 16,000 at the opening ceremony, led by official piper Roy Vickers, Scotland's players got off to a great start in the opening game against a Russian side packed with full internationals. Over 1,000 intrigued spectators saw Glaswegian full-back Barry Edgar steal the show in a 38-16 triumph.

But just two days later, Scotland bore the brunt of guest entrants New South Wales' backlash from their opening day thrashing by Wales, fading badly in a 42-18 defeat.

Another defeat by Wales meant Scotland finished second and met England in the semi-final. Despite being weakened by injury and having played a game more than England, the Scots started superbly, Clint Brown scoring from Andy Borthwick's offload in the 14th minute.

Edgar, who'd coped well under great English pressure, added a penalty before half-time and after the break, John McDonald drove to the line to give Scotland a 12-0 lead.

However, fatigue caught up with the Scots and the English scored two converted tries to level. Despite some tremendous runs by Whitehaven's Ryan Campbell, Scotland had to settle for extra-time. Exhausted, they went for the sudden death match-winning point when Edgar drop-kicked at goal but he was dismayed to see it rebound off both posts.

When the English successfully scored a drop goal at the other end to win the game 13-12, the Scots were heart-broken. But they could hold their heads high, knowing they had pushed the eventual winners all the way - England beat the hosts 34-16 in the final.

But it was undoubtedly the greatest trip in Scotland Students' 13-year history, one that included seeing Moscow's Red Square, being bombarded by autograph hunters, being invited by the mafia to play the pipes in nightclubs, gatecrashing a wedding, wearing cardboard neck braces and trying to lift a kaput BMW out of a mudbath while a Lada taxi cruised by.

"The trip was an experience of a lifetime that we will never forget and still struggle to comprehend," wrote a tour diarist in the tour brochure. "The country's culture, the matches, and most of all the astonishing friendliness and hospitality received - memories that we can always cherish."

What the players did learn was that Rugby League can certainly take you places and open your eyes to a wonderful world you would never have experienced without it.

Taking on the best

Arguably the best student Rugby League team in the world - Queensland - visited Scotland in December 2001. Unbeaten in seven years and containing most of the Australian Students team, Queensland had seen off European champions England 20-4 at a chilly Blackheath RFC, and then beaten Wales and Ireland before docking at Stranraer.

The Scots, concerned if they would cope after some late withdrawals and the Queenslanders' reputation for fast-flowing rugby, were led onto the field by a bagpipe procession and reacted with typical fervour, securing an early 9-0 lead thanks to a penalty, great individual try and conversion - all by Ryan Campbell - and a Ian Gilmour drop goal.

Queensland were in new territory having never been behind while on tour, but they responded with a barrage of attacks, seemingly unaffected by the heavy pitch conditions. Paul Horn (two), Dave Elliott (two), Brad Coey-Braddon and Kurt Richards all scored tries while Ian Brackstone kicked four goals.

Scotland valiantly attempted to stay in the game, but apart from a trademark weaving run and touchdown from centre Rob Clarke, failed to take their chances, going down to a 32-13 defeat.

But Scotland had shown they could hold their own against the world's best - a further indication of the progress made by the students since the early days in the 1980s.

Part 3: Internationals 1995 to 2001

1995 Emerging Nations World Cup: The Scotland and Russia squads
(Photo: David Williams)

6. 1995: Dublin debut and the Emerging Nations World Cup

Stena Sealink Challenge: Ireland 26 Scotland 22
13 August 1995, Royal Dublin Showgrounds, attendance: 5,716.
(Attendance figure for succeeding Charity Shield match: Wigan 45 Leeds 10)

Thirty one years after they appeared in the Halifax Sevens, Scotland finally fielded an open-age team for an international match thanks to two factors. One was concurrent development work going on in Ireland, led by Brian Corrigan, Neil Wood and Patrick Harkins. With both countries having had success with their students teams, possessing a smattering of amateur clubs with enthusiastic players, and knowing that their second generation emigrants playing professionally in England would love to represent their country, it made sense to form full international teams.

The second reason was that places at the Emerging Nations World Cup later that year were up for grabs, and the Scottish and Irish teams needed a warm-up match, to experience international Rugby League.

The RFL decided to revive the Charity Shield match in 1995, which had not been played since the 1992-93 season, and took the match to Ireland. However, the RFL had to be convinced to allow history to be made by the curtain-raiser and provided no financial support for either team. Scotland were sponsored for the ferry crossing and paid for their own basic accommodation.

Scotland's squad was primarily based on the Students side, with professionals Darrall Shelford (a New Zealander), Darren Shaw (an Australian) and Martin Ketteridge (from Yorkshire) playing for their ancestral homeland.

One of the student stalwarts was Graeme Thompson, who remembers the occasion fondly. He recalls: "What was remarkable about this was, that in the harsh financial world of professional Rugby League, these three players along with the rest of us, were prepared to pay the required £80 to cover transport and accommodation. In later years, and at the 2000 World Cup in particular, many observers were quick to accuse the Australian-born players of having no proper allegiance to the Scottish cause. This could never be said of Darren Shaw, who showed such commitment from the outset and there was no prouder and more deserving captain of Scotland when he finally took that role in the win over France in 2001.

The visit to Dublin was a typical student trip, with Youth Hostel accommodation, causing some confusion. We arrived in the early hours of the morning and were shown to spare beds in the dormitories. Everyone was tired and quick to sleep. Next morning, many players appeared at breakfast with the same comments, best summed up by one, who awoke and was coming round when he saw another person in a neighbouring bunk begin to rise and change their top. He woke up very quickly when he realised it was a Swedish girl. The dormitories were mixed."

At the last minute, the Irish RU prevented the teams from getting changed at Blackrock College as arranged and instead they had to change about half a mile from the ground and walk to the pitch in playing kit. "It was no bad thing really because it stimulated a lot of interest, marching to the ground in our kit behind the piper," admits Scotland coach John Risman. "The new lads like Darrall Shelford and Darren Shaw were absolutely emotionally drained by it. That was it for them - they were committed to Scotland."

The only try of the first half came just before the break through Ireland centre Lee Child. Scotland hit back with tries by Sean Cusack - Scotland's first in a senior international - and Gavin Manclark, but Ireland's Leo Casey squared things up on 55 minutes. When Seamus McCallion touched down for Ireland with 15 minutes left, it seemed all over, only for Scotland to score two tries in the 69th minute via Manclark and Shelford. Despite scoring four tries apiece, Ireland won thanks to full-back Ian Devery kicking five goals to Ketteridge's three.

Thompson remembers: "Unfortunately we lost but I was lucky enough to receive Man of the Match. The prize was a travel voucher provided by the sponsors, ferry company Stena Sealink. It was just a business card with a '£100' written on the back. The bloke gave it me and when I queried it he said: 'Don't worry, just turn up and present this and it will be accepted'. I handed it over to a friend six months later but still don't know if they were able to use it.

Alan Tait was playing for Leeds in the Charity Shield after our game and needed to borrow some studded boots because Taity only had moulded ones and the ground was heavy. Gavin Manclark, who had scored two tries for us, leant him his but they didn't have the same effect - Wigan thrashed them!"

Interestingly, the two hookers in the international came from the same club, Huddersfield amateurs Lindley Swifts. Scotland's Mark Burns was a student at the time, while Ireland's Seamus McCallion, the experienced former professional, was Lindley's physio.

Scotland: Thompson, Blee, Shelford, Cusack, Manclark, S. Tait, Murdock, Ketteridge, Burns, Waddell, Gamba, D. Shaw, Combe-Lilley.
Subs: Douglas, Walker, Hendry, Stranger, Knight.
Ireland: Devery, Joyce, R. Smith, Child, Comerford, Foy, McElhatton, Casey, McCallion, Horrigan, B. Smith, Nuttall, Owens.
Subs: Doyle, Slicker, McCartney, MacConann, Kerr.
Scorers:
Scotland: Tries: Cusack, Manclark 2, Shelford; Goals: Ketteridge 3.
Ireland: Tries: Child 2, Casey, McCallion; Goals: Devery 5.
Referee: Stuart Cummings (England)

Halifax Emerging Nations World Cup - Group One

Scotland 34 Russia 9
16 October 1995, Post Office Road, Featherstone, attendance: 3,133.

John Risman fulfilled his ambition of getting Scotland recognised on the world stage when they played their first match of the Emerging Nations World Cup, which ran parallel to the Centenary World Cup in October 1995, and was staged throughout England.

The Scotland side was a fascinating mixture of Risman's ever-improving students, a few expansive Union amateurs and a handful of League professionals, coached by George Fairbairn, with a love of Rugby League and Scottish roots their common themes. They had what Thompson called "a fantastic ten days" in Leeds.

"The mixture lent itself to a very positive environment, with the pros having few airs or graces," he explains. "This was probably helped by the first day when we all wanted to know who was rooming with the

41

The 1995 Scotland Emerging Nations Cup Squad (Photo: David Williams)

legendary Alan Tait. It turned out it was Stuart McCarthy, a student player. When Stuart went to his room, Tait was already there and introduced himself: 'Hello, Alan Tait from Leeds Rugby League'. Not taken aback, Stuart replied: 'Nice to meet you. Stuart McCarthy, Canvey Island second XV'!

"We'd all had kilts hired for us and their first outing was at the team meeting in the hotel before we left for the Russia game. Billy Gamba, one of the longest serving Scottish Students, stood up and announced that before the serious talk of the game, other important business had to be dealt with. He produced a cardboard box and declared: 'Anyone wearing pants under their kilt should now surrender them into the box.' Some embarrassed born and bred Scots came forward (and Tait) while a thoroughly bemused Charlie McAlister protested, complaining bitterly of the cold. Charlie, a huge Maori, was said to be the only winger in Rugby Union that the legendary All-Black John Kirwan had been scared of. However Billy was having none of it and Charlie duly became a 'true Scotsman'."

The match

Scotland were brimming with pride and it was no surprise when they took the lead after just four minutes, student James How scampering over from centre to score Scotland's first try in a competitive international. Two minutes later, the result was almost beyond doubt as Alan Tait, the main star on display and the man who drew much of the

42

crowd to Post Office Road that Monday night, doubled Scotland's lead.

However, Russia recovered well from that double whammy. On 13 minutes, stand-off Victor Netchaev of Moscow Magicians, who also scored in their win over the USA and went on to play in the 2000 tournament, pulled a try back and on the half-hour mark, Alexander Otradnov touched down again. But Scotland still led thanks to McAlister's experienced boot and Russia's failure to convert either try.

In the second half, Risman's men cut loose as their experience shone through. After just four minutes of the second period, former Great Britain international Hugh Waddell bundled over the line, shortly followed by a brace of tries from winger Ali Blee. When Tait got his second three minutes from time it was just a matter of how wide a margin Scotland would win by. McAlister's four goals and another from Thompson ensured that Andrey Scheglov's drop goal for the Bears was neither here nor there. Scotland were off to the perfect start.

Since then

Scotland and Russia have not met since, although they may meet in the proposed European Championship in 2002-03. Like Scotland, Russia were invited into the expanded senior World Cup in 2000, and similarly drew on some Australian-based players to strengthen their squad.

Of the class of 1995, Iliassov (who also played in the 1999 Student World Cup), stand-off Netchaev, centre Romanov, classy scrum-half Gavriline (who got a hat-trick against the USA) and veteran forward Garifoulline all remained in a squad that benefited from being captained by Sydney Roosters' Odessa-born Ian Rubin. He was joined by six other Aussies, with ex-Gold Coast Charger Robert Campbell the most illustrious – his qualification for Russia was almost as bizarre as Richard Horne's for Scotland. He always thought his grandparents were from Poland, but then discovered that one was born in a town that was, at the time, on the Russian side of the border.

Scotland: A. Tait (c) , Blee, Shelford, How, Manclark, Cameron, Rush, Waddell, Burns, Gamba, D Shaw, Cusack, McAlister.
Subs: Thompson, Smith, McCarthy, Stanger.

Russia: Iliassov, Otradnov, Romanov, Netchaev, Rozhkov, Scheglov, Gavriline, Garifoulline, Gridnev, Ermolaev, Sergeev, Koriabine (c), Kiryokov.
Subs: Kouton, Shein, Kolikov. Sub not used: Kizlov.
Scorers:
Scotland: Tries: How, Tait 2, Waddell, Blee 2; Goals: McAlister 4, Thompson.
Russia: Tries: Netchaev, Otradnov; Drop goal: Scheglov.
Referee: Tony Kuni (Papua New Guinea)

Scotland 38 USA 16
18 October 1995, Sixfields Stadium, Northampton, attendance: 2,088

Just two days after beating Russia, Scotland made the journey down the M1 from their hotel in Leeds to Sixfields Stadium in Northampton. It was another new venture for Scotland and Rugby League in general as the organisers took a double dose of the sport to a soccer ground in Rugby Union territory: Morocco played Moldova after the Scotland-USA match. More than 2,000 turned up to check it out and the response was positive enough for Super League to take a roadshow game to Northampton two years later.

Victory for Scotland would mean a winner-takes-all Group One clash with the Cook Islands for a place in the final just two days later but, despite having experienced top-class professionals in Tait, Shelford, Ketteridge, Waddell and McAlister, Scotland struggled to get going against an inexperienced USA side.

The Patriots consisted mainly of Union players, like healthcare manager Britton Coffman (of Houston Athletic); Fred Gruhler, now executive director of AMNRL champions Media Mantarays; and Dallas's Laau Afuhaamango, who played in the first ever Professional Arena Rugby League match (rugby sevens indoors on carpet), something that has not quite caught on either side of the Atlantic.

"The Patriots were a little greener in the finer arts - centre Greg Stelluti was playing only his second game of Rugby League - but the ritual slaughter that should have been never took place," reported *League Weekend*'s David Ballheimer. "In fact, the entertaining Americans were unlucky to be three tries to one down at the break."

David Kelso, reporting for the Scottish newspapers, admitted that it was not until USA Union winger Rory Lewis beat Ali Blee to touch down and put the US ahead after 12 minutes, that Scotland "sparked into life". Graeme Thompson, who'd opened the scoring with a simple penalty, "picked up a spilled ball [by Lewis] ten yards inside his own half and galloped in for a wonderful solo effort".

McAlister missed the conversion and a penalty but set up the next two tries which took Scotland into the comfort zone. First he dummied two Americans to set up Ketteridge, then chipped forwards for Mark Smith to gather and barge over.

Both sides exchanged tries in the second-half, Thompson creating a sitter for Shelford with a clever pass, former St George Dragons veteran David Niu gaining reward for sustained American pressure. Ironically, Niu could have played for either side. The Australian's mother was from Dunfermline and he represented Scotland in a World Stars XIII which played a fund-raiser for The September 11 terrorist attacks five years on.

Tait - who had "hardly been seen" according to Kelso - twice combined superbly with Shelford to see the big centre complete his hat-trick. Niu responded again with seven minutes left but it was a mere consolation as Scotland sub Steve Tait had the last word. Thompson's five goals gave the scoreline a flattering look for Scotland, although Ballheimer believed Tait, Shelford and Thompson all deserved praise for their displays. "Victory for Scotland; glory in defeat for the US", he proclaimed.

Mike Evergin remembers

One of the Patriots' late substitutes, Mike Evergin, became an important figure in Rugby League in the States, helping to introduce the game to the Pacific island of Hawaii from his base there in the Armed Forces.

"Those Patriots were just thrown together," Evergin recalled in Oahu in 2001. "We were a bunch of athletes - I was from an American Football background - and we played downs [planned moves] by numbers. That was good for Americans. We had four or five patterns practically written on our arms and when we were in possession we knew what to do. But the trouble came when we had to ad lib, on a turnover or something. It was not pretty."

The Scotland and USA teams (Photo: Courtesy Graeme Thompson)

Evergin, who also played against Scotland in the Nines tournament in Fiji and won 'Most Valuable Player' in the Americans' two-match series against Wales in 1996, recalls that the Scots did not take the Patriots lightly: "The Scots were tough, especially that Shelford. They tried to intimidate us but the USA don't mind mixing it up. It's the feints that fool us. We don't understand space. They'd outflank us in the backs and we were done for." That was certainly the case that night at Northampton as Scottish Rugby League took another step forward. But more importantly, the gospel of Rugby League was being spread in the right spirit.

"We had a good drink afterwards," reminisces Evergin. "I remember Shelford telling me about his Scottish grandfather and sharing some good scotch. I smile at the memories of that night."

Scotland: A. Tait (c) , Blee, Shelford, How, McCarthy, Thompson, Rush, Ketteridge, Burns, Waddell, Gamba, Smith, McAllister.
Subs: S. Tait, Cameron, Douglas, Killen.
USA: Maffie, Lewis, Stelluti, Wallace, Coffman, Ieriko, Niu, Bowe, Segers, Gruhler, Afuhaamango, Erickson, Preston.
Subs: Broussard, Taute, Evergin, McGough.
Scorers:
Scotland: Tries: Shelford 3, Thompson, Ketteridge, How, M. Smith; Goals: Thompson 5.
USA: Tries: Niu 2, Lewis; Goals: Niu 2.
Referee: Kelvin Jeffs (Australia)

Scotland versus the Cook Islands (Photo: David Williams)

Scotland 10 Cook Islands 21
20 October 1995, Wheldon Road, Castleford, attendance: 2,889.

Against the smallest nation with the strongest side in the competition, Scotland knew they would do well to beat the Cook Islands and therefore reach the final. And so it turned out.

Despite having just 14,000 inhabitants, Cook Islanders breed Rugby League players. Kevin and Tony Iro are among their most famous sons but, as with many Pacific nations, their best players often end up playing for New Zealand, where many grow up.

However, such is the draw of the motherland that even the most illustrious NRL stars return to play for the Cooks once they have done their time with the Kiwis. So much so that the island minnows

47

hammered world superpowers the USA and Russia in their first two matches, drawing media attention to the bizarre David v Goliath nature of these sporting encounters.

The match

Despite going ahead through a 15th minute penalty, struck from 35 metres by Thompson when Shelford was held down in the tackle, Scotland were soon trailing when winger Nigere Tariu slid over the try line in the corner.

But Alan Tait restored the lead just before the break with a superb try. Thompson spun the ball out to Shelford, who sent a perfectly weighted pass for Tait to blast through three tacklers and sneak in by the corner flag, leaving Thompson with too hard a task to add the two points.

Under almost constant pressure after half-time, Scotland eventually folded. The game hinged on a controversial, but magnificent try by the Cook Islands. At least seven players handled the ball in a tremendous team effort before centre Andrew Paitai fed winger Sonny Shepherd who darted over the line. Scotland protested that Shepherd, who played as a prop at the 2000 World Cup, had not grounded the ball properly but the try was given and it was close enough to the posts for Meti Noovao to convert. The lead was increased when Shepherd sneaked over from the play-the-ball after Scotland's defence had done well to stop Allan Tuara scoring.

The defeat - and Scotland's exit - was confirmed seven minutes from time when Tariu scored his second try and Noovao added the conversion. However, it was appropriate that Tait should score Scotland's last try of the tournament but unfortunate that his fellow star of the tournament, Graeme Thompson, could not add to his goals tally, leaving Cook Islands' scrum-half Ali Davys to knock over the final point with a drop goal.

The aftermath

The Cook Islands went on to beat Ireland, who thrashed Morocco on the same night as Scotland bowed out, in the final. For that they were rewarded with the promise of a place at the next World Cup. But that was not played until 2000, and by then, many of the players who had proved too much for Scotland had retired or were no longer at their peak. However, the Cooks did field several faces familiar to the Scots, in the defeats by Wales and New Zealand five years later, before salvaging some pride with a dramatic draw with Lebanon in Cardiff's Millennium Stadium. Workington and Illawarra star Anthony Samuel was still in the back-row behind ex Oldham, Hull and Newcastle prop Jason Temu; former Illawarra, South Queensland and Gold Coast star Craig Bowen remained impressive at stand-off; and Meti Noovao, who played for Adelaide Rams and Burleigh Bears, used his experience at loose-forward.

Facing so many pedigree players, it was no surprise Scotland lost, but they left the 1995 tournament with their heads held high. And thanks to the initial two wins and the efforts of journalists like David Kelso, Scottish Rugby League's cause was being raised in the media at home.

"The greatest disappointment in losing to the Cook Islands in what was in effect a semi-final," recalls Thompson, "was that this fantastic adventure and squad camaraderie was going to come to an end. To sum it up, Darrall Shelford, who had played at the top in both codes, describes to this day his time with Scotland at the Emerging Nations as his most enjoyable tour experience because of the unique mixture of people, and the spirit that prevailed. It was superb." Within four months, Risman's involvement with the senior Scotland side was over, apparently angry at the RFL's influence on proceedings. But he had played his part in history being made.

Scotland: A. Tait (c), Blee, Shelford, How, McCarthy, Thompson, S. Tait, Gamba, Burns, Waddell, Smith, Cusack, McAlister.
Subs: Manclark, Ketteridge, Killen, D. Shaw.
Cook Islands: Toa, Shepherd, Paita, Tuaru, Tariu, Bowen (c), Davys, Hunter, Cuthers, Temu, Kermonde, Henry, Noovao.
Subs: Tangimeta, Tini, Matapo, Jack.
Scorers:
Scotland: Tries: A. Tait 2; Goal: Thompson.
Cook Islands: Tries: Tariu 2, Shepherd 2; Goals: Noovao 2; Drop goal: Davys.
Referee: Colin Morris (England)

Group One final table:	P	W	L	F	A	Pts
Cooks Islands	3	3	0	143	36	6
Scotland	3	2	1	82	46	4
Russia	3	1	2	57	118	2
USA	3	0	3	48	130	0

Cook Islands beat Ireland 22-6 in the final at Bury.

7. Super League World Nines – an adventure into the unknown

With the 1995 Super League war splitting the world of Rugby League into two camps, one being paid by Rupert Murdoch and the other - the Australian Rugby League and a few others - by Kerry Packer, shows of supposed strength were on display wherever you looked. So much so that more international events took place in the mid-nineties than ever before. Sadly, by the end of the decade, international Rugby League was on its knees, with millions of pounds having been wasted.

But at least it gave Scotland an opportunity on the world stage. England's major clubs had signed up with Murdoch's Super League, and plans proceeded to re-launch the game in the summer of 1996 after an abridged Centenary Season in the winter. A few weeks before Super League (Europe) was due to start, the Scots were invited to Super League's World Nines in Fiji, in February 1996, their debut in a senior international tournament.

Manager George Fairbairn went with almost the same pick-and-mix squad which had gone so near to qualifying for the Emerging Nations final the previous year, a fine reward for all the hard work put in by volunteer players, coaches and officials. Alan Tait was the one big name absentee and with most of the world's top stars descending on the island, Scotland's international greenhorns knew they would be up against it.

Fairbairn's report of the trip in the RFL's *Scotland RL Newsletter* outlined: "It was the start of an historic adventure when, on a cold February day, the Scotland Rugby League players boarded a plane at London's Heathrow - destination Fiji. The long flight was helped by a 24-hour stopover in Los Angeles, where the boys took the opportunity to have a quick look at tinsel town's favourite sights on the Beverly Hills tour. We eventually reached Fiji after the 12-hour flight and, after a brief period of rest and relaxation, we got down to the serious business of training and preparation."

A very brief rest according to all reports. Scotland got off the plane, embarked on the trip from hell to the hotel in Suva - three hours in a rickety bus in the early hours of the morning on terrible roads with a driver unaware of the stress his driving abilities were causing his passengers - checked in and were immediately sent out to the training pitch to shake off the cobwebs. There was no need to warm-up - it was boiling.

"It was hell," Graeme Thompson told a Scottish newspaper. "Most of us have never felt such heat, let alone played in it." But they struggled on and Thompson was boosted by seeing himself on promotional posters for the event alongside Mal Meninga!

"We were well treated and George Graham in particular was well impressed. At one point lounging by the pool he expressed his incredulity at the beautiful surroundings. 'I cannae believe it all,' he exclaimed. I wonder if he could still not believe his even more salubrious treatment - staying in top hotels, plenty of free gear and being very well paid - when he became an international union player. Did he tell those team-mates that he 'couldnae believe it' then either?"

Fairbairn recalled: "Our aim was simple. We had three days in blistering 100 degree temperatures to be ready to face the best teams in the world. Then the big day arrived amid much pomp and ceremony."

Scotland got off to a great start with a hard-earned 12-6 victory over the similarly inexperienced USA Patriots, coached by former London Crusaders and New Zealand coach Tony Gordon and including only a few of the regular internationals who would play for the USA Tomahawks over the next five years. However, seven of their squad were familiar to the Scots, having lined up against them at Northampton a few months earlier in the Emerging Nations tournament: Terrance Wallace, Keith Cassidy, Fred Gruhler, David Bowe, Britton Coffman, Greg Stelluti and Mike Evergin.

"We had a scrub team virtually in those days," explained Evergin, when interviewed in Hawaii in 2001. "We didn't know that much but we had a Kiwi coach who got a good feeling going in the camp. In fact, he had us playing with a tennis ball - he wouldn't let us practice with a rugby ball! And you know what, we didn't drop the ball once in the tournament."

Western Samoa

The rain arrived as Scotland prepared to play Max McCamish's Western Samoa, which included the likes of Tea Ropati and Willie Poching.

Thompson remembered: "I was standing waiting to receive kick-off and I looked down and thought that the grass was moving as the green was jumping around. On a second look I released there were loads of frogs on the pitch jumping around. It was like a pond to them."

Despite putting in a fine, dogged display, Scotland were very unlucky to lose 8-4 against a very strong Samoan outfit.

Next up in their Group of Death, just an hour later, were Australia. Scotland versus Australia - for real. "This was a highlight for all of us as we got to play against some of the legends of the game," admitted Thompson. "They had Wendell Sailor, Ricky Stuart, Glen Lazarus, Laurie Daley and Steve Renouf. Thankfully Meninga was only the coach. I was on the wing and found myself, due to it being nines, 15 metres away from my nearest team-mate, Darrall Shelford inside me, and 15 metres outside me to touch, with the legendary Steve Renouf standing opposite me - a tricky situation.

Renouf got the ball and I tackled him. I was too involved to hear the referee shout that the tackle was complete that when he got up I tackled him again. Penalty against us and I think they scored a try from it. But to hang with that, I had tackled Steve Renouf!"

A 26-6 scoreline saw Scotland "beaten, but not disgraced" as Fairbairn put it. "It was realistic to expect Scotland to conceded 40-50 points but the team played their hearts out and really made the Australians work for their win". He was right to be pleased: Australia's squad also included legends Allan Langer and Andrew Ettingshausen, as well as test stars Brett Mullins, Jason Hetherington, Michael Hancock and David Furner. Renouf, who went on to star for Wigan at the turn of the century, scored two tries, Robbie Beckett, Lazarus, Stuart and Sailor one each. Furner kicked a goal.

Such was the nature of the Fiji Nines that world superstars rubbed shoulders with amateurs who had little Rugby League experience. This was epitomised by Scotland themselves, where students Thompson and Ali Blee lined up with famous names like Billy McGinty and Shelford.

"The big difference between us and the big boys is fitness," claims Mike Evergin. "These guys are like NFL athletes. And they run so low in the backs that you can't tackle them high or they'll go straight through you. When we played the top teams, we met up with them afterwards and realised they were million-dollar players. I'd only got my plane fare!"

After three games in five hours, Scotland - with several amateurs and part-timers in their ranks - were exhausted and were relieved to get the next day off because of the heavy downpours before coming back for finals day. "Unfortunately Ali Blee missed all three days," recalls Thompson. "He had been advising George Fairbairn what we should be eating during our time there. He was very exact about the type of food between matches. Unfortunately, he had eaten something dodgy and so our 'nutrition advisor' missed the games because of food poisoning!"

Fairbairn's boys were in the Plate Competition, for the teams that had finished third in each group, but a 4-14 defeat by Fiji meant they ended their trip with a play-off against Italy, a side consisting of Sydney-based Australians of Italian descent and Italians who played in France. Professional Rugby League has disappeared in Italy since development in the 1950s and early 1960s, to be superseded by Rugby Union.

Considering Italy had only lost 4-0 to England in their group, Scotland finished on a real high by spanking the Italians 34-0, Thompson touching down twice and Scott Gilmour, Sean Cusack and Danny Russell also scoring, with Steve Tait knocking over five goals. It was a fine note to end a tremendous eye-opening trip.

George Fairbairn concluded: "After three days' rest and relaxation, we headed home feeling reasonably satisfied with our efforts. Our attitude and commitment was superb, team spirit between professional players excellent. Everyone gave 100 percent - especially Darrall Shelford, who [as captain] led by example, always talking and encouraging his players. The future looks bright for Scotland Rugby League."

National Stadium, Suva City, Fiji
Thursday 22 February 1996: Pool A
Scotland 12 USA 6; Scotland 4 Western Samoa 8; Scotland 6 Australia 26
Saturday 24 February 1996
Plate Semi-finals: Scotland 4 Fiji 14; **Plate Play-off**: Scotland 34 Italy 0
Scotland squad: Chris Simmers, Alistair Blee, Nick Mardon, Darrall Shelford, James Cowan, Graeme Thompson, Darren Shaw, Danny Russell, Bill McGinty, Gary Murdock, Steve Tait, George Graham, Sean Cusack, Billy Gamba.
Coach: Scott Gilmour. Manager: George Fairbairn.

Training at the World 9s (Photo: Graeme Thompson)

World 9s team meeting, led by coach George Fairbairn. From left: Steve Tait, Ally Blee, George Graham, Chris Simmers, Darrall Shelford, Billy McGinty. (Photo: Graeme Thompson)

Scotland versus Ireland, Firhill Stadium, August 1996 (Photo: Mike Haddon)

Scotland versus France, Firhill Stadium, July 1997. Lord Provost of Glasgow, Pat Lally meets Phil Veivers. Introduction by skipper Danny Russell.
(Photo: Ian Watson)

8. Internationals 1996 to 1999

The decision by the International Federation to reward Scotland for their success at the 1995 Emerging Nations World Cup with full international status meant the RFL could begin organising senior internationals for Scotland for the first time.

Graeme Thompson recalls: "After the Super League Nines in Fiji - an attempt to show the new world order what Super League would offer when the Super League war was at its height - the final phase of this period of international exposure was the first ever home Scotland international. It was all part of continuing to raise the game's profile and it marked the return of Alan Tait to Scotland. Coupled with it being in the summer and therefore a lull in football and Rugby Union playing, we received great media coverage."

Indeed, the Scottish media gave the event extensive preview inches. 'We're Really Scrumthing! - RL Bravestart Cry' crowed *The Sun*; 'We'll Shel-Shock Irish' said the *Daily Record*.

With the eligibility rules being altered a couple of years earlier to allow third-generation descendants to represent the land of their grandparents, and no restrictions on the number of professionals who could play, Scotland coach George Fairbairn could have selected a new team of professionals. Instead he stuck by most of the players who had taken Scotland from a scratch student squad to an international outfit, for the inaugural official full international for both Scotland and Ireland.

Friendly: Scotland 26 Ireland 6
6 August 1996, Firhill Park, Glasgow, attendance: 1,147.

Fairbairn was fully vindicated in selecting six players who had no professional League experience as Scotland still had enough quality to see off Ireland on a damp Tuesday night at Firhill. Scotland led 14-0 at the break, having taken the lead after just five minutes when Alan Tait, the most illustrious player on view, touched down, with Sheffield Eagles' youngster Matt Crowther converting.

Ireland then settled down and kept the Scots at bay until the 21st minute when Carlisle hooker Danny Russell scored, followed on the stroke of half-time, by London Broncos' Australian-born forward Darren

Shaw, although Crowther failed to kick either goal. Shaw was then immediately replaced by Scott Gilmour of Dundee Institute, and a prime player for Scotland Students. History was made in the 52nd minute when Lee Hanlan scored Ireland's first official try, converted by winger Phelim Comerford. But Martin Ketteridge, by then playing prop for Halifax Blue Sox, kicked a penalty on 64 minutes and Scotland regained the initiative, mainly thanks to Irish indiscipline. Three Ireland players were sin-binned by referee Stuart Cummings; James Lowes for dissent, Bernard Dwyer for obstruction and Hanlan for deliberate offside.

Scotland took advantage with a flurry of points in the closing nine minutes as Darrall Shelford and Nick Mardon (soon to join Shaw at London Broncos) both touched down, Ketteridge converting the first try.

Lee Milner was voted 'man-of-the-match' after some powerful running and strong defence in Scotland's second row, while Tait was excellent at full-back, pulling off two spectacular try-saving tackles - increasing his profile after telling the Scottish media that he was unhappy at Leeds and wanted to join a professional Scottish Union club .

The crowd of just more than 1,000 was impressed, as was RFL chief executive Maurice Lindsay. He said afterwards: "We've got a genuine beginning and we'll build upon it."

Most Rugby Union writers were hugely impressed by the display. 'Scots in a different league' claimed *The Scotsman* in a back-page splash. 'On the evidence of last night's performance, rugby league has a future in Scotland,' wrote Alan Campbell in the *Daily Mail*. 'Even without a crowd, what we witnessed was a damn sight better than much of the winter entertainment served up at the same stadium.'

Scotland: A. Tait, Thompson, Shelford, Mardon, Cowan, Crowther, Keenan, Gamba, Ketteridge, D. Shaw, Russell, Milner, Cusack. Subs: Simes, Murdock, Blee, S. Gilmour.
Ireland: Foy, Comerford, Child, Hanlan, Gordon, Garth, Crompton (c), Casey, McCallion, Dwyer, Moffatt, Burgess, Lowes. Subs: Wyvill, Cleary, Doyle, Kennedy.
Scorers:
Scotland: Tries: Tait, Russell, Shelford, Mardon; Goals: Crowther 3, Ketteridge 2.
Ireland: Try: Hanlan; Goal: Comerford.
Referee: Stuart Cummings (England)

Graeme Thompson outlined the changes that had occurred in the Scottish set-up: "This game marked the last mixed team of students and professionals. Only Stuart McCarthy of the students played in the following season's international against France. This was always a natural progression. The period from summer 1995 to 1996 was the catalyst for the development of Rugby League in Scotland on many fronts. It was also a very exciting time for those involved and unique in the blend of people and their playing backgrounds that were brought together to represent Scotland on the international stage."

Friendly: Scotland 20 France 22
9 July 1997, Firhill Park, Glasgow, attendance: 2,233.

The headlines said it all: 'Referee blows time on Scots' history hopes' - *Daily Mail*. 'Scots in rage at bungling whistler' - *The Sun*. French ref Thierry Alibert was at the centre of controversy, after awarding a try to France that cruelly snatched the victory away from Scotland. He allowed Arnaud Dulac to score the match-winning try, with just seconds remaining on the clock, after a most blatant knock-on by a French player 25 metres from the Scots' line.

Although Scotland then fumbled the loose ball, a scrum should have been ordered for the first error. English touch judge Peter Walton signalled exactly that but Alibert ignored him.

Referees' director Greg McCallum said: "An obvious error took place which changed the outcome of the game. The touch judge clearly indicated an infringement, but in a moment of excitement, the referee decided to go with his own instincts. The guy's distraught about it and realises that he has made a mistake."

There were no suggestions of bias. Earlier in the game, Alibert, who was otherwise perfectly competent, disallowed a French try by forward Jacques Pech for a double movement.

Scotland, missing Alan Tait who strained a groin while starring on the British Lions Union tour of South Africa the previous week, had the better of the early exchanges, but failed to convert this into points and it was France who were first on the scoreboard when Wakefield's Freddie Banquet went under the posts in the 17th minute, after a Dulac break down the right wing.

59

Scotland hit back almost immediately, with two tries. Danny Russell began and ended a smart move involving debutant Jim McLaren, and three minutes later, Paul Carr and Nick Mardon combined cleverly to send in Gary Christie to touch down out wide.

But right on the stroke of half-time, substitute Jerome Guisset - later to play for Warrington in Super League – scored under the posts, to give the French a 12-10 lead at the break.

When Mardon dropped Pierre Chamorin's high kick allowing Fabien Devecchi to extend the lead to 18-10 just after the restart, France seemed to be taking control. But the Scots were not finished.

First, Stuart McCarthy crossed out wide, but crucially too far out for Matt Crowther to convert. Then, with just 10 minutes to go, Crowther went over and converted his own try to put Scotland 20-18 in front. Both tries were instigated by smart play by veteran Huddersfield stand-off Phil Veivers, making his Scotland debut at the age of 33. That was almost twice the age of fellow new boy John Duffy, making his international bow just seven days after his 17th birthday, a world record. But then came Dulac's dubious try, which gave coach Ivan Greseque's French side the victory at 22-20.

"The guys are all gutted about it and I am gutted for them," admitted Fairbairn. "They had come back so well after a mediocre first half. The way the guys played for each other, after only getting together for the first time yesterday, was really impressive." The history books will show this as a win for France, but the moral victory was certainly with Scotland.

Scotland: Mardon, McCarthy, Crowther, McLaren, Christie, Veivers, Duffy, Neill, Russell, Laughton, G. Bell, Carr, Solomon. Subs: Higgins, Dixon, McKelvie, Duncan.
France: Bourrel, Banquet, Dulac, Vergniol, Pastre-Courtine, Garcia, Devecchi, Teixido, Tena, Cabestany, Pech, Tallec, Chamorin. Subs: Cambres, El Khalouki, Guisset, Verges.
Scorers:
Scotland: Tries: Russell, Christie, McCarthy, Crowther. Goals: Crowther (2).
France: Tries: Banquet, Guisset, Devecchi, Dulac. Goals: Vergniol (3).
Referee: Thierry Alibert (France)

Scotland in European tournaments

Clash of the Nations 1998

When France collapsed to a record 73-6 defeat to England at Gateshead in 1996, it signalled the end - yet again - of the European Championship. France were no longer strong enough to give England's full-timers a worthy game and in 1997, the French were pointed in the direction of new boys Ireland and Scotland instead.

Unfortunately, but typically, because Ireland and Scotland did not meet in 1997 the opportunity to trumpet a new-look Euro Championship was missed, as England and Wales lay dormant.

The 'Clash of the Nations' was arranged to make November a month of international Rugby League, alongside the three-match series between Great Britain and New Zealand. Sadly, the RFL showed their usual vision. To avoid clashing with the glut of Rugby Union internationals, the League games were played at night. Thus, pitiful crowds in Dublin and Glasgow merely made League fans grateful that the media all-but ignored the matches, rather than mocking them. However, they did miss some classic encounters.

In the tournament's first game, on 4 November, Ireland lost 22-24 to France at Dublin's Tolka Park despite Irish debutant Shaun Edwards having a superb game for his 'new' nation. He had previously represented England.

Victory for France - who featured three of the Villeneuve side who had won the Treize Tournoi against Lancashire Lynx just four days before the Ireland game - would give them the title.

France 26 Scotland 22
11 November 1998, Stade Jean Laffon, Perpignan, attendance: 3,700.

Scotland's new coach Billy McGinty did his best to fulfil his promise in The Herald to field "the strongest ever Scotland squad", 16 months on from their last game, since which several players had joined Scotland's two professional union clubs. Only John Duffy, P. J. Solomon and skipper Danny Russell survived, and there were fewer late withdrawals because the Super League season was over. However, Dale Laughton was away, playing for Great Britain.

Despite being a new team, with a quarter of the game to go it appeared that Scotland were going to upset the form book with a surprise win and spoil the party for the crowd of nearly 4,000. They had gone ahead after just six minutes when one debutant - Lee Penny - created an opening for another, Jason Flowers, to score. Although Freddie Banquet, one of the Villeneuve champions and the match-winner against Ireland, drew France level four minutes later, man of the match Penny inspired Scotland to lead once more. The Warrington full back sent Danny Arnold on a scorching run to touch down with 18 minutes on the clock.

When Solomon's break created an opening for Jason Roach to make it 16-8 with less than half-an-hour gone, Scotland were on top.

However, French winger Claude Sirvent followed up a Banquet kick to narrow the lead to just four points just before the break, and Scotland tired in the face of an aggressive showing by the French forwards. With 25 minutes left, Jean-Marc Garcia, who had moved out to the centres, exploited that fatigue when he finished off a break by young winger Gilles Gironella to give France, coached by Gilles Dumas and Patrick Pedrazzani, the lead for the first time.

That was short-lived as Roach touched down again to put Scotland's noses in front on the hour mark but when Eric Vergniol scored three minutes later, Scotland had no reply. Garcia's try 10 minutes from time confirmed a home victory.

Most of the Scots had not played for at least six weeks while the French were surprisingly sharp despite playing a fourth game in 10 days. "Fatigue took its toll and a few of our players switched off," admitted McGinty to *Open Rugby* magazine. "I was pleased by our first-half performance when we tackled well and attacked well. But in the second half we didn't control the ball, had a poor kicking game and didn't defend all that well."

Scotland: Penny, Roach, Campbell, Arnold, Flowers, Orr, Duffy, D. Shaw, Russell, Berry, Wainwright, Solomon, N. Graham. Subs: Hewitt, G. Shaw, Knox, Wilson.
France: Banquet, Sirvent, Vergniol, Dulac, Gironella, Garcia, Devecchi, Sands, Wulf, El Khalouki, Sort, Frayssinet, Jampy. Subs: Banet, Carrasco, Tamghart, Teixido.
Scorers:

Scotland: Tries: Roach (2), Flowers, Arnold; Goals: Duffy (3).
France: Tries: Garcia (2), Banquet, Sirvent, Vergniol; Goals: Banquet (3).
Referee: Bob Connolly (England)

Scotland 10 Ireland 17
18 November 1998, Firhill, Glasgow, attendance: 1,028.

France had shown what rewards you could get from working as a close squad. Many of them had been together since Paris St Germain's Super League days, including their two 'imports', Aussie prop Jason Sands and Samoan-Kiwi hooker Vincent Wulf - while Scotland and Ireland had been almost thrown together in the off-season.

A week after France lifted the title, Scotland met Ireland for the first time since their inaugural official international two years earlier. Scotland were still without Laughton, who was injured in Great Britain's drawn third test with the Kiwis at Watford just four days earlier, but Ireland were able to give a long-awaited debut to Terry O'Connor and included Wigan flier Gary Connolly, both of whom had played in the New Zealand test series.

Instead of playing the 'Clash of the Nations' in-between the Lions internationals to keep the nation's sporting mind on Rugby League, or even before them as an international aperitif, the decision to play the deciding game after the Lord Mayor's Show was a major mistake.

Only a thousand intrigued spectators turned up at Firhill, a hugely disappointing figure given the increased profile of the Scotland team. Indeed, the game itself was an anticlimax for the home fans, who had been treated to the rare sight of a mute swan rising from the Forth and Clyde Canal behind the city-end terrace and flying the length of

Match Publicity (Courtesy RFL)

63

the pitch just before kick-off - and to think the Americans pay a fortune to put on pre-match displays of considerably less beauty and dignity.

With Scottish development officer Graeme Thompson having recently left for London Broncos, ticket sales were poor. Throw in the usual appalling weather, and a pre-match fire alarm caused by a chip pan blaze under a stand and the walk-up crowd was minimal. However, the show went on, not that there was much to celebrate from Scotland's point of view. Despite a battling first-half display in which they put the star-studded Irish under severe pressure, Scotland went in 6-0 down thanks to centre Richard Smith's try and Tommy Martyn's conversion. Scotland would have been on the board, though, had it not been for a fantastic piece of defending by Connolly after Joe Berry chased his own grubber kick.

By the time Duffy dummied his way through to the try-line on the hour mark, Scotland were playing catch-up football, Martyn having regathered his own kick six minutes after the break to put the Irish 10 points clear and on their way to their first official senior victory. Martyn and Smith combined to put Mark Foster in for another Irish try and Martin Crompton's field goal sealed victory for the visitors.

But it was fitting that Scotland sent their few fans home happy with a superb consolation try in injury time, Logan Campbell finishing off P. J. Solomon's pass to give the scoreline more respectability. O'Connor won the *Open Rugby*-sponsored Man of the Match award in a game perhaps most significant, retrospectively, for the debut of Colin Wilson. When the Linlithgow Lions man replaced Mike Wainwright on 31 minutes and played until 15 minutes into the second half, he became the first Scottish Conference player to represent his country at the highest level.

Scotland: Penny, Roach, N. Graham, Campbell, Arnold, Orr, Duffy, D. Shaw, Russell, Berry, Knox, Solomon, Wainwright. Subs: Dixon, G. Shaw, Flowers, Wilson.
Ireland: Prescott, Carney, Connolly, R. Smith, Forster, Martyn, Crompton, O'Connor, Lawless, McDermott, Harmon, Cassidy, Burgess. Subs: Child, Eccles, O'Sullivan, Gray.
Scorers:
Scotland: Tries: Duffy, Campbell ; Goal: Duffy.
Ireland: Tries: Smith, Martyn, Foster; Goals: Martyn (2); Drop Goal: Crompton.
Referee: John Connolly (England)

Lincoln Financial Group Triangular Challenge 1999

A year after the last tri-nations tournament which had been a great success on the pitch but a flop off it, it would have been fair to expect the RFL to plan the follow-up diligently and avoid making the same mistakes. Instead, they made even more naive, inexcusable decisions.

With England, minus their Great Britain contingent, playing France home and away before the French hosted the World Cup qualifiers, that left the Celtic nations to play a round-robin tournament.

The three international matches were arranged to coincide with Great Britain's trip down under, an understandable idea, knowing that only Dale Laughton would be missing from the Scotland squad (although Wales and Ireland suffered heavier withdrawals). But Super League had ended three weeks earlier, the football and Rugby Union seasons were in full swing, League fans were hardly on a high after watching Great Britain get heavily defeated in Australia that morning, and playing on a Friday night may work on balmy summer evenings, but there are many other attractions in Glasgow in October when the weekend starts.

Scotland 36 Wales 16
22 October 1999, Firhill, Glasgow, attendance 667.

Just 667 on-lookers were found rattling around Partick Thistle's neat stadium, lying beneath Ruchill Park in the north of the city. At Glasgow Bulls' Hillhead ground, just 10 minutes drive away, that number would have looked respectable rather than embarrassing. Instead, the players did well to put on a show in front of a crowd familiar in size only to those who had played Alliance rugby recently. And yet, according to the BBC, RFL officials declared themselves satisfied with the turnout!

Thankfully for Scotland, the game was far more successful than the event. Despite new coach Shaun McRae fielding eight new faces, six of them from the start, Scotland had the upper hand from the off. Wales, who were without Iestyn Harris and Keiron Cunningham on Great Britain duty, had lost the competition's opening game against Ireland in Swansea the previous week (watched by a tiny figure of 812, just four years after 15,385 saw them beat Western Samoa there in the World Cup - sadly that 812 was the highest crowd of this competition). Wales showed their familiar spirit and took some killing off before Scotland pulled away to leave Wales with the wooden spoon. The more experienced Scotland side were the most creative, but it was Leeds' teenager Scott Rhodes, showing incredible confidence at halfback, who dictated play despite never having played a Rhinos' first team game.

Scotland took a deserved lead when Danny Arnold took Andy Craig's inside pass to cut in from the wing and race over the try line. But Wales drew level for the first of three times when Martin Pearson evaded the cover after halfback partner Lee Briers had sent him clear.

Rival skippers Danny Russell and Neil Cowie crossed within two minutes of each other to maintain parity, although Scotland led at the interval courtesy of an injury-time try from substitute Andrew Lambert.

Seven minutes after the re-start, Wales came back yet again, Briers dummying his way over from close range. But they could not keep Scotland at bay, Mike Wainwright finishing off a move which started in the Scottish half and passed through the hands of debut-making Queenslander David Maiden, Jason Roach and Nathan Graham before Wainwright finished off with a 20- metre sprint to the line.

For the first time, Wales had no response. The battle had taken it out of them and the excellent Matt Crowther nabbed the next try, following his own kick-through and beating Pearson to the final touch. Crowther also kicked four goals, while a second try for Workington youngster Lambert - promoted from the Scottish Students side - ensured Scotland went past Ireland's seven point victory margin in Swansea. A draw in Dublin would give the Scots the title on points difference. As Wales faded, Arnold widened the margin to 20 points, pouncing to touch down as the ball dribbled towards the dead-ball line.

Scotland: N. Graham, Roach, Maiden, Craig, Arnold, Crowther, S. Rhodes, Cram, Russell, McDonald, D. Shaw, Anderson, Wainwright. Subs: Lambert, Duffy, Berry, Lowe.
Wales: Davis, Smith, Gibson, Thomas, Lee, Pearson, Briers, Makin, Watson, Cowie, Morley, Highton, Hammond. Subs: Eaton, Price, Eyres, Lockwell.
Scorers:
Scotland: Tries: Arnold 2, Lambert 2, Crowther, Russell, Wainwright; Goals: Crowther 4.
Wales: Tries: Briers, Cowie, Pearson; Goals: Briers 2.
Referee: John Connolly (England)

Ireland 31 Scotland 10
31 October 1999, Tolka Park, Dublin, attendance 385.

Having seen the World Cup draw only days earlier, both countries knew that not only the Triangular Challenge title, but a psychological boost ahead of their World Cup clash was at stake. Incredible then, that the Irish fans vanished into hiding. A pitiful 385 turned up at Tolka, an embarrassing attendance at Ireland's Rugby League home.

Ireland included Terry O'Connor and Mick Cassidy, who were getting some international rugby after missing out with the hapless Great Britain squad down under, but the most amazing appearances were that of Gary Connolly and Barrie McDermott, both of whom had played in the 26-4 defeat by the Kiwis in Auckland just two days earlier. The time difference allowed both players to make the 24-hour flight home straight after that game and be in Dublin for Sunday, albeit jet-lagged and stiff.

Both sides were without one player each who had faced the Kiwis. Scotland were missing Dale Laughton again while Ryan Sheridan did not appear for Ireland. Having rehearsed *Flower of Scotland* for the first time, Scotland's players were dismayed to hear the high school marching band, with triangles and kazoos, launch into *Scotland the Brave*. Most players were flummoxed. Perhaps they never recovered.

Ireland took the initiative and never let go, with Super League stars Tommy Martyn, alongside Martin Crompton at halfback, O'Connor and Cassidy outstanding. O'Connor's fantastic display, which ended when he was injured 20 minutes from time, was all the more impressive in that he heard his brother had broken a vertebrae in his neck in a car crash just a couple of hours before kick-off.

Scotland were by no means disgraced. Indeed, thanks to tries from Russell and Arnold and a Crowther conversion, they were level at 10-10 with an hour gone and the game was there for the taking, although it was always likely that Ireland's team of stars would pull through. In the event, they roared away, blitzing Scotland for 21 points in the final quarter.

However, coach McRae was not despondent. "It has given us a great indication of who can handle it at this level," he told *Rugby League World*, a warning as to his axe-wielding ahead of the World Cup. "We were up against a more determined and intense team than against Wales and, at crucial times where we might have scored against Wales, we didn't against Ireland. I saw a lot of things [against Wales] which I didn't see again. But we are still on a learning curve and the players know how hard it is to back up from a winning performance. I was more disappointed in the scoreline because we had the opportunities to win, even when we were 21-10 down."

Scotland: N. Graham, Roach, Maiden, Craig, Arnold, Crowther, S. Rhodes, Cram, Russell, Neill, D. Shaw, W. McDonald, Wainwright. Subs: Lambert, Anderson, Berry, Lowe.
Ireland: Prescott, Carney, Connolly, Smith, Forster, Martyn, Crompton, O'Connor, Lawless, McDermott, Harmon, Cassidy, Burgess. Subs: Child, Eccles, O'Sullivan, Gray .
Scorers:
Scotland: Tries: Russell, Arnold; Goal: Crowther.
Ireland: Tries: Lawless, Harmon, Prescott, Carney, Forster, Smyth; Goals: Martyn (2), Harmon; Drop Goal: Martyn.
Referee: Karl Kirkpatrick (England)

9. The 2000 Rugby League World Cup: spreading the net

If it were not for the Super League war, Scotland would not have competed at the twelfth World Cup. Despite their impressive showing at the Emerging Nations tournament in 1995, and in internationals immediately afterwards, Scotland were initially excluded. But when the tournament was delayed while the ARL and Super League patched up their differences and organised the launch of the NRL, Scotland were invited to an expanded, 16-team, World Cup in autumn 2000. Although the news made little impact north of the border, the RFL made plans to field a Scotland team capable of competing with the best in the world.

They re-appointed the most successful coach in Super League to take on the task of leading Scotland: Shaun McRae. He had achieved tremendous success with St Helens, winning three trophies in two seasons before being replaced by Ellery Hanley. He then launched Gateshead Thunder into Super League with fellow Australian Shane Richardson as chief executive. 'Richo' became Scotland manager.

McRae, who played cricket with Warrington fan Neil Fairbrother while coaching at Canberra Raiders, had previously coached on two Kangaroos tours, been assistant to the Kiwis at the 1995 World Cup and Great Britain in the 1997 Super League Ashes series. His first two games with Scotland in November 1999 had been low key, and he kept it that way in the build-up to the World Cup.

McRae and Richardson trawled through the NRL and Super League for Scottish-qualified players who had previously had no involvement, hoping to increase the standard of the squad to compete in a tough group which had no clear favourite and no make-weights: Scotland faced Samoa, Ireland and the New Zealand Maori.

"Maybe we haven't been quite as proactive (as Ireland) in terms of meeting as a group, but that's deliberate," McRae told *Rugby League World* magazine. "My view is that there's no point meeting as a group of 40 when some of the guys aren't going to make it." McRae failed to add that many of his initial 38-man preliminary pool were based down under and could not meet up in Britain anyway!

When McRae revealed his hand, many League fans were shocked at its strength. His new-look Scotland squad contained nine top grade players who had never represented the country before: NRL-based Australians Geoff Bell, Daniel Heckenberg and Scott Logan; Super League Australians Mat Daylight, Graham Mackay and Adrian Vowles; English born and bred Lee Gilmour, Richard Horne and Richard Fletcher. Only Darren Shaw survived from inaugural game in 1995.

McRae had earmarked even more NRL stars for selection only to see them pull out, several in order to get themselves fit for the 2001 campaign. After all, in this game, club comes before country. He had to replace former Kangaroos Paul McGregor of St George-Illawarra and Tim Brasher of North Queensland Cowboys (who thought he had an outside chance of an Australia call-up), Newcastle Knights's Billy Peden, Parramatta Eels' starlet Ian Hindmarsh (brother of Kangaroo Nathan) and Steve Carter, who later joined Widnes Vikings from Penrith Panthers. Wests Tigers' Mark Stimson was also out of the equation, along with Hull's Logan Campbell. Instead, McRae was working with talented young players from the Northern Ford Premiership, like Featherstone's Brisbaner Michael Rhodes.

"It's opened the door for some of the younger players to make a real name for themselves," wrote McRae optimistically on *PlayTheBall.com*. "I've got an 18-year-old in Richard Horne, two 19-year-olds in Scott Rhodes and Richard Fletcher – what a great occasion for those guys if they manage to get on the field. And even if they don't, what a great learning curve, a tremendous way for them to benefit them as individual players."

While the Irish Rugby League were given a certain degree of autonomy from the RFL, and support from their local media, Scotland's team was seen as an impostor on Scottish culture, a fake, a fraud. The reason? The final squad for the tournament included not one player born in Scotland, not one with a Scottish accent, playing for an Australian coach and manager.

Understandably, the Scottish media had a couple of digs at the set-up and then walked away, wanting nothing to do with a team purporting to represent their readers and yet full of Sassanachs.

That all these players bar one – the highly-dubious selection of Horne, whose grandfather was born in the Isle of Man – had Scottish blood from either parents or grandparents was not deemed qualification enough. Even without Horne and the other condemned selection, Graham Mackay, who had been capped by Australia, Scotland would not have been accepted by the Scottish. The eligibility envelope may have been pushed too far.

David Hopps, writing in *The Guardian's* World Cup Preview, claimed: "the only Glen most (Scotland players) have ever come into contact with is the bonzer bloke they crack a tinnie with down the boozer". But after seeing the squad rehearse *Flower of Scotland* at their West Yorkshire training camp, Mackay told Hopps that: "if you are picked for a representative side, you do your best. To the older blokes it is a nice little bonus, to the youngsters it is a chance to make an impact".

Clearly, no players raised on the Scottish game were of high enough standard to play in the World Cup. However, the RFL made another bad call when allowing McRae to pick his strongest possible squad, hoping the public would get behind them for a high profile clash with either Australia or England in the quarter-finals.

Scottish sports fans tolerate imported players but not when they make up the *whole* team. If McRae had picked the best two players with Scottish accents – probably from the Students squad – and taken them along for the ride, their presence at media events would have created an entirely different public perception of the Scotland team. They would also have benefited hugely from the experience. The same goes for Wales and Ireland, who had only a couple of home-grown players each. The Celtic nations should have been allowed larger squads in order to include some local talent. The cost of carrying a couple of extra players would have far outweighed the media value and public interest they would have gained. Scottish Development Officer Mark Senter admitted that visits by the Scotland team to local schools during the tournament would have done more harm than good. "The kids wouldn't have understood them," he said. "They'd have wondered who these Aussies are pretending to be Scottish." Instead, the Samoans went down a treat. That Gowanbank Primary, whose pupils were mascots at both matches in Scotland, have pictures on their wall of Samoa lining up before the Tynecastle clash rather than Scotland says it all.

However, the lambasting the 'Jockeroos' got in the press was hypocritical. At the time, Scotland's football team was captained by a

(The RLWC publicity leaflet. Courtesy RFL)

Geordie and included two Londoners, a Midlander, and a Scouser who was a former England Under-21 international. English accents were common and only the selection of Jamaican international, David Johnson (who was raised in Shropshire and had played for England Schoolboys) drew criticism for manager Craig Brown's recruitment policy.

Even worse was the Scottish Rugby Union squad, which included 11 'foreigners': among them captain Budge Pountney, a former England Under-21 international from Southampton, qualified for Scotland thanks to a grandma born in the Channel Islands; David Hilton, who played 41 times for Scotland before discovering his grandfather was from Bristol, not Edinburgh; and Shaun Longstaff, one of five 'Kilted Kiwis', who had no Scottish relatives, but still qualified through the ludicrous three-year residency rule (under which some of McRae's Australians had lived in England long enough to 'qualify' as Brits). There was no major complaint until 2001 when, having already added five more non-Scots (including Aussie Andrew Mower who had trained with England), coach Ian McGeechan (from Leeds) went a step too far, selecting New

Zealander Brendan Laney against the All Blacks just 10 days after arriving in the UK. The SRU had to close their own online chat rooms after it was jammed with protests. However, the presence of some true Scots in the side allowed the SRU to market the team as Scotland's own with flag-waving conviction, something denied the League team.

Scotland's chances

One constant in the Scotland Rugby League World Cup squad was captain Danny Russell, who would become Scotland's most capped player in senior internationals during the tournament: his last top grade rugby before retiring. He thought that "with the quality of players in the Scotland squad, there's no reason why we can't make the quarter-finals". It was a fair proposition. McRae believed that limited interchange and the freezing wet weather would hamper the southern hemisphere sides and give Scotland an advantage.

"I don't envy the Maoris and the Samoans," he said. "They are going to be coming to a cold day that will probably be wet as well. And the guys who have been playing in the NRL are going to have to play a lot more than they have been used to. Both these teams have some big players who are used to playing in bursts of eight, 10 or 12 minutes. With 10 or 12 interchanges in a match including bloodbins, they're going to have to play much longer bursts"

Staying at home

While England went to Florida, Ireland to Spain and Wales to South Africa, McRae opted to keep his squad in the UK rather than spend his limited budget on a warm weather training camp. Whisking the seven Australia-based players off on another flight as soon as they arrived in the UK, to play on the same hard grounds they had been playing on at home seemed pointless, especially as conditions would be entirely different during the World Cup.

McRae also declined the opportunity to play any warm-up matches, meaning Scotland had not played for a year. "I think we can stimulate enough drills and game-related activities to compensate," he reasoned in his *PlayTheBall* column. "My fear with playing games was that if you lose a player, you'll probably never forgive yourself.

"We've already had a number of pull-outs and can't afford any more. Of course, that can still happen in training but the chances are far less. And if you don't go into a practice match playing 100%, what's the point anyway?" With several players having been involved in the play-offs, Scotland's preparation time was limited but McRae arranged sessions for the English-based players before the whole squad headed to the training camp at Murrayfield a week before the tournament began.

Amid the limited media hype for the event, Danny Arnold accompanied the appallingly-named World Cup mascot Bluke Tryscorer on a promotional trip to Glasgow and Edinburgh shopping centres, and TV actress Samantha Janus, on the basis of her appearance in the Rugby League film *Up 'n Under*, was the star model at the kit launch, accompanying Lee Penny and Danny Russell for Scotland's photoshoot. The fact that all the home nations' kits were launched by the RFL in Leeds merely underlined the fact that Scotland could be seen as England's puppets on the international stage.

Now it was time for Scotland to break free.

Lincoln Financial Group Rugby League World Cup Group Four

Scotland 16 Aotearoa Maori 17
29 October 2000, Firhill Park, Glasgow, attendance: 2,008.

As well as being an extremely tough opening match for Scotland, the Maori's appearance at the World Cup made many fans uncomfortable. There were concerns at the presence of a racial group rather than a national team, although a similar claim could be made of Ireland, Lebanon, Italy (in the Emerging Nations) and even Scotland, all of whom had few players from their homeland but who were descendants of that nation's people, representing their 'blood ties'.

Known in New Zealand as Aotearoa Maori - "the people of the land of the long white cloud" - the Maori have been competing in the Pacific Cup since 1975, but they have never been granted full international status. Instead, they play tour matches, providing a high calibre of opposition, as a hapless Great Britain found in 1999 when they just squeezed past a below-strength Maori side 22-12 at the end of their disastrous Tri-Nations trip.

Part of the deal to get many of the finest Kiwis to sign for Rupert Murdoch's Super League clubs in the mid-1990s was that the Maori team would be at the next World Cup. Little did anyone know that unity in the game would mean all the top sides were at the next World Cup anyway, but the game's leaders felt that promises had to be kept.

"The determination of Maoris to play will be written in blood," predicted coach Cameron Bell, who was assisted by his son Dean (the former Kiwi star) and went on to coach Barrow after the tournament. With former Kiwi internationals Tawera Nikau, Gene Ngamu, Sean Hoppe, Terry Hermansson and Tyran Smith in their squad, plus 12 more former junior New Zealand internationals, this was basically the Kiwi second string. Scotland were in for a tough opening game.

The match

A physical battle between two closely-matched teams ended with Gene Ngamu's drop goal in the dying stages breaking Scottish hearts at a wet and windy Firhill. With the scores locked at 16-all and only seven minutes left, Ngamu coolly slotted a field goal from 20 metres out to give the Maori a 17-16 win after a superb Scottish fightback.

A mistake ridden and ill-tempered display by the Maori enabled Scotland to take a half-time lead, albeit only 6-4, but immediately after the break the Maori put in a surging performance, scoring two tries through impressive debutante Clinton Toopi and imposing centre David Kidwell to send them out to a 16-6 lead.

However, a gallant Scotland side didn't lie down and replied with two tries of their own to David Maiden and Geoff Bell; the latter making his debut, which tied the scores before Ngamu shattered Scotland's dream.

"We're devastated," said Scotland captain Danny Russell. "I think a draw would have been a fair result but we made too many mistakes which cost us in the end. We lost too much ball and we didn't use the conditions to our advantage."

Indeed. Despite the wintry weather which must have contributed to a lacklustre display from the Maori side, Scotland could not open up a defendable lead. Both sides made cautious but extremely physical starts with the forward packs putting in some thunderous hits in the pack. The Maori were denied a try by the video referee after Tahi Reihana was caught short of the line but two tackles later they opened the scoring through full-back Toopi. The young Auckland Warrior took advantage of some slack Scotland marking to crash over in the left hand corner, despite the best intentions of winger Lee Gilmour.

Scotland's full-back, Lee Penny, soon had his team level as he waltzed over the whitewash following an excellent passage of football close to the Maori line, orchestrated by teenager Richard Horne making his international debut. Graham Mackay slotted over the conversion for his only points in his one appearance for Scotland.

The slippery surface and stiff breeze made handling difficult and both sides struggled early on. Tempers also got the better of the Maori and at the end of the first-half, captain Tawera Nikau of Warrington Wolves was sin-binned along with Wayne McDonald for a bust-up that had threatened to flare for most of the first 40 minutes.

Although without their skipper, the Maori came out firing in the second spell and immediately Kidwell strolled over for the second try after being put through a huge gap by Ngamu. Just minutes later Toopi's impressive debut continued when he crossed for his second try after another well-worked move that had the Scotland defence bamboozled. Ngamu scored his second goal to give the Maori a ten-point lead.

Scotland refused to lie down, Maiden leading the comeback with a try that Mackay converted and then, moments later, the impressive loose-forward Vowles put Bell through to tie the scores. Scotland had the opportunity to take the lead but Crowther's conversion fell short, leaving Ngamu to complete the scoring with his match-winning drop-goal.

Scotland: Penny, Daylight, Mackay, G. Bell, L. Gilmour, Purcell, Horne, Heckenberg, Russell (c), Laughton, Logan, Cram, Vowles. Subs: Maiden, Crowther, W. McDonald, Shaw.
Aotearoa Maori: Toopi, Manuel, Kohe-Love, Kidwell, Hoppe, Ngamu, Te Rangi, Rauhihi, Perenara, Hermansson, Koopu, Smith, Nikau (c). Subs: Moana, Leuluai, Nahi, Reihana.
Scorers:
Scotland: Tries: Penny, Maiden, G. Bell; Goals: Mackay 2.
Aotearoa Maori: Tries: Toopi 2, Kidwell; Goals: Ngamu 2; Drop goal: Ngamu.
Referee: Stuart Cummings (England)

Ireland 18 Scotland 6
1 November 2000, Tolka Park, Dublin, attendance: 1,782.

Scotland's hopes of a dream quarter-final tie - a first-ever meeting with either Australia or England - all but disappeared with a hugely-disappointing performance at Shelbourne's football ground in Dublin. Scotland's second straight defeat meant they would be grasping at straws even if they beat the Samoans in their final group game.

"We did not play well but we still have a chance," admitted McRae on *PlayTheBall*. "We turned over a hell of a lot of football, far too much. We did not control the play and the penalty count was against us. I think there was something of a hangover from Sunday's game, no doubt whatsoever."

The turning point of the match came when the inspirational Adrian Vowles was sent to the sin-bin midway through the second-half for persistent offside. Moments earlier, Lee Gilmour knocked on with the Irish try line begging. Seconds later, Michael Withers struck with a try that gave Ireland a ten-point lead and killed Scotland off.

Scrum-half Ryan Sheridan had given Ireland the perfect start inside the first three minutes when Leeds club-mate and opposite number Scott Rhodes saw his attempt at a relieving kick rebound off the legs of Ireland loose-forward Luke Ricketson. The youngster attempted to recover the ball but could not stop it being kicked ahead for Sheridan to pounce for the try which Prescott converted.

Prescott then struck two penalties - the first for encroaching, the second for a high tackle - in the space of seven minutes to put the home side into a comfortable 10-point lead. But if Ireland had any thoughts they would cruise into the knock-out stage they were shattered by a Scots comeback.

Rhodes atoned for his early error to spearhead the fight back for the injury-hit visitors who knew defeat could spell the end of their campaign. Huddersfield full-back Danny Arnold, in for Lee Penny who, along with Andrew Purcell, failed a late fitness test, rounded off a stunning move. Vowles created the space for Gilmour, who expertly drew the defence before sending Arnold in for an uncontested try.

Left-wing Matt Crowther, playing instead of the injured Graham Mackay, added the conversion to cut the half-time deficit to just four points with Prescott missing a late penalty.

Ireland were clearly stung and dominated possession at the start of the second-half. It took a brave catch from Hull wing Mat Daylight on his own line to deny a clutch of Irishmen who were waiting to pounce on any dropped ball. Scotland need to score next but instead Ireland increased their advantage when Prescott rediscovered his direction to convert a penalty. For Scotland, the game was up.

Prescott added his fourth penalty minutes from the end to round off victory for Ireland, who had improved on their showing in the win over Samoa in Belfast the previous weekend, and left the Bravehearts pointless. "Having three games in a week has taken its toll, as predicted," McRae reflected. "Our sport does not allow you to play three games in a week and expect the standards to improve when you have got so many guys taking the field with bumps, bruises and knocks. I'd have liked to see the group games spread over 10 days or two weeks.

"Young Scott Rhodes was thrown in at the deep end, made a few mistakes early on but came good in the end. But with him at seven and Richard Horne at six, we had a 20-year-old and an 18-year-old and you are expecting them to run the game for you.

"We're not in a group like Australia and England where they have had their tough game and can now sit back. We have no respite from such physical encounters. There were a lot of guys out there who were not just physically but mentally tired as well," he outlined.

"We scored a tremendous try, it was a great bit of rugby, and unfortunately Ireland scored off our errors. The guys are disappointed. We thought after Sunday [against the Maori] we were unlucky and we could get something out of this group."

Scotland: Arnold, Daylight, L. Gilmour, G. Bell, Crowther, Horne, S. Rhodes, Heckenberg, Russell (c), Laughton, Logan, Cram, Vowles. Subs: N. Graham, Maiden, W. McDonald, Shaw.
Ireland: Prescott, Carney, Withers, Eager, Herron, Martyn, Sheridan, O'Connor, Lawless, McDermott (c), Joynt, Campion, Ricketson. Subs: Williams, Mathiou, Barnhill, Bradbury.
Scorers:
Scotland: Try: Arnold ; Goal: Crowther.
Ireland: Tries: Sheridan, Withers; Goals: Prescott 5.
Referee: Russell Smith (England)

The 2000 Rugby League World Cup Scotland team (Photo: David Williams)

Scotland 12 Samoa 20
5 November 2000, Tynecastle, Edinburgh, attendance: 1,579.

The Maori's surprise defeat by Samoa meant that despite losing their first two games, a win by two points would be enough to see Scotland into the quarter-finals and a clash with Australia at Watford. That carrot could have put some players off - terrified at the prospect of facing the world champions or too excited - because Scotland failed to take their chances and went down to a third straight defeat.

Samoa were now familiar with the weather and the interchange rules after losing the opening game of the tournament against Ireland in Belfast (a damp squib of an occasion broadcast live on BBC's *Grandstand* which set the tone for the rest of the World Cup: fantastic rugby played before empty stands in pouring rain). Having beaten the Maoris 21-16 in a thriller at Workington, culminating with two renditions of the haka for the exuberant crowd, Samoa were also one win away from the last eight.

Their young side bore little resemblance to the Samoans beaten in a ferocious battle by Wales at Swansea in the 1995 World Cup. Va'aiga Tuigamala, and Apollo Perelini had returned to Union, and only Hunslet's Willie Swann and Wakefield duo Willie Poching and Tony Tatupu survived from that classic.

They came into this tournament on the back of a series whitewashing by Fiji, but did add Poching and the exciting dreadlocked David Solomona to a squad which remains a source of talent for the Kiwis.

However, Samoa did have the experienced former Kiwi international Anthony Swann, who pounced on a mistake by Mat Daylight to send Penrith Panthers winger Bryan Leauma over for the first try after 17 minutes. That dropped catch by Daylight wiped out the good work done by Matt Crowther's 30 metre penalty in the third minute which should have settled Scotland's nerves.

When Solomona, one of the stars of the tournament, blasted through the Scottish cover with ease four minutes later, alarm bells started ringing in the home team's camp.

Ten minutes later the game seemed almost over when Wests Tigers' full-back Loa Milford got his reward for a superb display with a breakaway try to make it 14-2. Daylight had chased Adrian Vowles' chip down the left only to be caught by Leauma, allowing Milford to gather and fly down the touchline to score at the other end.

However, the break did Scotland wonders. Fired-up by the prospect of elimination, McRae's side showed real passion, hammering at the Samoan forwards and dominating possession as they forced a string of penalties. Vowles sneaked in by the left corner flag after a Wayne McDonald offload just four minutes in, and Scott Rhodes danced his way through after Darren Shaw had been held up short of the line. Crowther's conversion left just two points in it.

But when Scott Cram was penalised at the ruck and Shane Laloata kicked the penalty from an acute angle, Scotland needed a try. Rhodes almost got it, but then disaster struck. Danny Arnold missed Fa'afili's 40-20 attempt, Leauma pounced on the loose ball, hacked ahead and won the chase to touch down and all but win the game. Vowles's fantastic tackle stopped former Australian Schoolboy International Albert Talapeau, now of Sydney Roosters, increasing the margin but, when Richard Horne was held up in a tackle two minutes from time, the dream was over and Scotland were out.

McRae thought that the series of results unfair on his team.. "It just proved what a tough group it was," he said. "The guys' efforts should have been rewarded with a win somewhere." Only Ireland had a comfortable win over Scotland and few teams would end up with nothing from a points tally over three games of scored 34, against 55. But it's winning that counts and Scotland had won just two of nine games since being given full international status in 1996.

Scotland: Arnold, Crowther, L. Gilmour, G. Bell, Daylight, Purcell, Horne, Heckenberg, Russell (c), Laughton, Logan, Cram, Vowles. Subs: Maiden, S. Rhodes, W. McDonald, Shaw.

Samoa: Milford, Leauma, Anthony Swann, Lasloata, Lima, Fa'afili, Talapeau, Puletua, Betham, Seu Seu, Solomona, Tatupu, Poching (c). Subs: W. Swann, Leuluai, Leafa, Fala.

Scorers:

Scotland: Tries: Vowles, S. Rhodes; Goals: Crowther (2).

Samoa: Tries: Leauma (2), Solomona, Milford; Goals: Laloata (2).

Referee: David Pakieto (New Zealand)

World Cup reflections

Scotland's cause in the media and even among Rugby League cognoscenti was not helped by their three defeats. On paper, it looked like a disastrous World Cup campaign for the expansion team: no points, appalling attendances, and very little impact.

In reality, Scotland raised Rugby League's profile in Glasgow and Edinburgh. However, an opening day win over the Samoans could have made all the difference to exactly how much, as Shaun McRae admitted: "Had we won I think it would have spurred us on to bigger and better things," he wrote on *PlayTheBall.* "We were very, very disappointed and that took a lot out of us.

"The biggest disappointment is that we did not win games but teams in other groups would not have won games in our group either. I think Ireland had to work very hard to qualify [for the quarter-finals] whereas I don't think Papua New Guinea or France were in a strong group. I find it very hard to believe the rankings have put Scotland 14th, behind Fiji, Lebanon and the Cook Islands. You've got to take the group situation into account. I was very proud of the players' efforts and I think they answered some of their cynics and critics.

The question is: 'Where does Scotland go from here?' I hope we don't just leave it at that and say: 'Thanks Scotland, see you in four years' time'."

Unfortunately, that's almost what happened. Only one fixture was arranged for the whole of 2001 - away to France - by the financially-troubled RFL, compared to a full programme of events organised by the Scottish RL and Scotland Students. Shaun McRae's contract was up at the end of 2000, so he was left to concentrate on coaching Hull, to great success. And when the 2005 World Cup was confirmed, there was talk of it being just eight teams, which would certainly exclude Scotland, as well as half a dozen other League-playing nations.

However, that may please *Open Rugby* founder and international League fan Harry Edgar who said: "We should stop deluding ourselves that the Scottish team are Scottish."

Much of the World Cup debt was incurred due to a shambolic ticketing system which saw games advertised as 'sold out' in the national press just because ticket agencies had sold their initial few thousand allocation, only to be played out in front of virtually empty stands. Tom Edwards of marketing company World Rugby Ltd, called it "catastrophic", Phil Thomas, writing in *The Sun*, "abysmal".

The RFL's decision to use impressive stadia, despite empty seats looking dreadful on television, backfired. Instead of 2,000 creating a great atmosphere at somewhere intimate like Hillhead, Scotland played at Firhill and Tynecastle where the crowd rattled round seemingly sparsely populated stadiums.

Danny Kazandijian, editor of website *13world*, hoped the World Cup would be the launch pad for a senior Home Nations championship, something the RFL's Neil Tunnicliffe said in 1997 would be in place by 1999. It wasn't, and still isn't.

"If the organisers say this World Cup was a success, they're wrong," claimed Kazandijian. "But if they use it as a building block to get a Home Nations Championship in place then something will have come from it."

10. Triumph in France 2001

France 24 Scotland 40 - Home International
Tuesday 3 July 2001, Lezignan, attendance: 3,200.

Scotland shocked 2000 World Cup quarter-finalists France with a stunning performance, despite going into the game with half their first choice team missing, a new coach and playing at unfamiliar temperatures. But with newcomers Richard Fletcher, Ryan McDonald, Neil Lowe and Leeds teenager Gareth Morton coming into the squad, the Scots produced a passionate performance to end their four-match losing run in style with the biggest win in their history against all odds.

Scotland, wearing a new all navy kit, were inspired by Adrian Vowles, who created three of their tries with towering kicks to France's left-hand corner before retiring with a groin injury. Matt Crowther scored a try and kicked seven goals from eight attempts to break his own Scotland record for goals and points in a match. It was also an historic day for Darren Shaw, who captained the side for the first time.

"I'm just so proud of them," said coach Billy McGinty, returning to take charge of the side after the end of Shaun McRae's reign. "I wanted them to play with passion and I kept reminding them of who they were playing for. It wasn't just another game. It had to mean something special and they all went out and gave their all." A formidable display by the pack, with Wayne McDonald and Scott Cram well above their counterparts, laid the platform for the Scottish backs to show their skills.

Vowles helped Scotland get off to a flier in 30°C plus temperatures, sending two kicks to the right corner that the French failed to deal with. First, David Maiden got a touch to the ball as it bounced around the in-goal area after two French backs collided, then Danny Arnold rose highest to claim an almost identical try minutes later. The lively Scots were scoring at more than a point a minute when Jason Flowers supported a half-break by Fletcher to score, with Crowther converting.

France, urged on by a vociferous crowd, hit back with an unchallenged 20th-minute try from Sort, Dulac adding the goal to cut the lead to 10 points. However, Scotland defied the stifling conditions to claim their fourth try just before the break when another Vowles kick bounced horrendously for full-back Renaud Guigue, allowing Arnold to claim his second try, to which Crowther added his third goal.

McGinty could hardly have hoped for a better start after just three training sessions with his patched-up squad, but with Lowe, Dixon and Higgins impressing, they were good value for their interval lead.

France made a series of handling errors in the perfect conditions, but kept their hopes alive when Jampy touched down early in the second half, a cruel reward for young Morton who'd made a last-ditch tackle on Guisset in the previous play to rescue some poor Scottish defending. But the skilful Vowles crafted a crucial try, moving the ball from right to left for Lowe to finish behind the posts, and, although Houles pulled a try back on 58 minutes after a Devecchi grubber kick, Scotland ensured their win when Flowers took Ryan McDonald's pass to claim his second try.

Winger Michael van Snick went in for France's fourth try, but Scotland finished in command and in injury time Lowe and Arnold combined in a sweeping move from their own half for Crowther to grab his side's seventh try. "It was difficult with the preparation and I had doubts because of the amount of match fitness some of our players had had, players like Scott Cram, Mattie Crowther and Mike Dixon," said McGinty. "But they showed up really well and stuck in there. But that's what international rugby is all about, passion. It's probably the first time I've seen a Scotland team that has been proud to play for Scotland."

After leading a rendition of *Scotland the Brave* with his jubilant team-mates, skipper Shaw said: "We made it pretty tough on ourselves. We got off to a good start but we tended to slip the ball away and force too many passes and we had a lot of dropped ball. We let them back into it at one stage." Maybe, but everyone involved rightly considered this Scotland's finest moment since fielding an all-professional team. It was just a shame that so few Scots saw it, as television exposure was limited to only a few minutes of highlights on Sky Sports.

Scotland: Flowers, Arnold, Maiden, Higgins, Crowther, Vowles, S. Rhodes, W. McDonald, Dixon, Cram, Fletcher, D. Shaw (c), Lowe. Subs: N. Graham, Berry, R. McDonald, Morton.

France: Guigue, Noguera, Houles, Dulac, van Snick, Frayssinous, Devecchi (c), Guisset, Wulf, Gagliazzo, Jampy, Shead, Carrasco. Subs: Teixido, Anselme, Sort, Cornut.

Scorers:

Scotland: Tries: Flowers 2, Arnold 2, Maiden, Lowe, Crowther; Goals: Crowther 7

France: Tries: Houles, van Snick, Jampy, Sort; Goal: Dulac.

Referee: Ian Smith (England).

Part 4: Scotland's players

Dave Valentine (Photo: Courtesy Robert Gate)

11. Interviews: Scotland's recent players

Alasdair Blee

Ali made all his Scotland appearances before turning professional and now flies into war zones for a living

Changing to League

I was playing Union but there were some rifts in the club at Loughborough University and, at the same time, I met Zoe [daughter of Trevor Smith - *Smith's of Wigan* bookshop owner], who is from Wigan and talked a lot about Rugby League. We started going out and she took me to some games, including Great Britain versus Australia and that was it. When I went back to uni after the holidays, I joined the Rugby League club instead. I played on the wing for their second team and was soon in the firsts. I loved it.

Getting the Scotland Students call

Bev Risman was co-ordinator for England and Great Britain Students and he approached me, via some team-mates, about playing for England. But I told him I wanted to play for Scotland - if they had a team. I found out that they did so I went for trials and got in the side, around 1993. We had training sessions with John Risman [the Scottish Students coach] in Cumbria.

Senior honours

Most of the student side then played in the first senior game against Ireland in 1995 and I played in the Emerging Nations later that year. I've lost touch with the Scotland players although I was at London with Darren Shaw.

Mixing it in the real world

I graduated in June 1995 and was invited to train pre-season with Salford, which was great because I needed to keep playing before the Emerging Nations. I was there for a few months, including when the league stopped for the World Cup. We had a trainer over from Australia who was great and then I went off to join the Scotland squad.

I went back to Salford afterwards and was in the squad but never played a first-team game. We had lads like Scott Naylor and Nathan McAvoy and won the league (First Division) but didn't go up because it was the Centenary season before Super League was launched.

I couldn't agree terms with coach Andy Gregory and left. I still see Andy around Wigan - he sent me a copy of his book, actually, which explained a lot about his problems at that time.

London calling

Bev Risman arranged for me to go down to London Broncos. I trained with them and played in the second team, then I found out I'd been picked to go to the World Nines in Fiji the following February with Scotland, so I had to fill the gap and keep playing. I got a job working for a healthcare company but I didn't enjoy it, and that's when I decided I wanted to join the Army.

Fiji fever

I missed the Australia game in Fiji because of food poisoning. I was in bed feeling dreadful when they carried Billy McGinty in. He'd got crunched on the head and had severe concussion. They brought him into my room and said: "Keep an eye on him - he's acting funny". I was in no fit state to look after him! He never played again.

Bowing out

I was living in Richmond and the Broncos were training at Crystal Palace, so it was a nightmare journey. By sheer chance I met Scott Quinnell in a pub with Ben Clarke and Scott said: "Why don't you come along to training at Richmond (Rugby Union)?" By now, I actually had a date for when I'd be starting my army training at Sandhurst so I knew I'd have to give up rugby. But the Rugby League Student World Cup was during Easter 1996 - I was still eligible because I'd left within the last year - and I wanted to keep my hand in until then so I knew I had to keep playing rugby.

In the Army now

When I went to Sandhurst, I basically retired from rugby because you can't risk any injury whatsoever. But I found it easy to make that decision. I felt that I had achieved a lot. I'm very proud of having played

88

for my country at student, amateur and professional level, and being with Salford when they won the league and London when they finished fourth in Super League. I'd always wanted to fly in the military - it was always a matter of 'when'. Pilot training took me two years, until I was 25. Now I spend about nine months a year abroad, all over the place - the jungle, desert, South America, the Balkans - and I might be going back to Kosovo. I'm about the only member of 16th Brigade not in Afghanistan at the moment.

Suffolk, March 2002

Scott Cram

Scott Cram started playing for Scotland soon after joining London Broncos, having been a young star in the NRL in Australia.

Going from 'teenage sensation' to 'surplus to requirements'
Basically, things were going all right at Illawarra. I was NRL Rookie of the Year in 1997 and in 1998 I played most of the year. Then the merger came around with St George and I wasn't part of it. But I knew I could compete with any of the people who were picked. Then London got hold of me and I thought, "I'm only 22, I can come over and experience another part of the world, play in another country and see how it goes".

Being coached by Ian Millward
Ian coached me at Steelers since I was 19. One reason he's such a good coach is that he's so personable. He's been around good coaches in the past and picked things up off them. He's adapted and been fantastic. London looked at him when they replaced Dan Stains and I said you can't go wrong with 'Basil', but they went for John Monie instead.

Qualifying for Scotland
My mum's father was from Scotland. He emigrated to Oz but mum brought me up as being Scottish and I used to have fights with kids at school about it. One mate had English family - he was the Pom and I was the Jock! After the World Cup, mum and I hired a car and drove around Scotland, visiting relatives. We went to the very house where grandfather was born, in Lesmahagow. Standing there in his old house was an awesome feeling for mum. I'm very proud of my roots.

Iain Higgins and Scott Cram (Photo: Gavin Willacy)

Needing more internationals

There's talk of a European Championship and I hope it comes off. It would be great because you need those sort of games to promote Rugby League in those countries. It would be absolutely awesome to have two groups producing two top teams to play in a sort of grand final.

Perhaps it would be best at the start of the year, when you're fresher, than in mid-season when a few injuries are catching up with you. That's when you risk people dropping out to give their bodies a rest. If we kept the week free and then played on Saturdays that would be perfect. Apart from the World Cup, we've not had a lot of time to prepare for Scotland games, to get the game plan sorted. If we had a week to prepare we could look at the opposition and work out on a few moves on our own to do it properly. It's only going to make it a better game and a better spectacle for everyone.

Scotland's Aussie-dominated World Cup squad

It backfired really, but only because of the way we performed. On paper we had a good team, a bloody good team. We just didn't put it together. We just didn't perform and that may be one of the reasons why: we just didn't know each other. But I don't want to make excuses - we just didn't gel.

Going back to the NRL

When my contract's up at London I'll be 26. Ideally I'd like to go back to Australia for a couple of years and see how things go. The NRL is recognised as the best competition in the world and you want to be part of that. The likes of Wigan, Bradford and St Helens would all be in the top eight in the NRL but the skills levels are a bit higher there. If it didn't work out, I'd come back here for a couple of years. I'll be 30 then and quite happy to put my boots over my shoulder and say "thanks for the memories."

London, August 2001

Billy Gamba

An Aberdonian with an Italian grandfather ,Billy Gamba played for Scotland in their first five games, as well as several years with the Scottish Students. Now a dentist, he plays for Aberdeen Grammar School Former Pupils RFC.

Getting into League

I was at Dundee University, playing Union for the first XV and someone told me I'd be quite good at League. Mal Reid was coaching the Scottish Students League team and they sent me down to a trial in Edinburgh. I just got hooked! I must have played 20 to 30 matches for Scottish Students because it takes six years to qualify in dentistry.

Playing with the professionals

I'd only ever played Union but we were very well coached in the Scotland League side. The pros were very understanding of us amateurs and very considerate, which helped everybody. The fact that we'd played Union was actually used to our advantage because we'd do unusual and unpredictable things. For instance, we'd do Union-style kick-offs, and we'd challenge in the scrums. We'd take the ball against the head and drive the scrum. We got a few tries by driving the scrum over the line. We'd also take on wingers on the outside like they do in Union. We had great success.

Seeing the world

Being involved with Scotland Students was wonderful because we went to the World Cup in Australia in 1992, where we beat the English to finish fifth. We had players like Nick Mardon and Bob Baxendale, who used to play for Sheffield Eagles and became a Marines officer. We went on tours to France and I also went to British Students training camps.

Full Scotland honours

I actually captained Scotland in the first international we played in Ireland, and I played in the Emerging Nations and World Nines. I played either second-row or loose-forward in League, back-row in Union, but I never scored a try for Scotland. My last game for the full team was against Ireland at Firhill in 1996. Once more pros started playing, I dropped out of it.

The 2000 World Cup

The World Cup was disappointing, I thought. Picking no Scottish-born players was a negative move. It meant the team didn't attract support or coverage in the media and so it backfired, especially when they lost every game. It might have been different if they'd started off winning. When we played, we were the underdogs, a real bunch of misfits, yet we did very well.

Aberdeen, September 2001

Daniel Heckenberg

Daniel Heckenberg had his 21st birthday two days before making his Scotland debut at the 2000 World Cup. The front-rower moved from St George-Illawarra to Parramatta Eels for the 2002 NRL season

Growing up in Australia

I was born in Camden, which is about 50 kilometres south-west of Sydney. I started playing Rugby League when I was about 10 in junior clubs and then I joined the Magpies (Western Suburbs). When I left school at 17 I joined St George Dragons, eventually went full-time there and got in first grade in 1999. But it was tougher to get a game after the merger (with Illawarra).

Brought up a Scot

My mother's from Edinburgh. She moved over when she was about 12. She'd only been back once since then I think. But she considers herself a Scot and so do I, Scottish through and through. Pop's brothers are still over there (in Scotland). We stayed with two of my cousins just outside Edinburgh after the World Cup, once we'd been knocked out.

The World Cup: a mixed bag

The World Cup was good. But the biggest thing about it for me was the weather. When we were in Scotland, it rained every single day – but we just got used to it. The weather was actually okay when we played apart from against the Maori.

But it was a good experience and I enjoyed going to that part of the world. The other guys were great, too. They gave me a birthday cake at training on the Friday and then on the Monday, when we didn't have a game, we had a party in a pub in Edinburgh. I can't remember much about that - they got me pissed.

Working with Shaun McRae

He's a good laid-back Aussie bloke. He's a simple communicator. He told me what he wanted and there was no bullshit. We spoke a few times before I came over and we met as soon as I arrived and got on very well.

A lot of the Scotland boys have played for him at Hull or Gateshead. In fact, I could have gone over to play for him this year but I wanted to stay here. If ever I need someone to talk to about the British game, I can talk to Shaun or Shane Richardson.

Playing for Scotland

The problem with internationals is that it's too far for me to come to play one-off games. It's not fair on my team in Australia or the Scotland team if I was to come straight in and take someone else's place. The logistics aren't easy. If the games were at the end of the year, I'd definitely go.

Coming back to Britain

I'd only ever been abroad once before the World Cup and that was to play footy against the Warriors in New Zealand. I'd like to get back to Scotland, go on a holiday and play a bit of footy, in a couple of years.

When the time comes I can get a British passport – it doesn't take long – and be off-quota. My brother is only 20 but we may go overseas together some time. That would be fun. We could get a club in England and play for Scotland again.

It would be great because you're only a hop, skip and a jump from Europe and you're not far from the States either, compared to us. Here it takes a day to fly anywhere. I never even see the other Scotland boys.

Casola - New South Wales, October 2001

Iain Higgins

A proud Scot from Nottingham, Higgins became the second solicitor - following Struan Douglas - to play for Scotland during a renaissance in his career in 2001

Explaining the accent
It's a strange one because I was born in Nottingham but we moved back to Glasgow, where my parents are from, when I was 12 and I went to school there. That's my home – just north of Glasgow in Perthshire. I played for Scottish Schools at Union at under-15 and under-16 and then for Scottish Exiles under-21s when I was at Cambridge [University]. That was where I had my first game of Rugby League.

Switching codes
The way it works at Cambridge is they support a load of postgraduates to come in and play Rugby (Union) - they are basically rugby professionals, lots of them from overseas - and they train full-time up to the time of the Varsity match, then realise they haven't done any academic work, which is why there is no structured Rugby Union after Christmas. I wanted to keep playing so I went to the League club and loved it from the very start.

The great attraction
As a winger or centre you just love the involvement you get in League. In Union you can be standing out there in the cold and rain - especially in Scotland - waiting for a touch of the ball for half an hour, freezing to death. In League, even if you are a creative player you have to make 20 tackles a game and make 20 hit-ups.

Varsity colours

I played both Union and League for all three years at Cambridge and got to play in two League Varsity matches and was on the bench for one Union match, but didn't get on. We won both League games which was brilliant. We played one at London Welsh and one at Richmond, I think, in front of about 3,000 but it was great fun. They were similar to the Under-21 union games. The Union one at Twickenham is a bit different! In fact, it was the Varsity match that got me my chance at the Broncos. Tony Currie, who was London coach at the time, and was judging man-of-the-match, gave it to me, then asked me down for a trial for a month, so I went that Easter.

At the bar

Part of the reason for moving north was to continue qualifying as a lawyer. I went on loan to Hunslet halfway through the 1998 season. Then I went to law school in Leeds for a year while playing full-time for Hunslet, which was when we won the Northern Ford Premiership Grand Final. The following season I didn't play - I came back to London to do my first year of qualifying and worked in an office. The second year I went back to work in the same firm's Leeds office and played part-time for Hunslet. I qualified at Christmas and it seemed a natural time to either go on with my law career or have a break and have a go at playing Super League again.

Scotland calls

I was very surprised when I was called up for the Scotland Rugby League team in 1997 against France at Partick. I'd only played about six games of League, including the Varsity match. I had so little experience and I wasn't really ready for it but I was very proud. It helped that there were a couple of other Broncos in the Scotland squad - Andrew Duncan and Nick Mardon. We were robbed in the last minute by a dodgy refereeing decision [see match report]. I was much happier to be involved in 2001 - it was more justified as I'd had a good season.

International rescue

That game in France was a key moment for my career, a big day. In retrospect, it could be the turning point. I loved it and it made me want to come back to London and make a go of it again. We'd had a poor year with Hunslet and not been in the play-offs, so it was the last game I played for six months. It was brilliant to be involved, to start and to make a contribution to an historic win. Everyone played with a lot of passion. It gave me inspiration - I enjoyed training with the Super League boys, guys like Crammie, and I realised I wanted to get back into this again.

Brentford, February 2002

Mike Hubbard
The Honourable Michael Hubbard's background is of landed gentry from Buckinghamshire. He is now project manager for a London interior design company. He played for Scottish Students at the 1989 Student World Cup

Getting into League
I was at De La Salle teacher training college in Manchester and although I was a Union player, I played Rugby League in a 10-a-side competition. We won it and I got Man-of-the-Tournament. We were small in number but we had an amazing little team - we even beat Leeds, which was incredible.

A flirtation with the big time
After that tournament, a guy from Salford Reds took me into the stand and started spinning stories about how much money I could make if I turned professional and I believed him, being a wide-eyed idiot. But I'd got badly injured in that last match and was hobbling around all summer.

I was never really fit, but I went down to Salford for pre-season training. I'd graduated that summer and was working in Manchester, so I kept my foot in the door. I was playing at a higher level but it was less enjoyable to be honest. It was all train, train, train and never play. It was all far more serious than student Rugby League, of course. Everyone was more cynical.

I played for the Alliance side (second grade), but the first team were in the First Division with players like Adrian Hadley, so I was never going to walk into that team. After a few months I had the usual "things are not working out" conversation and they let me go. I'd flirted with greatness!

Playing for Scotland

I had no idea about the Scottish Students team until Dominic (Lord Addington, Hubbard's brother) told me. He'd had a conversation with Mal Reid at Aberdeen and the information trickled through to me while I was at Manchester. Mal was scouting around and because Salford scouts had taken an interest in me, I was in contention. I qualified because our mother was Scottish, although she was born in Burma.

I'd gradually come to understand the elements of Rugby League, like the different timing and the angles, and it suited me. So Dom introduced me to Mal and I went to the try-outs with a very strange bunch of people. I'd say there were only about 40 per cent Scottish accents there. It was a bit embarrassing for me when Mal was trying to rile the team up on a nationalistic basis to play against England, the "old enemy", when I was English myself to all intents and purposes.

The World Student stage

We had training camps and orientation courses in Cumbria and Mal gradually got a team together. The Student World Cup in York was great. There was an interesting comparison between the big physical teams with not much idea what they were doing, and the experts, like the Aussies. England were typical: 17-stone with wide foreheads and thighs like tree trunks; the Aussies were silky and calm; and the Dutch were just brutes, basically. One of them smacked me in the nose, the bastard.

There were some classic stories, though. One of our tall, athletic guys picked up a real mutton-dressed-as-lamb bird, about 45 years old, at a club. But once he saw her under the corridor lights in the halls, he screamed and ran off, locking himself in his room. Her pride was severely damaged and she went on the rampage, kicking the doors in and yelling. Superb.

Life after Rugby League

I went to Leicester Poly (now De Montfort University) to do a masters in interior design for two years and played League there. We had another good side there, too. But I've not played since then, apart from a couple of games for Dominic's [Lord Addington] Lords/Commons team but they're under Union rules. I miss Rugby League, actually. But there were no teams around here and I'm not fit enough to play anymore anyway.

Luton, January 2002

David Maiden

David Maiden played six times for Scotland during his time in England with Gateshead Thunder and Hull FC before heading back to Queensland at the end of a highly successful 2001 season.

Growing up around Cairns
Rugby League is the predominant sport there, although it's hard to know in Australia these days because there are so many sports. But there's a lot of junior League played and a 10-team league.

Qualifying for Scotland
I've got feet in four camps. My Dad's Australian but his parents are Scottish, from Cooperangus, near Perth. My Mum's English – her family are all around Widnes, but her Dad's called Glyn Jones – he's Welsh, as you can tell. But I chose to play for Scotland and it was a great honour.

Getting the call
Shaun McRae was responsible for me playing for Scotland, rather than Wales. He was coach and Richo (Shane Richardson, then Hull chief executive) was manager back in 1999 and they were asking around to see if anyone had Scottish ancestry. When I was first asked if I wanted to play, I thought it was just another game. Then I got into camp and saw everyone's pride and their backgrounds and it was something special.

The best moments with Scotland
Winning that international cap was the highlight of my career. I love playing for Scotland – going to France and winning this year was the high point. Singing *Flower of Scotland* in our funny accents was a fantastic moment. I've told the Scotland coaches: "If you need me I'll come back and play for you - I'll pay my own air fare".

The future

We're going back to the bush, to Atherton, inland from Cairns. I'm going to play for Atherton Roosters there and coach the Under-18s. It's semi-pro': you train on Tuesdays and Thursdays, unless it's raining, then you go to the pub! My wife, Jackie, is doing a fitness instruction course at the moment and we're going to open a gym there. I'm a surveyor by trade but I reckon between us we know enough about fitness to make a go of that instead.

Hull, October 2001

Lee Penny

It took full-back Penny seven years to clock up three appearances for Scotland, missing half of the internationals through injury during a decade at Warrington.

How a Wiganer plays for Scotland

My grandparents on my dad's side are from Hamilton. They moved to St Helens when they got married, when they were 21. My dad was brought up as a bit of both - Scottish and English - they called him Jimmy McPenny and a few Warrington fans shout at me: "Oi, McPenny."

I knew from an early age that if I was going to make it and get to play international rugby, I was qualified for Scotland. My granddad made sure I would play for Scotland given the chance. I go to Glasgow and Edinburgh whenever I can - it's good to know I've got family roots up there.

Making his Scotland debut

When the first games were played, I was involved with the Great Britain Academy and the Under-21s and I didn't get to play for Scotland. I made my debut in 1998 in Perpignan and I was 'Man of the Match'. We just lost out to a try in the last five minutes, but at the reception afterwards I got a plaque as Man of the Match. We had to vote for their best player and they voted for ours, so I was made up with that. I've still got it somewhere.

Sticking together

I remember getting well beaten by Ireland in Scotland (in 1998), but there were no problems whatsoever in the squad, none of the cliques and little groups of players which you usually get. We all bonded and stuck together. You've got to: get it right off the pitch and it all comes together on it.

It's a bit strange playing for Scotland against blokes you play with for your club but on the field you are enemies. Off the field, you have a drink and a talk about the game. But you're not mates on the field, you are all trying to win, always giving 100 per cent. You do get to make friends with more people though going away with Scotland.

The World Cup squad

We had a few Australians come into the squad for the World Cup, but they got into it and Shaun McRae was superb at getting the team bonding going. We had a few meetings and a few socials. We got together at training camps at Castleford and Warrington and so we knew each other. There was a good atmosphere. It's just a pity we didn't perform on the day.

A frustrating tournament

I pulled my hamstring in the last 15 minutes against Samoa and was out for two months. It was so frustrating and I'd been looking forward to the World Cup all year. I knew straightaway what I'd done and the physio and doctor told me I'd play no more part in it. But I didn't want to go home. I stayed with the lads to push them on.

We were in a really tough group, to be honest, but we thought we could get through. We should have beaten Samoa but we missed a few penalties and conversions. We lost to the group favourites (Maori) by a point but I still thought we'd qualify. But we had injuries to major players - Graham Mackay and Scott Logan hardly played - and we had to fetch the kids in. But you can't beat experience. That plus the bad luck turned it against us.

Injury-hit international career

I've not had a lot of luck with Scotland. Injuries just seem to come to me when Scotland games are coming up. I missed the games in 1999 through injury and then broke my thumb the day before we were going to France this year. It was a good win though, especially as France had given Ireland a good hiding the week before.

The international future
They are trying to get a Five Nations going, which has never been done before. That would be good, to play England or Wales, as we only seem to play France and Ireland. If that comes off, it would be a great experience for me in my testimonial year. I think Scotland would be up there with Ireland, challenging England for it.

Wigan, November 2001

Darren Shaw
Darren Shaw has had a successful career in Great Britain since joining the London Broncos in 1994. In 2001, while with Castleford Tigers, he captained Scotland for the first time.

Captaining Scotland for the record win against France in 2001
That was up there with my best moments in the game. During the week, we had a lot of players pulling out injured but the guys who played really put their hands up and got stuck in. Leading the team out was fantastic, singing the national anthem and all that. It was a great honour.

Billy McGinty said it was the first time he'd seen a Scotland side play with pride. Well I think I've played with pride every game for Scotland but I know what he means. I felt it too. There was a different atmosphere among the players. Perhaps it was because they were mainly British guys rather than in the World Cup when we had 15 Aussies or something. There were more home-grown players who gelled and knitted quickly.

How a Victorian-born Queenslander qualifies for Scotland
I was born in Melbourne and grew up in Queensland. My Mum's from Lanark but I didn't have any connection with Scotland until I found out about them in around 1995. Someone in London told me they were putting a team together (for the Emerging Nations Cup). I've played ever since.

But it's very frustrating only playing one international a season. We play a lot of Rugby League but they should organise a couple of weeks off for a Tri-Nations tournament or something every year. It would be good to have a break, get away from our clubs in mid-season. It's up to the clubs but I think it would add some excitement to the season for the fans and the players. It would re-ignite your season and you'd come back fresher.

Career highlights
Winning the Challenge Cup with Sheffield in 1998 was by far and away the number one highlight for me. It's hard to explain how it (beating Wigan) happened or why. We just all clicked on the day, put our hands up and gave it everything. I really enjoyed my time at London too. I had three great seasons there before my chance came to go back with Canberra.

Not making it in the NRL
I've no regrets really. I played for two great clubs in Brisbane Broncos and Canberra Raiders and I learned a lot when I was there. I just had limited opportunities at Canberra so I sent a few CVs out and, by chance, Sheffield picked one up and invited me back over. I've been here ever since. I'm off-quota having lived here for most of the last seven years and I've got a 'Right of Abode', which gives me most of the same rights as a British passport.

West Yorkshire, August 2001

12. Scotland's international players

Despite these matches not being listed as full internationals, this chapter includes players who played in 1995 for Scotland against Ireland and/or in the Emerging Nations Cup, and at the World Nines(W9) in Fiji the following year, even if they never played in a full official international. Players who only played for Scottish Students are not included because that is not considered a senior all-Scottish team. All details are correct up to end of March 2002.

Paul Anderson
Born: 2 April 1977

Paul came through the St Helens academy, making his first team debut as a teenager in the 1995-96 Centenary Season. He played at Old Trafford in Saints' Premiership defeat by Wigan in 1997 and was a regular off the bench but, having made only two appearances in 1998, moved to Sheffield Eagles, where he won his Scotland caps.

Released when they merged with Huddersfield Giants, Paul moved to Leigh Centurions in 2000 and was ever-present, scoring 16 tries, as they reached the NFP Grand Final. But with defeat by Dewsbury, and another by Oldham in the semi-finals a year later, Paul (and Leigh) missed out on a potential return to Super League two seasons in succession.
1999 v Ireland (sub), Wales.

Danny Arnold
Born: 15 April 1977

Danny first appeared on the national stage in 1987 when he played for Warrington Under-11s in the curtain-raiser to the Challenge Cup Final between Halifax and Saints at Wembley. He was clearly undaunted by the big time.

In two amazing seasons with St Helens in the mid 1990s, Danny achieved more than most professionals in their whole careers. In 1996, aged just 18, he scored two tries in the Challenge Cup Final win over Bradford and lifted the inaugural Super League title. He also broke three individual Great Britain Academy records in the 72-10 hammering of France: most tries (four), most goals (eight) and most points (32). A year later, he returned to Wembley for another triumph over the Bulls. Two successive losing Premiership finals faded into insignificance in comparison.

His record of 33 tries in 41 Super League appearances for Saints is among the very best, but his career went downhill for a while after moving to Huddersfield Giants. He had short spells with Castleford Tigers and Wakefield Trinity before dropping into the Premiership with Oldham Roughyeds after the 2000 World Cup. Six months later he was back in the big-time, signing for Salford City Reds.

Throughout his club career, Danny has been a regular try-scorer for Scotland, his seven touchdowns in his first seven full internationals making him the most prolific try-scorer in Scotland's brief history.

1998 v France - try, Ireland; 1999 v Wales - 2 tries, Ireland - try; 2000 v Ireland - try, Samoa; 2001 v France - 2 tries.

Geoff Bell
Born: 1 June 1973

A fast and skilful winger or centre from Australia, Geoff started his career at Cairns Brothers club before becoming a star at Cronulla, where he played against Scotland's Nathan Graham and Simon Knox when the Sharks comprehensively beat Bradford Bulls in the 1997 World Club Championship. That was a big year for Geoff: he played for Queensland in the Super League State of Origin and appeared in the Super League Grand Final defeat by Brisbane Broncos.

He moved to North Queensland Cowboys in 1999 but, after becoming one of only four Cowboys to score an NRL hat-trick, his time there was ruined by injuries. He appeared for Scotland at the 2000 World Cup - continuing his career-long record of scoring a try every three games - before joining wooden-spoonists Penrith Panthers for 2002.

Geoff qualifies for Scotland through his Glaswegian grandmother, Agnus Blackwood Holmes ('Black Agy' to her friends), whose father quit his bakery and moved the family from Morrison Street to Australia on *SS Paparoa* in 1912. A committed Christian who has also found time to complete a Bachelor of Teaching degree, Geoff aptly says his favourite film is *Braveheart*.

2000 v Maori - try, Ireland, Samoa.

Glen Bell

Born: 26 March 1965

Glen came to England from New Zealand in August 1991, joining fellow Scotland internationals Nathan Graham and Danny McKelvie at Dewsbury. The high point of his time there was probably the 1992-93 season when Dewsbury reached the Premiership semi-finals after finishing third in the Third Division.

A second-row forward, Glen was capped by Scotland as he reached the end of his career with the Rams. He is related to fellow Maori Bell family members, Wigan legend Dean and Dean's father, Barrow coach Cameron.

1997 v France.

Joe Berry

Born: 7 May 1974

Berry first played professionally with Keighley Cougars, where he was used mainly as a substitute, before joining Huddersfield Giants in 1997, just in time to win the First Division Premiership at Old Trafford and promotion to Super League.

Despite being a Scotland regular, Joe made just six starts in the Giants forward line in Super League, before being released when they merged with Sheffield. He signed for Doncaster Dragons, with whom he'd spent part of 1999, but rejoined Keighley just six games into the 2000-01 season. A couple of months later he was on the move again, Keighley's dire financial problems seeing him jump ship to Rochdale Hornets.

1998 v France, Ireland; 1999 v Ireland (sub), Wales (sub); 2001 v France (sub).

Alasdair Blee

Born: 12 August 1973

Alasdair was born in Elgin, where he lived until going to board at Keswick School in the Lake District, during which time his Stirling-born father moved the family to Oxford. Despite being very close to the Rugby League centres on Cumbria's west coast, Ali played Union until going to Loughborough University to study sports science and physics. There he converted to the 13-a-side code, winning selection for Scottish Students and making his senior debut against Ireland in 1995.

Ali was still at Loughborough when he made his full Scotland debut in 1996, having played every minute of the Emerging Nations Cup the previous season. A speedy if slight winger, he scored two tries and had another disallowed in the win over Russia, a game in which he voted was man of the match.

1995 v Ireland, Russia-2 tries, USA, Cooks Is; 1996 v W9, Ireland (sub).

Mark Burns

Nicknamed 'McBurns' by his fellow students, Mark was hooker in Scotland's first ever game in Dublin before the 1995 Charity Shield. Having graduated from the Scottish Students side, which he captained at the 1996 World Cup, Mark remained in the senior side for the Emerging Nations competition later that year.

After graduating from Lancaster University, Mark continued playing for Lindley Swifts, the historic amateur club from Huddersfield. One of the Pennine League's top sides, Lindley won the Yorkshire Cup in 2000.

1995 v Ireland, Russia, USA, Cooks Is.

Graham Cameron

Born: 15 September 1962

A fine goal-kicking winger, Graham was born and bred in Whitehaven and started his career with the Cumbrian club before moving to Barrow in December 1992, where he played with fellow Scottish international Gary Murdock. Cameron, who worked in the medical industry, added a Cumbria RL selection to honours won at school and Under-21 level during an impressive spell in Union with the Moresby and Fylde clubs.

Kurt Sorensen brought Graham back to Whitehaven in 1994-95, but he had retired from the professional game by the time he won his first international cap, appearing in Scotland's three-quarter line in the 1995 Emerging Nations Cup.

1995 v Russia, USA (sub).

Logan Campbell

Born: 23 May 1971

Sharing a name with the 19th-century Scottish emigrant who was known as 'the father of Auckland', it's fitting that Logan should have been brought up there before representing Scotland. Born in Samoa, Logan spent most of his professional career in England after learning the game with Auckland club Northcote Tigers.

After a spell in Newcastle Knights' reserve grade, he joined London Crusaders in 1993 and was immediately effective, starring in his first season as the Broncos. He scored a try in every round of the Division Two Premiership, including the final when London lost to Workington at Old Trafford.

Logan quit his job as a garage engineer to join Workington Town, where the club won promotion, but he only played eight times in Super League for the Cumbrians before their relegation. He followed coach Peter Walsh to Hull Sharks in 1997 where he was a regular but, after the merger with Gateshead, Logan went from one 'Scottish enclave' to another - Castleford - for the 2000 season, commuting from Humberside with Andrew Purcell.

After missing the 2000 World Cup through injury, Shaun McRae brought Logan back to Hull where he played his part in their excellent run to third place in Super League VI.

1998 v France, Ireland - try.

Paul Carr
Born: 13 May 1967

Originally from Sydney, Paul started his career in Britain with Hunslet before joining Sheffield Eagles in July 1992. In his first season with the Eagles, when he played with Scots Hugh Waddell, Dale Laughton, Charlie McAlister and Matt Crowther, Paul scored 14 tries in 28 appearances, and played in Sheffield's only Yorkshire Cup Final appearance, a defeat by Wakefield Trinity. Despite playing in the second-row, he managed to average a try almost every two games during his time in the English game. A workaholic forward and loyal servant to the Eagles, Paul starred in their incredible Challenge Cup Final win over Wigan at Wembley in 1998. Along with fellow Crowther, Laughton and Darren Shaw, he enjoyed one of the all-time classic upsets. But an ankle injury ended his career at Don Valley and he returned to Sydney without adding to his one Scotland cap against France.

1997 v France.

Gary Christie
Born: 23 January 1972

An amateur with Widnes Tigers, Gary turned professional at Oldham in 1991 before moving on to Wakefield Trinity in August 1993. That year he won Great Britain Under-21 honours alongside Scotland's Lee Penny and the likes of Jason Robinson, Chris Joynt and Mick Cassidy in the side that played France.

By November the following year, Gary was on his way to Bradford, where he was a prolific try-scorer, touching down 11 times in his first 17 games. Not surprisingly he was capped by Scotland while with the Bulls, although he got less game time as the years went by, playing just four times in Bradford's 1997 Super League title triumph and not appearing in either of the club's Challenge Cup Final defeats by Saints. He scored as many tries for Scotland as he did in Super League - one, in his only international.

1997 v France - try.

John Coumbe-Lilley
Born: 1 February 1971

Born in Lewisham, south London, John was a Rugby Union player with London Scottish and London Irish before attending Crewe & Alsager College, where became involved with League, coaching the college teams.

He continued to play Union, for Wrexham and Rugby Lions, but became a regular for Scottish Students at League, playing 16 times, before earning a place on the Great Britain Students tour to Morocco in 1994. A year later he made his Scotland RL senior debut against Ireland in Dublin, but sadly broke his ankle very badly just 10 minutes into the match, requiring seven screws and a metal plate. He never played for Scotland again, although he did return to the student side in the World Cup the next year, when he graduated from Manchester Metropolitan University.

John then qualified as a police constable with Kent Police but soon emigrated to the USA, where he ran a sports development company and studied for a masters degree in Sports Psychology at the University of Illinois. He concentrated on coaching rugby, first with Chicago Westside Condors and then Chicago Rugby Union. He also coached goalkeepers in youth football.

1995 v Ireland.

James Cowan

Born: 4 December 1975

Jimmy joined Oldham from Waterhead ARLFC in May 1995, making his top flight debut in the Centenary Season of 1995-96, and was soon capped by Scotland at just 20 years old. A full-back or three-quarter, Jimmy was mainly confined to Oldham's Alliance team, making just 10 appearances in Super League in two seasons, and left the professional game the following year after the collapse of the Oldham Bears club.

1996 v W9, Ireland.

Andy Craig

Born: 16 March 1976

Once one of the most promising youngsters in the country, Andy played for Great Britain Academy and signed for Wigan despite coming from St Helens - his great grandad played for both. He won a championship medal with Wigan in 1995-96, but in 1996 was in the side beaten by Salford to bring their 43-match unbeaten Challenge Cup run to an end.

After just 10 appearances in the inaugural Super League season, Andy went part-time with Swinton Lions but after a prolific try-scoring season in 1998, was called back into the big time with Halifax Blue Sox in 1999, the year in which he won his first caps for Scotland.

He returned to Swinton in 2000, switching successfully from centre to stand-off under Scotland assistant coach Mike Gregory as he scored an impressive 14 tries in 23 NFP starts. That earned him a late call-up to the Scotland World Cup squad in 2000, although he did not play.

Andy spent the 2000-01 winter season playing Union for Orrell before following his great uncle, Peter Molyneux, in signing for Widnes Vikings, in April 2001. Three months later they won the NFP Grand Final. He spent 2001-02 back in the Wigan organisation: captaining the likes of Gary Connolly and Wes Davies as they played for Orrell RFC, which had become Wigan RLC's new sister club. He was called into the Scotland RU training squad in May 2002

1999 v Wales, Ireland.

Scott Cram

Born: 30 January 1977

Born in Wollongong, about 30 miles south of Sydney, Scott first played for West Devils at the age of 12. He spent seven years with the ARL's

Illawarra Steelers, where he reached a semi-final in 1997, the year he was voted ARL Rookie-of-the-Year. Having developed into a 6ft 2in forward, Scott came to London in May 1999 after being left out of the Illawara/St George merger squad, and was a great success in the Broncos' front row.

Scott, whose maternal grandfather emigrated from Lanarkshire to New South Wales, made his Scotland debut in 1999. He and his mother toured Scotland after the World Cup, visiting relatives and his grandfather's original house in Lesmahagow.

1999 v Wales, Ireland; 2000 v Maori, Ireland, Samoa; 2001 v France.

Matt Crowther
Born: 6 May 1974

Scotland's record points-scorer was born in Pontefract to a Scottish father and started his career with the Kippax amateur club. Surprisingly he joined Sheffield Eagles in 1991 rather than any of his local professional clubs, and was a great success at Don Valley.

A speedy stand-off or wing, Matt's biggest moment in the game came when he scored a try in the Eagles' amazing Challenge Cup Final win over Wigan in 1998. He had a blistering start to that season having missed most of 1997 through injury, so it was doubly cruel on him when he suffered terrible knee damage a few days after the glory of Wembley.

Out for almost a year, Matt drew encouragement from his team-mate for club and country Dale Laughton, who had fully recovered from the same injury. Once fit, Matt found himself at Huddersfield when the Giants and Eagles clubs merged, but it was not until the 2001 season, when he moved to Hull - the former club of his uncle, Sammy Lloyd - to play for Scotland boss, Shaun McRae, that Crowther flourished.

He starred in their march to third place, kicking 69 goals and scoring 10 tries in just 23 appearances. That came as no surprise to McRae, who said: "Matt's an enormously talented athlete but has suffered a lot from injuries. I worked with him in the Scotland squad and Matt impressed me with his attitude and professionalism."

A proud Scot, Matt has scored points in every appearance for Scotland since his debut in 1996, with the one blip being his missed late conversion attempt against the Maori in the 2000 Rugby League World Cup which subsequently cost Scotland a place in the quarter-finals.

Matt, who had a spell in Australia with South Newcastle, is nicknamed 'Malcolm' after the character on the *Mrs Merton* TV show - because he still lives with his mum in Castleford.

1996 v Ireland - 3 goals; 1997 v France - try & 2 goals; 1999 v Wales - try & 4 goals, Ireland - goal; 2000 v Maori (sub) - goal, Ireland - goal, Samoa - 2 goals; 2001 v France - try & 7 goals.

Sean Cusack
Born: 27 January 1966

Sean scored Scotland's first ever try - in Dublin in 1995 - while still a player for Cumberland League side Broughton Red Rose. A loose-forward, he went on to win a contract with Carlisle Border Raiders after impressing at the Emerging Nations tournament that same year and played in the first full Scottish international the following August as a replacement for the injured Terry Matterson.

However, he had made more appearances for Scotland than he did for Carlisle in 1997 - just two - and left the club when they merged with Barrow the following season. Indeed, only six Carlisle players survived what was in effect the closure of professional League in Carlisle after 16 years of struggle. Sean was one of five Carlisle players to then join Workington Town, but made no appearances after signing in May 1998.

1995 v Ireland - try, Russia, Cook Is; 1996 v W9, Ireland.

Mat Daylight
Born: 2 March 1974

An Australian by birth, winger Mat had spells at Cronulla Sharks, Perth Reds and Adelaide Rams before coming to England when Perth and Adelaide both folded. His luck appeared to have turned in Super League when he scored Gateshead Thunder's first ever try - seven minutes into a friendly at Castleford in January 1999 - and got two more in the historic league win over Wigan. He clocked up exactly 100 points for the club and was Super League IV's joint top try-scorer with 25 in 30 appearances. Not surprisingly, he was selected in the Super League Dream Team and won the Thunder's first Player-of-the-Year award.

But Gateshead failed to last and Mat joined Hull under the subsequent merger. After one less explosive season on Humberside, his club coach, Shaun McRae, drafted him into Scotland's World Cup squad. They were to be Mat's last games in Britain - he was wanted back in Cronulla. But a few weeks into his second spell with the Sharks, Mat broke his leg and was released, joining Port Kembler in the Illawarra Carlton League.

2000 v Maori, Ireland, Samoa.

Mike Dixon

Born: 6 April 1971

An English-born hooker who made his Scottish debut while with Hull, 'Mighty Atom' started his career at East Park amateurs before joining the Hull Kingston Rovers academy. However, he turned professional at city rivals Hull, winning a Great Britain Under-21 cap against Papua New Guinea in 1991 while with the Airlie Birds, and played in the 1997 First Division Premiership defeat by Huddersfield at Old Trafford. But when Sharks coach Peter Walsh claimed Mike was too small for Super League at 5ft 6in, he returned to Craven Park and became a firm crowd favourite at Hull KR, impressing with his bursts from dummy-half.

Incidentally, at Rovers he plays with Bob Everitt, the only professional player who almost qualifies for Scotland on residency grounds. Everitt spent two years, between 1997 and 1999, in Scotland, doing missionary work on behalf of the Mormons.

1997 v France (sub); 1998 v Ireland (sub); 2001 v France.

Struan Douglas

Born: 18 September 1966

Struan made history when he became the third generation of his family to play rugby for Scotland when he made his SRL debut in 1995. His maternal grandfather, Alec Brown, played for Scotland at Rugby Union and later became president of the SRU, while his father, John Douglas, was a Union star for Scotland and the British Lions. Struan reports that his father was "delighted" by his son's Scotland Rugby League call-up. Unfortunately his grandfather died before seeing history made.

A scrum-half in both codes, Struan was born and bred in Edinburgh where he played for the Academicals RU club. But at Dundee University he was invited to trials for the fledgling Scottish Students Rugby League team and made his debut in the 1989 Student World Cup.

Having graduated and become a solicitor in the Scots' capital, Struan was playing Union for the Accies when he made a brief return to the 13-

a-side game. After coming on as substitute for the injured John Coumbe-Lilley just 10 minutes into Scotland's first international at the Royal Dublin Showgrounds in 1995, Struan was selected for the Emerging Nations Cup. Unfortunately, he was injured on his debut against the USA and has hardly played a game of rugby in either code since.

1995 v Ireland (sub), USA (sub).

John Duffy
Born: 2 July 1980

The youngest international of all time, this former Wigan St Patrick's half-back made his Scotland debut, thanks to his Glaswegian father, aged just 17. John made his Warrington debut at 16, and played in Wolves' humiliating World Club Championship matches in 1997.

But, after just 13 Super League games for Warrington, the stand-off joined Salford in 2000. A season later, John dropped into the Northern Ford Premiership to play for Leigh Centurions.

He was recalled to the Scotland squad in 2001, but did not play. However, he did play in the NFP Under-21s win over their Super League counterparts in October 2001, just before signing for the resurgent Chorley Lynx, the fifth Leigh player to move to Victory Park that winter. Three successful months later, he quit the Lynx and, ironically, re-signed for Leigh after working to install new turnstiles at Hilton Park ahead of their Challenge Cup quarter-final with Wigan.

1997 v France; 1998 v France-3 goals, Ireland-try & goal; 1999 v Wales (sub).

Andrew Duncan
Born: 13 September 1972

A few months after leaving Brisbane Easts for London Broncos, full-back Andrew won his one and only Scotland cap. After scoring three tries in just eight appearances for London, he joined Warrington on 12 July 1997, the same day as Ireland's Michael Eager arrived from South Queensland. It meant a summer down under playing in the World Club Championships, as Andrew scored a try for London in the opening game, (a defeat at London's former owners, Brisbane Broncos) and then played for the Wolves when they were heavily beaten by Cronulla and lost in Auckland.

Andrew only made four appearances in Super League for Warrington before returning to Australia, playing in the Bundy Gold Cup for Brisbane's Northern Suburbs Devils, with Ireland's Liam Tallon.
1997 v France (sub).

Richard Fletcher
Born: 17 May 1981
Richard signed professional for Hull FC in 1999 from amateurs Ideal Isberg, after starting with Fish Trades ARLFC. A strong-running back-row forward who makes huge hits in defence, Richard won honours for Yorkshire Academy and Great Britain & Ireland Academy against the Australians.

Having appeared for Great Britain Under-21s against France in October 1999, he was voted Alliance Player of the Year in 2000 and made it into the Scotland World Cup squad but did not play. After some fine performances when called upon from the bench by title-chasing Hull in 2001, he was selected for the England Under-21 squad which toured South Africa (funding from Sport England meant the British team played as 'England'). He scored two tries and kicked a goal in the 74-14 second test victory. A former judo player, Richard became the 17th full international on the Airlie Birds' books when he played for Scotland against France in 2001, six of those internationals being Scottish: Logan, Crowther, Maiden, Horne, Campbell and Fletcher himself.
2001 v France.

Jason Flowers
Born: 30 January 1975
The Pontefract-born full-back started with Red Hill amateurs and won two Great Britain Academy caps in 1994 after joining Castleford, his local club. But Jason did not quite fulfil his potential. He did score a try at the WACA in the Tigers' narrow defeat by Perth Reds in the World Club Championship of 1997, earning himself a place in the Great Britain training squad for the Super League Ashes Series, but he was cut from the final squad and never got close again.

Jason missed most of the 2000 and 2001 campaigns with a long-term shoulder injury, meaning he did not make the Scotland World Cup squad either. He was then released by Castleford coach Graham Steadman - his childhood hero - after more than 200 appearances for the club at the end of 2001, his ninth season at Wheldon Road. Ironically, his first game after signing for Halifax Blue Sox in January 2002 was against Castleford.

1998 v France, Ireland (sub); 2001 v France.

Billy Gamba

Born: 14 October 1967

Mal Reid spotted Billy playing Union for Dundee University and sent him for League trials in Edinburgh. He was soon hooked and played for Scottish Students nearly 30 times in six years, including in the 1992 Student World Cup in Australia, when Billy was man-of-the-match in the win over England.

St Andrews-born Gamba, who played second-row in both codes, captained Scotland in the first senior international in Ireland in 1995, and his last game was the first official full international against Ireland at Firhill the following year. In between, the hefty forward - described in one programme as "outstanding as a runner, support player and tackler" - played at the Emerging Nations World Cup, where he was vice-captain, and the World Nines in Fiji. Into his thirties, he continued to play Union for his only club, Aberdeen Grammar School Former Pupils, while running a dentists' clinic in the city.

1995 v Ireland, Russia, USA, Cook Is; 1996 v W9, Ireland.

Lee Gilmour

Born: 12 March 1978

Lee was selected for Scotland at the 2000 World Cup, having been persuaded by coach Shaun McRae to use his Scottish ancestry to appear in the tournament after being left out of the England squad, two years after appearing for Emerging England. Indeed, October 2000 was a strange time for Lee because he also made a surprise move from Wigan, where he had experienced outstanding success, to Bradford Bulls.

A loose-forward, Lee was spotted by legendary Wigan scout Eric Hawley, playing for Dewsbury Moor ARLFC and he was soon a teenage starlet at Central Park, winning Great Britain Academy caps in 1996 and 1997, under Mike Gregory's coaching.

In 1998, his first full season as a professional, Lee played in the Challenge Cup Final and was voted Super League Young Player of the Year as Wigan won the inaugural Grand Final at Old Trafford. He couldn't join in the party, though, because he had to join up with the Great Britain squad the next day.

Having played in the series defeat by New Zealand, Lee could have expected to become one of Super League's top players over the next two years. Instead, he struggled to get in the Wigan starting line-up and that problem continued at Bradford, cutting a forlorn figure as the Bulls rampaged to Grand Final glory without him. However, he made a winning return to the side in the 2002 World Club Championship thrashing of Newcastle Knights.

Nicknamed 'Gilroy', 6ft 2in Lee is proud of his sister, Natalie, who plays League for Wakefield Panthers and Great Britain and has played hockey for England Under-16s and football for Leeds United ladies.

2000 v Maori, Ireland, Samoa.

Scott Gilmour

Born: 15 April 1971

Capped while a student at Abertay University, Dundee, Scott played League for the Scottish Students - including at the 1996 World Cup - and also for the Great Britain Students over several seasons.

His first senior appearance was in the 1996 World Nines, after which he also appeared in the inaugural official international against Ireland.

A hefty prop or second row, 6ft 2in and 16 stone Scott spent nine years playing Union for Heriots Former Pupils, winning the Scottish championship in 1998-99. Rumour has it he was once selected for the Scotland A Union side, but didn't attend because he thought it was a wind-up.

A software engineer, Scott moved to Bath for work and continued to play Union for Keynsham RFC in South-West Division One.

1996 v W9, Ireland (sub).

George Graham

Born: 19 January 1966

Graham played his early rugby with his local Union side, Stirling County, winning Scotland honours at Under-21 and B team level and touring Zimbabwe with the full side, France and Ireland in 1988. A former Army team-mate of top Union coach Dean Ryan, Graham then turned to professional Rugby League with Carlisle, and played in the first ever Scotland Rugby League match, against the North-East XIII at

Meadowbank in 1994. He was initially named in the team to play Ireland in 1995, but did not play again for Scotland until the Fiji World Nines.

With Union turning openly professional, George transferred to Newcastle Falcons, and eventually won his first full cap at either code in 1997, as a replacement against Australia at Murrayfield. He toured South Africa with Scotland in 1999 and played in the Union World Cup that autumn. George was injured scoring his first international try - on his 16th appearance - in the last minute against Wales in 2000.
1996: W9.

Nathan Graham
Born: 23 November 1971
Despite being born in Chipping Sodbury in the Cotswolds, Nathan grew up in the Heavy Woollen district of West Yorkshire, playing at the Mirfield and Hanging Heaton amateur clubs before making his Dewsbury debut while still a student in the 1988-89 season. He spent six years there before moving to Bradford Northern for the 1995-96 season.

His time at Odsal was undermined by the 1996 Challenge Cup Final when his dropped catches from high kicks enabled St Helens to complete an extraordinary 40-32 victory. After spending another season mainly on the bench, Nathan returned to Dewsbury for 1998-99, having a sensational season. He was also capped by Scotland, courtesy of his ancestry, and has represented them every year since. After a 12-11 NFP Grand Final defeat by Hunslet in 1999, Nathan captained Dewsbury to Grand Final and Trans-Pennine Cup triumphs a year later, scoring 17 tries along the way. He was rightly nominated for the NFP Player of the Year award and was rated one of the best players outside of the top flight. Nathan left the Rams in November 2001, joining several other Scotland players at Featherstone. He also had a spell with North Sydney.
1998 v France, Ireland; 1999 v Wales, Ireland; 2000 v Ireland (sub); 2001 v France (sub).

Daniel Heckenberg
Born: 27 October 1979
A front-row forward with the Australian Schoolboys who beat the touring BARLA Young Lions in 1997, Daniel started his career at Western Suburbs Magpies but joined St George in 1998. He made only five appearances for the merged St George/Illawarra club in 2000 but

still won a call-up from Scotland for the World Cup - Daniel qualifies through his mother, who is from Edinburgh.

The prop spent most of 2001 playing in the Dragons' successful second grade team in the NSWRL, but he missed their First Division Grand Final triumph over Parramatta Eels having only just recovered from injury. However, he had shown enough ability during the season to be given a contract by the Eels after being released by the Dragons.
2000 v Maori, Ireland, Samoa.

Gareth Hewitt
Born: 5 January 1979
Born and bred in Bradford, Leeds Academy centre Gareth informed Scotland coach Billy McGinty of his eligibility - his father's mother is from Aberdeen - and got a surprise call-up for the 1998 Tri-Nations. He played just 10 minutes of international rugby - as a first-half replacement while Logan Campbell visited the blood bin - before losing his place to Mike Dixon the following week and has yet to regain it. He left Headingley without a first-team appearance and played just three times for Salford City Reds before dropping into the NFP with Sheffield Eagles for the 2000-01 season, where he became a regular.
1998 v France (sub).

Iain Higgins
Born: 14 September 1976
Robert Iain Higgins was born in Nottingham to Glaswegian parents but moved to Perthshire when he was 12. He began playing League at Cambridge University before joining London Broncos in June 1997. He was soon making his Scotland debut, alongside Broncos team-mates Nick Mardon and Andrew Duncan.

A stocky centre or winger, he only made one start for London in two seasons, but scored two tries in seven appearances off the bench, including one with his first touch of the ball in the first team. So Higgins dropped into the NFP and had a hugely successful 1998-99 season with Hunslet Hawks, scoring a try in their thrilling 12-11 win over Dewsbury in the NFP Grand Final. But when they failed to win a place in Super League, he took a year out to complete his qualification as a solicitor before returning to Hunslet in 2000-01. Iain's displays won him a surprise Scotland recall and, when his Hunslet contract expired, at the

beginning of 2002 he succeeded in getting a three-month deal to play again for the Broncos in Super League VII after impressing at their training camp in Gosford, NSW. However, he did not get a Super League chance with the Broncos and in May 2002 joined Rochdale.
1997 v France (sub); 2001 v France.

Richard Horne
Born: 16 July 1982
Arguably the most controversial of all Rugby League World Cup 2000 selections, Richard has no Scottish connections. A grandfather born in the Isle of Man made him eligible for all four home nations and he was chosen by his club boss at Hull FC, Shaun McRae, to play for Scotland.

This exceptionally talented scrum-half joined Hull from local amateurs Ideal ABI and won honours with Yorkshire Academy, Great Britain Academy, and Great Britain Under-21s. He became a Hull FC first-team regular in 2000 and won his Scotland caps in the World Cup.

After a tremendous 2001 season, in which he helped Hull to third place, Horne was selected for Great Britain & Ireland for the Ashes series, making his debut against France and coming on as a substitute in the stunning win over the Kangaroos at Huddersfield.
2000 v Maori, Ireland, Samoa.

James How
Born: 20 January 1975
James was born in London, but qualified for Scotland through residency. A big forward who played centre for Scottish Students while representing Edinburgh University, How kicked a goal in the historic 10-6 win over England in the 1996 Student World Cup. The previous year, James scored a try against Russia on his senior debut and another against the USA, in the Emerging Nations Cup. He also played Union at university, and stopped playing League after moving to London to work in the city. He played Union for Saracens and Rosslyn Park before dropping down to Surrey League level with the Law Society RFC.
1995 v Russia - try, USA - try, Cook Is.

Mark Keenan
Born: 11 November 1975
Mark came through the academy at Workington Town, making his top

flight debut at 19, playing under Kiwi legend Kurt Sorensen. He made seven Super League appearances in 1996, the year he was capped by Scotland, but his emergence was ill-timed as soon-to-be-relegated Workington were struggling on and off the pitch. After another dismal campaign, in 1998, half-back Keenan joined local rivals Whitehaven Warriors. But he made just 10 NFP appearances for them before moving into the amateur game. He spent 2001 with Widnes St Maries ARLFC. *1996 v Ireland.*

Martin Ketteridge
Born: 2 October 1964
Dundee-born, but brought up in Doncaster, prop-forward Martin joined Castleford from Moorends ARLFC in June 1983, having won Yorkshire Colts honours and played Union for South Yorkshire boys.

During 12 years at Wheldon Road, arguably Martin's biggest moment

came in 1986 when his two points won the Challenge Cup for Castleford as they beat Hull KR 15-14 in front of more than 82,000 at Wembley. However, his two missed conversions in the second half almost cost Castleford dear. Martin, who kicked all 17 of the team's goals in the four games en route to Wembley, was also man-of-the-match in the incredible 1994 Regal Trophy final slaughter of mighty Wigan.

He then joined Halifax and, while at Thrum Hall, got the chance to represent his country, playing in Scotland's first ever international and scoring a try in the win over

Martin Ketteridge with Darrall Shelford in background (Photo: David Williams)

USA in the Emerging Nations competition. He was near the end of his career when he made 12 appearances in the first Super League season for Halifax.

He spent 2000 with his first club, Redhill ARLFC, before joining Castleford Lock Lane as player-coach.

1995 v Ireland – 3 goals, USA – try, Cook Is (sub); 1996 v Ireland - 2 goals.

Alex Killen

A sergeant in the RAF, Alex represented Scotland in the 1995 Emerging Nations Cup while playing rugby for Peterborough. As Rugby League became officially acknowledged in the forces, Alex played at prop for the RAF throughout the late 1990s against the likes of Royal Navy, Army and GB Students.

Bizarrely, despite all his experience, he appeared for the RAF Emerging Players against Emerging Welsh Students in 2000.

1995 v USA (sub), Cook Is (sub).

Andy Knight

Born: 27 February 1972

Born in Stirling and raised near Thurso in Caithness, after representing North Scotland Schools RU Andy went to Napier College in Edinburgh to study hospitality and management, something he has now taken into the bar/restaurant trade. At college he took up League, appearing for Scotland in the first ever match against the North-East at Meadowbank and the inaugural (unofficial) international in Ireland in 1995.

With no serious League being played in Scotland, Andy returned to Union with Boroughmuir RFC, where he had scored 48 points from stand-off on his debut in a 104-0 win. He has been there since 1990, clocking up a Scottish Cup Final appearance in 1997, a trip to the Dubai Sevens and captaining Boroughmuir in 1999-2000, around which time Andy helped coach both Scotland Students and amateurs.

1995 v Ireland.

Simon Knox

Born: 14 October 1972

Cumbrian Simon, who can play second-row or centre, started his career with Hensingham ARL before joining Carlisle Border Raiders in December 1991. He moved on to Whitehaven Warriors before getting his first chance in Super League with Bradford Bulls in 1996. He spent two years mainly coming off the bench but did score seven tries before brief spells with Salford Reds, Workington and Halifax Blue Sox. He played for Scotland in 1998.

Simon returned to the NFP with Widnes in April 2000 and went on to win the Grand Final with the Vikings in an outstanding 2001 season. He was rewarded with a recall to the Scotland squad (but did not play) and earned a place in the NFP Team of the Year.

One of the best props in the NFP, Simon did not play with Widnes in Super League, but joined Oldham so he could continue his day job. But after just three games there, he signed for Leigh in February 2002.
1998 v France (sub), Ireland.

Andrew Lambert
Born: 11 August 1976
Australian-born, but with Scottish paternal grandparents who emigrated to Sydney in 1933, Andrew impressed so much for Scotland Students in the 1999 World Cup that Shaun McRae promoted him to the full squad for the Tri-Nations matches that year. He moved from Workington to Barrow and appeared set for a career in England. But, after just two games for York Wasps later that season, he returned to Australia in January 2000 to be with his ill mother. After her death, he returned to play another 18 times for York, scoring five of his six tries in the final month of the NFP season, again alerting scouts to his talents. But after a few games for London Broncos Alliance side injuries forced him to return to Sydney, where he had once been on the books of Manly Sea Eagles. He is now playing for Wentworthville in Sydney's Metro Cup.
1999 v Wales (sub) - 2 tries, Ireland (sub).

Dale Laughton
Born: 10 January 1971
Dale was a trialist goalkeeper with his local soccer club Barnsley FC until dragged out of bed one morning by his brother Ronnie (now a senior referee) to make up the numbers for their village team, Dodworth, in a South Yorkshire Cup Final against deadly rivals Grimethorpe. Dale claims he did not even know the rules but they won and he was hooked. "If ever anyone stumbled into a career then I was the man," he admitted.

Five months later, Dale was snapped up by Sheffield Eagles, where he spent 10 years, broken only by four games on loan at Wakefield Trinity in 1997. After helping the Eagles win the Second Division Premiership at Old Trafford in 1992, Dale gave up his job as a miner to go full-time. He made his Scotland debut in 1997 against France. The 6ft 1in forward was rewarded in 1998 with the ultimate prizes in the game: a Challenge Cup winners' medal after the Eagles stunned Wigan, and Great Britain honours.

"I know that if I had stuck at football and made it to the top I could have been picking up 20 grand a week but there were no guarantees I'd have made it," admits Dale, the son of a professional boxer. "So I know I made the right choice."

Dale captained the newly-merged Huddersfield-Sheffield Giants to the wooden spoon in 2000, after which he made some rare appearances for Scotland at the World Cup. Great Britain commitments had made him miss the 1998 and 1999 matches. After an injury-wrecked 2001, Dale left relegated Huddersfield and signed for Warrington.

1997 v France; 2000 v Maori, Ireland, Samoa.

Scott Logan

Born: 22 June 1976

Scott was born in Wollongong to a Scottish father, who tragically died aged just 44, in early 2002. Scott played junior Rugby League at Brisbane Easts but returned to New South Wales to start his pro career with the Sydney City Roosters, making his debut in 1996. He became a star prop at the Sydney Football Stadium, although a broken cheekbone forced him to miss the 2000 Grand Final defeat by Brisbane Broncos. He recovered to make his Scotland debut at the World Cup a month later.

Scott's British passport made him particularly attractive to Super League clubs but it was still a surprise when his international boss, Shaun McRae, persuaded Sydney Roosters to let Logan join Hull midway through the 2001 NRL season.

No relation to former Scotland Rugby Union captain Kenny Logan, Scott is a keen golfer and intends to play far more when he retires to Queensland's Gold Coast.

2000 v Maori, Ireland, Samoa.

Neil Lowe

Born: 20 December 1978

Neil joined Featherstone Rovers from Hunslet Parkside in 1997 and was selected for Mike Gregory's Great Britain Academy side, playing against France Under-21s alongside Scotland's Lee Gilmour.

A try-scoring second-rower, Neil played for Featherstone in the 1998 First Division Grand Final against Wakefield Trinity. When he left the field after 50 minutes, Rovers were 18-12 up, only to lose 24-22 in a thriller. He made his Scotland debut in 1999, coming on twice as a substitute. Neil failed to fulfil his potential at that stage, missing the World Cup in 2000. But he had a good season after that and returned to Billy McGinty's Scotland team for the 2001 trip to France, scoring his first international try.

1999 v Ireland (sub), Wales (sub); 2001 v France - try.

Graham Mackay

Born: 12 October 1968

Probably one of the strangest selections ever for Scotland, Graham was an Australian Rugby League international playing Union for Leeds Tykes when he made his one and only appearance for Scotland RL in the World Cup. His Scottish grandfather, who once played bagpipes for the Queen, qualified him for Scotland under the RLIF qualification rules.

The Scotland episode fits well with Mackay's bizarre CV. The Sydneysider, who scored two tries in his only appearance for the Kangaroos - against Papua New Guinea in the 1992 World Cup – has played for 11 clubs in a nomadic cross-code career. He also represented his native New South Wales at Rugby League four times while with Penrith Panthers, for whom he played in the World Club Challenge defeat by Wigan.

In Australia, Mackay also played for Western Suburbs, Sydney City, South Queensland Crushers, Gold Coast Chargers and Manly, and then played Union with Bezier in South West France in 1999.

Mackay soon joined Leeds Rugby Club in a deal which would see him play both codes. The bulldozing 6ft 2in, 17-and-a-half stone winger had an explosive spell at Leeds Rhinos in the second half of the 2000 season, earning a place in the Super League Dream Team and the Scotland squad. By that time he was the [Union] Tykes' top try-scorer as they won promotion to the Premiership.

But before clinching the title, Mackay announced he was making a shock move down the road to Bradford Bulls, having had a short spell at Odsal as a precocious youngster in 1989-90. This time he was magnificent, contributing a dozen touchdowns as they romped to the minor Premiership. He capped his League career by scoring the final try in the Bulls' hammering of Wigan in the 2001 Grand Final and Henry Paul allowed him to convert it, precisely 10 years after winning the Australian Grand Final with Penrith.

He returned to Leeds Tykes for his sixth back-to-back season before planning to retire to Queensland's Gold Coast. However, he changed his mind in January 2002, quitting Union to sign for his Scotland boss Shaun McRae at Hull FC.

2000 v Maori - goal.

David Maiden
Born: 7 August 1971

'Maido' became a crowd favourite in two seasons at Hull FC but was still released at the end of an excellent 2001 campaign in a cost-cutting measure. Despite an offer to stay in Super League with Wakefield, he went back home to the Atherton Tablelands in northern Queensland, where he grew up, playing in the Cairns District 'Bush' League.

David was returning to his roots having spent most of his career playing at that level with the likes of South Townsville, Pittsworth, Mareeba Gladiators and Cairns Cyclones. His only top-grade experience was a few games for South Queensland Crushers, and after scoring two tries in the Country-City match in 1998, he headed to Britain to see his relatives in the Widnes area. But before he'd visited anyone, he'd signed for expansion franchise Gateshead Thunder.

A strong and quick back-row or centre, Maiden had three enjoyable years in England, all with coach Shaun McRae, who used him as an impact player off the bench at Gateshead, but rated him so highly that he kept Maiden when he had to release 12 import players for the merger with Hull. With English, Welsh and Scottish roots, Gateshead chief executive Shane Richardson, who was Scotland manager, moved fast to persuade David to make his Scotland debut in the 1999 Home Nations.

1999 v Wales, Ireland; 2000 v Maori (sub) - try, Ireland (sub), Samoa (sub); 2001 v France - try.

Gavin Manclark

A Currie RFC Union player, Gavin played at centre against Ireland in the Stena Sealink Challenge match in 1995 - he had to lend Alan Tait a spare pair of boots - and scored two tries. He was also in the Emerging Nations squad later that year, representing Edinburgh University. He later played Union for Leith.

1995 v Ireland – 2 tries, Russia, Cook Is (sub).

Nick Mardon

Born: 24 September 1971

A former captain of Scottish Students, Nick played in the 1992 Student World Cup in Australia while studying economics and maths at Edinburgh University, where he first learned the game. He also played for Scotland Schoolboys at basketball, football and cricket.

In Union, full-back Nick played for Scotland Universities, Districts, Edinburgh and then Scotland A (against South Africa in 1995), eventually making the full squad without being capped. But he went a step further in League, making his SRL debut in 1996 while with Boroughmuir RUFC.

After impressing at international level, Nick was recommended to the London Broncos by Bev Risman and moved south in January 1997 to join the London club. He made only 23 appearances in two injury-effected seasons at the club, although he did play in the famous win over Canberra Raiders at The Stoop. His place at London was taken by Andrew Duncan, who then joined him in the Scotland set-up.

Nick, now based in Staines, was one of only two Scottish-born players in the squad for the 1998 Tri-Nations but did not play. He moved to London Welsh Union club for the 1998-99 season, while working as a chartered accountant.

1996 v W9, Ireland - try; 1997 v France.

Charlie McAlister

Born: 17 March 1963

Charlie was born in Waitera in New Zealand and played union for NZ Maori and the All Blacks Under-18 team. Indeed, he played Union, for Bradford & Bingley, when he first moved to Yorkshire.

A prodigious goalkicker, 6ft 2in, 17-stone Charlie took up League and knocked over 14 goals and scored three tries in the last four games of the 1987-88 season for Oldham – whose team included Scotland colleague Hugh Waddell - as they won the Second Division and the Premiership. His last gasp conversion saw off Featherstone in a 28-26 thriller at Old Trafford, having thrown away a 22-0 lead to trail 22-26.

Charlie played in the top flight with Sheffield Eagles before dropping into Division Three for a spell with Whitehaven. During a loan period with Keighley Cougars, he scored five tries in 10 games - all of them won - as Keighley clinched the divisional title in 1993.

Short spells with Oldham and Rochdale Hornets came before Charlie made his Scotland debut in 1995, kicking four goals in the win over Russia at the Emerging Nations tournament. By then he had retired from the professional game and was with Oldham amateur club Higginshaw in the North West Counties League. He later returned to New Zealand.

1995 v Russia – 4 goals, USA, Cook Is.

Stuart McCarthy
Born: 28 March 1973

An Anglia (Leicester) University graduate, Stuart first appeared for Scotland in the 1995 Emerging Nations tournament, returning from Zimbabwe, where he was living, to play for the land of his forefathers. As well as the legendary meeting with room-mate Alan Tait, Stuart was captured on video psyching up his team-mates before a game telling them they were going to win "because they were Scottish" – all said in a broad Essex accent.

Stuart scored the winning try for Scottish Students against England in the 1996 Student World Cup, and impressed on the wing for London Broncos' second team during a brief spell at The Stoop. But after playing for Scotland against France in 1997, he returned to his initial code, playing again for Canvey Island RUFC.

In 2000, Stuart moved to New York City through his work with HSBC - he was back in Britain during the terrorist attacks on 11 September 2001 - and played for New York Rugby Union Club.

1995 v Russia (sub), USA, Cook Is; 1997 v France - try.

Ryan McDonald

Born: 24 February 1978

Ryan started his career at Leeds before spending the 1998 season on loan at Bramley, playing alongside Barrie McDermott in the front row. Still a teenager, prop Ryan did enough in Academy rugby for Leeds to be named in George Fairbairn's Scotland squad for the game against France in 1997 but did not play until four years later.

In search of first-team Rugby League, Ryan joined Dewsbury and, as he had for most of that season, came off the bench for the Rams in their 2000 NFP Grand Final win over Leigh. But he really came of age the following season in a struggling Dewsbury side. Soon after making his Scotland debut, he achieved his aim of becoming a full-time player when he signed a one-year deal with Widnes Vikings for their Super League debut season. Coach Neil Kelly knew Ryan well from his days as Dewsbury boss and thought he could develop far more if full-time.

2001 v France (sub).

Wayne McDonald

Born: 3 September 1975

The giant prop forward - the tallest player in Super League at 6ft 7in - was ever-present for Scotland for three seasons after making his debut, albeit over only six matches. Wayne turned professional for Wakefield Trinity from Middleton ARLFC in 1993-94, representing Great Britain at Academy level. He came on for the last 10 minutes of Wakefield's dramatic 24-22 First Division Grand Final win over Featherstone in 1998, in time for the try which sent the Wildcats into Super League.

One successful year later, having been capped by Scotland for the first time, 'Big Mac' joined Scotland boss Shaun McRae at Hull FC but the previously prolific try scorer had a mixed 2000 there: he grabbed the touchdown which bundled Wigan out of the Challenge Cup and scored four tries in 5 Super League starts in a season ruined by a knee injury.

That was enough for St Helens to sign Wayne but, frustrated by the lack of opportunities at Saints, he moved to Leeds Rhinos in October 2001, making it four different Super League clubs in four seasons. He soon appeared in *The Sun* newspaper posing with new team-mate Rob Burrows – a full 15 inches smaller than him.

1999 v Wales, Ireland; 2000 v Maori (sub), Ireland (sub), Samoa (sub); 2001 v France.

Billy McGinty

Born: 6 December 1964

Born in Springburn, Billy is a proud Scot with a bizarre accent courtesy of spending his first six years in Glasgow before moving to Johannesburg, then Widnes. Billy's potential was clear when he was playing for Widnes Tigers Under-13s when he was just 8. Having captained Lancashire Under-17s, he joined Warrington in 1982, playing part-time for the first team while working as a labourer.

Billy, who won full Lancashire honours, played in the historic international development match against Wigan in Milwaukee in June 1989 despite having passport problems en route to the USA because his real surname is Paton after his natural father, rather than McGinty, his stepfather.

A year later, Billy came off the bench in the Wire's 1990 Challenge Cup defeat by Wigan but returned to Wembley two years later playing now for the victorious Wigan side - and an infamous televised meeting with Prime Minister John Major in the showers afterwards.

Billy spent four fantastic years at Central Park in which he won three championship medals and played in three successive World Club Challenges, including arguably the greatest result of all time by an English club when the Cherry-and-Whites won 20-14 in front of 50,000 Broncos fans in Brisbane in 1993-94. Billy also played a part in the greatest British Lions victory of his generation: the 33-10 win over the Kangaroos in the second test in Melbourne in June 1992, battling away in the second-row for an hour of that stunning win.

After adding a second Regal Trophy winners' medal in 1993 to the one he won with Warrington two years earlier, Billy left Wigan for Workington where he stayed for two years before retiring. Billy went into coaching at Wigan and took charge of Scotland in 1998 and 2001 when he led them to a record win in France. But he never played a full international for his homeland, however, because he received a career-ending head injury against Australia at the World Nines in Fiji, making his final senior - and only Super League - appearance in 1996.

After coaching the winning 2001 Alliance Grand Final team, Billy left Wigan to become skills coach at Sale Sharks RUFC.

1996 v W9.

Danny McKelvie
Born: 10 October 1969

Danny's fleeting international appearance came while he was with Dewsbury Rams, having joined the club from Ryedale-York in October 1994. His 27 minutes for Scotland came when he replaced Dewsbury team-mate Glenn Bell in the game at Firhill against France in 1997. He spent his final season at Dewsbury often on the bench with Scotland colleague Lee Milner.

Danny's last big game was the Challenge Cup Fifth Round tie with Wigan in 1998, when Jason Robinson scored a hat-trick of tries in the 30 minutes Danny was on the pitch. However, McKelvie's display in the 56-0 hammering was enough to earn him man-of-the-match nominations.
1997 v France (sub).

Jim McLaren
Born: 28 June 1972

Born in Stirling, James Gerard McLaren learned much of his rugby in Australia, having moved to Bathurst in New South Wales with his family as a seven-year-old. He came over to play Union for Stirling County and Glasgow Under-21s but returned to Australia to attend university, and switched to League, playing for Canberra Raiders in the ARL.

However, he won his one Scotland RL cap while with Wakefield Trinity, for whom he scored eight tries in 20 appearances in 1997. He was playing under the cloud of a six month ban from the Scottish Rugby Union for kicking Melrose's Craig Chalmers in the face while playing for Stirling County. Despite that misdemeanour, the 6ft 3in, 17 stone 4 pounds giant spent the following winter playing for the SRU's professional side Glasgow Caledonians and Scotland A. Jim then spent two seasons with Bourgoin-Jallieu in France but still made his full Scotland RU debut, at centre against Argentina, in August 1999. He earned himself a World Cup place and became a Scotland regular in 2000, returning to play for the Glasgow Caledonians side. He was joined at the club by his bother Tom.
1997 v France.

Lee Milner

Born: 26 February 1977

A second-row forward, Yorkshireman Lee broke into the Huddersfield Giants first team, aged just 19, and was soon capped by Scotland - he qualifies via a grandparent from Musselburgh. After being named man- of- the-match in the inaugural full international against Ireland, the Great Britain Academy tourist was much sought after. But his professional career did not go according to plan. He was hoping to win his first Scotland cap against France in 1997 - a new nation can only award caps from their second game onwards - but did not play. Lee joined Dewsbury in 1998, but was then sacked by the Rams in February 1999 after playing for his old amateur club, Greetland, under an assumed name. He joined Halifax Blue Sox, but after one appearance returned to Greetland.
1996 v Ireland.

Gareth Morton

Born: 21 October 1982

Although born in Scotland, Gareth grew up in Widnes and joined Leeds from Leigh East amateur club. A crucial player for the Rhinos' Alliance team in the 2000 season, he can play at loose-forward or stand-off. He made his full international debut before he had even played in Super League, coming on in Scotland's win in Lezignan in 2001. But after scoring four tries in Great Britain Academy's two tests in New Zealand, he made an impressive debut in the Rhinos' last Super League game of 2001 - a defeat at Bradford.
2001 v France (sub).

Gary Murdock

Born: 6 January 1968

Gary turned to Rugby League with Carlisle Border Raiders in June 1987 and was one of seven Scots at the club at one stage. Capped by Cumbria against the touring Australians, Kiwis and France, Gary won his first international honour with Scotland in 1995 after moving to Workington Town but he missed the Emerging Nations tournament later that year through injury. He returned for the Fiji World Nines the following year, during which Gary moved into coaching, first with amateur club Ellenborough, then as player-coach of the struggling Lancashire Lynx in 1999. He returned to Workington Town as player-coach but hung up his boots at the turn of the millennium and left the club in April 2002. At the time of writing he is scouting for Wakefield Trinity Wildcats.

1995 v Ireland; 1996 v W9, Ireland (sub).

Jon Neill

Born: 19 December 1968

Originally from Whitehaven, prop Jonathan was a painter and decorator who played part-time with St Helens after joining them in July 1987 from Kells ARLFC. Capped by Cumbria in 1994-95 and by Great Britain Colts, Neill had played in the 1992 and 1993 Challenge Cup Finals at Wembley, winning the second, before leaving Saints for Huddersfield Giants in 1996 after just one appearance in Super League.

After helping the Giants to the Premiership title and promotion to Super League, Jon made his international debut against France.

After the Huddersfield-Sheffield merger in 2000, he moved to Swinton to continue working with Scotland assistant coach Mike Gregory and despite only playing six games that season due to injury, signed a new contract in September 2001.

1997 v France; 1999 v Ireland.

Chris Orr

Born: 18 November 1973

Capped after being released by Huddersfield Giants, scrum-half Orr was born in Sydney, but has a Scottish grandfather. Chris was so keen to make his Scotland debut that he paid his own airfare from Australia to play. Having played League for Manly, Cronulla Sharks and Gold Coast Chargers, Chris joined Huddersfield in November 1997. He made 22 appearances for the Giants in Super League, kicking 38 goals. However, he turned down the chance to captain Oldham to return to Australia, signing for Gold Coast Breakers Union club in the Brisbane Premiership.

In February 1999 he offered his kicking services to Scotland RU coach Jim Telfer: Orr claimed a RL goalkicking success rate of 75%. Telfer did not take him up on the offer.

1998 v France, Ireland.

Lee Penny
Born: 24 September 1974

This Wigan-born and bred full-back signed for Warrington from Orrell St James and made his professional debut in 1992-93. Lee was soon capped by Great Britain at Under-21 level playing alongside Scotland's Gary Christie and Lions stars Jason Robinson and Chris Joynt, before touring Australia in 1994 with John Kear's GB Academy side along with the likes of Iestyn Harris and Andy Farrell - "an amazing experience I'll never forget," he said.

Lee's next international experience came when he made his Scotland debut in 1998 but he missed all but the one of Scotland's next six internationals through a series of injuries.

He was part of the Warrington side humiliated by Australian clubs in the World Club Championship in 1997, a few months after he was transfer-listed for £120,000, but he remained at Wilderspool, receiving a testimonial in 2002. Lee scored a club record four tries in a Super League game against Leeds on 23 June 2000.
1998 v France, Ireland; 2000 v Maori - try.

Andrew Purcell
Born: 20 May 1971

Queensland-born Andrew was a regular alongside Scott Cram in the 1998 Illawarra Steelers side but, like Cram, found himself surplus to requirements after they merged with St George. Purcell had impressed former Workington coach Peter Walsh when he spent the 1994-95 season as a winger or centre with Swinton and then Batley, before returning to challenge for a place in Illawarra's first grade. Now coach at Hull Sharks, Walsh recruited Purcell, who was by now a hooker who could also play stand-off or loose-forward, in 1999.

But after a season on Humberside ruined by a back injury, Purcell moved to Castleford along with fellow Scots Darren Shaw and Logan Campbell - Castleford boss Stuart Raper knew Andrew from their time together at Cronulla. Tigers' supporters rarely saw the best of Purcell due to injuries, although he was fit in time to play for Scotland - land of his grandfather - in the World Cup. They were his last appearances in Britain before going home to attend university in Cronulla.
2000 v Maori, Samoa.

Scott Rhodes

Born: 21 June 1980

Like Gareth Morton, this half-back made his Scotland debut in 1999 while still a teenager and before he had even played a first team game for Leeds Rhinos. Scott is from York, where he played as a junior with Heworth, although his Dad is from Aberdeen.

Scotland boss Shaun McRae tried to take Scott to Gateshead Thunder in 1999 and finally signed him on loan at Hull, where he played twice in 2000. But, unable to get past GB international Ryan Sheridan into the Leeds side, he moved to Sheffield Eagles at the start of 2001. He spent 2000-01 working part-time on the flood damage scheme in his home city.

1999 v Wales, Ireland; 2000 v Samoa (sub) - try; 2001 v France.

Jason Roach

Born: 2 May 1971

Much-travelled Jason has rarely spent more than one season at any club since leaving hometown team St Helens for London Broncos in March 1995. He lived up to his reputation as a prolific try-scoring winger in brief spells in the capital and at Swinton, Castleford Tigers and then was on the move again, joining Warrington Wolves in 1998.

During two seasons at Wilderspool, he made his Scotland debut, qualifying through his grandfather, a proud Scot who regularly wore his kilt in Lancashire. Jason rejoined Swinton Lions in 1999-2000 and, despite scoring 16 tries in one season, was on the move again, to Oldham. He then spent a winter playing Rugby Union with Orrell before signing for Whitehaven in May 2001 but only squeezed in six league appearances, touching down twice. After a spell in Union with Birmingham RFC, he signed for a third time with Swinton in October 2001 to play under Scotland assistant coach Mike Gregory. At the start of 2002, he had scored 96 tries in 155 senior career appearances.

1998 v France - 2 tries, Ireland; 1999 v Ireland, Wales

Michael Rush

Born: 2 March 1976

Mike, a scrum-half from St Helens, was brought up playing League for Blackbrook amateurs with fellow Scottish international Andy Craig, before turning professional with Huddersfield. He played in their Alliance side for coaches Alex Murphy and George Fairbairn.

After a short spell at Leigh Centurions, he returned to education, spending two years at Edge Hill College in Ormskirk. There he represented Scottish Students, qualifying through his grandparents, and was elevated to the senior side for the Emerging Nations Cup. After playing at the 1996 Student World Cup, Mike took up development work at Wigan Warriors, before gaining invaluable experience with Brisbane Broncos. He returned to his home town to become development officer for St Helens RLFC.

1995 v Russia, USA.

Danny Russell

Born: 24 December 1969

Scotland's captain and ever-present from the first full international began in 1996 to the end of the 2000 World Cup, Danny won nine caps before retiring after the World Cup. Born in Brisbane but with a grandma from Wick, the hooker learned the game with Sandgate Sharks and was man-of-the-match when he represented Queensland in the Under-21 State of Origin series.

After playing for Aussie giants Manly, he came to England to be player-coach at third division Carlisle Border Raiders in 1996, when he made his Scotland debut in the Fiji World Nines. He moved to Huddersfield Giants the following season, where he was virtually ever-present in three years at Fartown, winning the 1997 First Division Premiership and promotion to Super League

He went on to coach Huddersfield YMCA in the Pennine League and in 2002 became coach of the Giants' Academy Under-17 side.

1996 v W9, Ireland - try; 1997 v France - try; 1998 v France, Ireland; 1999 v Wales - try, Ireland - try; 2000 v Maori, Ireland, Samoa

Darren Shaw

Born: 5 October 1971

This hard-working, stocky front-rower was born in Melbourne but qualifies for Scotland through his mother, who's from Lanark. He began playing League as a six year old after his family moved to Queensland, playing with West End juniors before going semi-professional with Ipswich Jets.

He signed for Brisbane Broncos, but was loaned to their sister club in London in 1994, where he failed to score a point in his first 33 league appearances. He volunteered for Scotland's first trip - to Ireland in 1995 - and became a loyal servant for the team, and London's first Scotland international. He captained the side for the first time in the win in France in July 2001.

After a brief spell back in the NRL with Canberra Raiders, Darren achieved his greatest moment in the game: winning the Challenge Cup with Sheffield Eagles in that incredible final triumph over Wigan in 1998. When the Eagles merged with Huddersfield, Darren moved to Castleford, where he had a successful 2000 season. He joined Salford City Reds for 2002.

1995 v Ireland, Russia, Cook Is (sub);1996 v Ireland, W9;1998 v France, Ireland; 1999 v Wales, Ireland; 2000 v Maori (sub), Ireland (sub), Samoa (sub); 2001 v France.

Graeme Shaw
Born: 13 June 1975

A second-row forward, Graeme joined the Oldham Roughyeds from Bradford Bulls early in the 1998 season having failed to make a regular first team spot his own at Odsal. A former BARLA Young Lions international, Graeme picked up his Scotland caps when he came off the bench in the 1998 Tri-Nations tournament. After three years with Oldham, Graeme moved onto Keighley Cougars in May 2001.

1998 v France (sub), Ireland (sub).

Darrall Shelford
Born: 29 July 1972

Darrall comes from Rotorua in New Zealand, a Maori area with many tourists visiting the volcanic springs, which send steam pouring from every nook and cranny. However, Darrall came to Britain to play professional Rugby League.

He arrived at Bradford Northern in 1990 with a splendid pedigree, having represented the NZ Maori and the All Blacks B team while playing club Rugby Union for Bay of Plenty, with whom he faced the British Lions in 1983, and the historic Ngongotaha League club. Darrall's brother, Wayne, captained the All Blacks.

A powerful centre, Darrall was a full-time player at Bradford when most top flight players still had day jobs. He played in the 1991 Regal Trophy Final but unfortunately won nothing before moving onto

Huddersfield Giants in August 1994, missing Bradford's rebirth as the Bulls. Once at Fartown, his losing run continued in the 1995 Second Division Premiership at Old Trafford.

However, having qualified for Scotland through Highland grandparents, Darrall was one of the three permitted professionals in the Emerging Nations Cup of 1995, becoming Scotland's first hat-trick hero with three tries against the USA at Northampton's Sixfields Stadium.

After retiring as a player, he rejoined the Bulls' coaching staff, also coaching Scotland amateurs in 1998.

1995 v Ireland - try, Russia, USA – 3 tries, Cook Is; 1996 v W9, Ireland - try.

Chris Simmers
Born: 17 October 1969

Glaswegian Chris was brought up in one of Scotland's most illustrious Rugby Union families. His father, Brian, and grandfather, Max, both played for Scotland, and went on to become chairman of Glasgow Hawks RUFC and Scottish RU president respectively. While Chris never won full Union honours, he did represent Scotland in the Super League World Nines in Fiji in 1996 - the only senior League he played.

Chris earned selection for the Nines after a trial game at Lancaster while playing for Edinburgh Accies Union side. Soon after he signed for Australian Rugby Union club Manly, where he spent a season playing alongside five full internationals, including Willy Ofahengaue.

Returning to Union in Scotland in 1997, Chris - a centre - won the Scottish Cup and Division 2 titles with Glasgow Hawks and, after turning professional with Glasgow Caledonians played for Scotland A. He also represented Scottish Students at two Rugby Union Student World Cups.

Back at the Hawks - where Scotland Rugby League Students played Queensland in 2001 - he played in the 2000 Scottish Cup Final at Murrayfield before leaving to take up a marketing job with Westpac back in Sydney.

1996 v W9.

Mark Smith
Mark, a huge, hard-working second-row forward, played for Scottish Students in 1995 while at Dundee University and was elevated to the senior side for the Emerging Nations Cup, scoring a try against the USA.

Nicknamed 'Thumper', he was Irish but qualified for Scotland through his family. He returned to Northern Ireland after his studies.

1995 v Russia, USA – try, Cook Is.

Pehi James Solomon

Born: 17 August 1976

Originally from New Zealand, 'PJ' joined Lancashire Lynx in March 1997 from Wellington Dukes and spent three seasons with the club, winning the Second Division in 1998 and reaching the final of the Treize Tournoi, only to lose to Villeneuve. He won his first Scotland cap in 1997, and played twice in 1998.

He left the struggling Chorley-based club in 1999 to play Union north of the border with Gala RFC, and was not selected for Scotland RL again, although he did make a guest Rugby League appearance for Edinburgh Eagles in their Challenge Cup game with Woolston in December that year.

PJ represented the SRU's Scottish Thistles development squad in Sevens tournaments in 2001 and starred for London-based ex-pats side, the New Zealand Wekas.

1997 v France; 1998 v France, Ireland.

Iain Stanger

Born: 28 September 1970

Originally from Inverness, Iain first played League while at Moray House College of Education in Edinburgh. He had played Union for Highland, but attended Mal Reid's trials for Scottish Students at Heriots and within three years was playing in the 1992 Student World Cup - and was described in the programme as "a chunky barnstorming prop".

After four years in the student squad, he appeared in all Scotland's historic early matches: the first ever one against the North-East at Meadowbank, despite protests about him playing League from the SRU - "Rugby League had been good to me so I was going to play" he said - the clash with Ireland in Dublin in 1995; and the Emerging Nations Cup. He also captained GB Students.

A PE teacher, Iain's League career ended when he moved to Aberdeen. Instead he spent nearly a decade playing Union with Aberdeen Grammar School Former Pupils in Scottish Premier 1.

1995 v Ireland (sub), Russia (sub).

Jason Syme

Born: 27 June 1973

Jason played District Rugby Union at all age levels before appearing for Dunfermline. He started playing League while at the University of Abertay in Dundee and first represented his country with Scotland Students in 1994. In the next five years he also played internationals for Scotland Amateurs RL and Union for Scottish Universities. When he was capped in the amateur's inaugural 1997 game against Ireland, while with Central Centurions, Jason became (along with Graeme Thompson) the only Scot to play for all three international league teams: students, amateurs and seniors. At that time he was playing Union for Heriots FP.

Jason went on to captain Kirkcaldy RUFC in Scottish Premier 1 and then skippered Caledonia Reds in 2000. He has also represented the Samurai's International Sevens Select.

1996 v Ireland (sub).

Alan Tait

Born: 2 July 1964

Alan has the rare distinction of being capped by the British Lions in both codes, and being capped by Scotland RU. He was born in Kelso, but brought up in Workington after his father moved to Cumbria to play Rugby League when Alan was just three. When he was 15 and his father's professional career was over, they returned to Kelso.

Alan started his illustrious career with the town's Union club and, after winning six caps for Scotland B, made his full Scotland debut against France in the 1987 World Cup. After winning eight caps he decided to follow his father's career path and turn professional, signing for the all-conquering Widnes in 1988.

With a record of more than one try every two games for Kelso, Tait was brought in by Douggie Laughton to add even more points-scoring potential to the Chemics side and, sure enough, Tait made history in the first few couple of weeks, winning a medal without starting a game in the sport. Alan came on as a substitute after nine minutes of the Premiership Final at Old Trafford in 1988 - his third appearance off the bench - and even scored a try as Widnes beat St Helens in front of more than 35,000.

Alan Tait with fellow Scottish legend George Fairbairn
(Photo: David Williams)

Part of Laughton's great side with the likes of Jonathan Davies and
Martin Offiah, Alan won a championship medal in 1989 and a year later
was a World Club Challenge winner after Widnes beat Canberra Raiders
30-18 at Old Trafford.

Among his many other honours were two Premiership triumphs in
which he won the Harry Sunderland Trophy for man of the match in
1989, when he was exemplary at full-back against Hull, and again a year
later, when Alan scored two tries against Bradford. He also played in the
1989 JPS Trophy final, won the Charity Shield three times and the
Lancashire Cup once.

Not surprisingly, Alan became a Great Britain regular, winning 14
caps between 1989 and 1993. It was with the Lions that Tait says his
career took a major turn as he learned more from playing and training
alongside Ellery Hanley than from anyone else in his career despite Tait
already being 28. Among his greatest achievements with the Lions was
playing as a second half substitute in the 1992 World Cup Final in which
Australia scraped a 10-6 win in front of 77,000 at Wembley. He was
denied a late winning try when held up over the line by Tim Brasher.

He was selected for England to play Wales in the 1994-95 season but
withdrew, feeling it would compromise his loyalties to his fatherland,
where he had built a house at Stichill. Soon, Scotland would have its
own League team for him to lead.

Having scored 55 tries in 136 appearances for Widnes, Tait moved to
Leeds in 1992, spending four years at Headingley, playing twice in
losing Challenge Cup Final teams, defeats by Wigan in 1994 and 1995.

Later that year Tait was the star attraction for Scotland in the Emerging Nations World Cup, scoring four tries in three games. He then captained Scotland against Ireland in their first full international.

After six games for Leeds in the inaugural Super League season, Alan returned to Union but remained in the north of England, signing for Newcastle Falcons RUFC. He was immediately a star again, winning the Premiership in 1998-99, scoring 17 tries in 27 appearances for Scotland and being a hero for the British Lions. He scored two tries as they historically won the first two tests and the series in South Africa in 1997.

He last played Union for Scotland in the 1999 World Cup quarter-final defeat by the All Blacks, when he received an emotional farewell from a packed Murrayfield. After finishing playing at Edinburgh Reivers, Alan went into coaching with the SRU.

1995: v Russia - 2 tries, USA, Cook Is— 2 tries; 1996 v Ireland - try.

Steve Tait

Steve was a regular for Scottish Students while studying business at Leeds Metropolitan University, playing in the 1992 Student World Cup in Sydney. Nicknamed 'Magic' for his scheming at scrum-half, he was described in the programme as having "the ability to change the shape of a game with his eye for an opening and astute reading of the game".

That talent saw him sign for hometown club Leeds from local amateurs Milford in November 1994, captaining their second string but he did not break through into the first team. One of the three permitted professionals in the Emerging Nations, Steve also played against Ireland in 1995. No relation to team-mate Alan Tait, Steve gave up the professional game but remained working as an accountant in Leeds.

1995 v Ireland, USA (sub), Cook Is; 1996 v W9.

Graeme Thompson

Born: 25 August 1972

Born and brought up in Edinburgh, Graeme was one of the country's most promising Union players, the back-up to Gregor Townsend in the Scotland Schoolboys side and Gavin Hastings at Watsonians. When some of his mates at Moray House College went down to Gateshead for a Rugby League trial, he went along. He played for Scottish Students in the 1992 World Cup and progressed to Great Britain Students.

In 1995, Graeme made his senior debut in the game in Dublin before impressing hugely in the Emerging Nations competition. Workington Town took him on trial, but he turned down the chance to join the top-flight club because of their financial position. Having been appointed Scottish Development Officer by the RFL, Graeme played for Lomond Valley Raiders and Glasgow Bulls while playing for West of Scotland RUFC in Scotland's Union top flight and coaching League's Scottish Students. After being appointed player development manager for London Broncos in 1998, Graeme retired through injury and concentrated on coaching Crawley Jets to the Summer Conference title, and his work with the Broncos' Academy. Graeme continued to work as co-manager of the full Scotland team. He moved to Leeds in November 2001 as the RFL's Head of Player Development.

1995 v Ireland, Russia (sub) - goal; USA - try & 5 goals; Cook Is - goal; 1996 v W9, Ireland.

Phil Veivers

Born: 25 May 1964

Born in Beaudesert, Australia, this veteran loose-forward was capped while with Huddersfield Giants, who he briefly coached during the 2000 season. He was coaxed out of retirement by Swinton and Scotland assistant coach Mike Gregory to play for the Lions in 2001, adding his experience to a young side. He retired at the end of the season. He then played Union for Cleckheaton.

Phil arrived at St Helens from Brisbane Souths as an unknown, and spent an eventful decade at Knowsley Road, making 381 appearances for Saints. He was very versatile, playing anywhere in midfield. He made three losing appearances at Wembley for Saints, but enjoyed success when he scored a try in the Premiership Final win over Hull KR in 1985.

Phil, who represented Queensland Schools at Union, left Saints to guide Huddersfield into the Super League in 1997, captaining them to a Premiership triumph at Old Trafford on the way. He then won his sole Scotland cap - he was in the 1998 Tri-Nations squad, but did not play. He played for Huddersfield in 1998 in Super League. In May 2002, he became coach at Swinton.

1997 v France.

Adrian Vowles

Born: 30 May 1971

Born in Cunnamulla, in the outback of south Queensland, Adrian first played the game at Charleville All Whites amateur club, 125 miles further north. He turned professional with Gold Coast Seagulls in 1992, before joining North Queensland Cowboys. He made one State of Origin appearance for Queensland, off the bench in 1994, but was still seen in Australia as being not big, strong or fast enough for the top level.

He proved the critics wrong after signing for Castleford in 1997. Two years later he became only the third non-Briton to win the Man of the Steel award for his inspirational displays at loose-forward which helped the Tigers reach the final hurdle of the play-offs in 1999, and the knockout stages a year later. Arguably Stuart Raper's greatest signing, Vowles's ancestry led to him representing Scotland in the 2000 World Cup. He joined Leeds Rhinos for the 2002 season.

2000 v Maori, Ireland, Samoa - try; 2001 v France

Hugh Waddell

Born: 1 September 1959

Born in Ayrshire, but brought up in Burton-on-Trent, Hugh was unusual for a professional rugby player: he was also a florist and a teetotaller. Having switched from Union in September 1983, Hugh played one international for England, against Wales in 1984, while with Blackpool.

At only 5ft 11in, but 16 stone 8 pounds, Hugh was a stocky, powerful prop whose displays for Oldham earned him a Great Britain debut against France in 1987 and, a few weeks after winning the Second Division Premiership in 1988, a place on the Ashes tour. He played for the Lions in their extraordinary third test win over Australia in Sydney. That performance may have tempted Manly to sign Hugh the following close season, joining other English world class players in Australia.

Back home, Hugh moved to Leeds and won the Premiership again in 1992, then spent time with Sheffield Eagles, where he played in the Yorkshire Cup Final in 1992, coming on to replace Dale Laughton.

He moved to Carlisle Border Raiders in January 1994, where he was a one of five Scottish League internationals. After an eight-month spell as player-coach, Hugh went on loan to Whitehaven in 1995. Later that year when he won his first Scotland cap at the Emerging Nations Cup.

He was playing for amateurs Egremont when he signed for Third Division newcomers South Wales in 1996, but his professional career ended when the club folded at the end of the season.

His last medal was for the Scottish Rugby League Championship which he won with Border Eagles in 1998. He was remembered in 2001 when Ian Millward compared the stature of Saints' barrel-shaped Australian signing Barry Ward to Hugh.

1995 v Ireland, Russia – try, USA, Cook Is.

Michael Wainwright

Born: 25 May 1975

A loose-forward, Mike started at amateur club Woolston Rovers before joining Warrington in 1992. It was a dream come true for the Wire fan, whose childhood hero was Mike Gregory. Wainwright made two trips down under early in his career, with Great Britain Academy and Warrington for their World Club Championship defeats at Penrith, Auckland and Cronulla. A giant at 6ft 4in, 'Wedge' played for Scotland in all four 1998 and 1999 fixtures before joining Salford City Reds. He was in the Scotland 2000 World Cup squad but did not play due to a lingering injury. Mike, who is not to be confused with Hunslet's Mike Wainwright and is no relation to former Scotland Union skipper Rob, qualifies for Scotland thanks to grandparents from Partick.

1998 v France, Ireland; 1999 v Wales - try, Ireland.

Colin Wilson

After watching Rugby League avidly on television for years, Colin took up the code in 1997 when he joined Linlithgow Lions. Later that season he was the only home-based player in the full Scotland squad, and made his debut a year later in the 1998 Tri-Nations. A winger for Glasgow Union side Hillhead Jordanhill, Colin switched to prop in the 13-man code. After skippering Scotland in the amateur internationals in 1998, coach Darrall Shelford recommended him for the full team. Colin then had a brief spell in the professional game with Hull KR, aged 29, before moving to Scottish Rugby League side Border Eagles.

1998 v France (sub), Ireland (sub).

13. Scots in Rugby League: 1895 to 1995

In Rugby League's first century - 1895 to 1995 - 230 full internationals from the British Isles crossed codes from Rugby Union to League, 51 of them going on to win full caps in the 13-a-side game. About 150 of those players were Welsh, while only 14 were Scottish Rugby Union internationals, heading south in search of a living from their sport. For most of Scotland, Rugby Union was a middle-class pastime, played by men with regular incomes from professional jobs and therefore no need to be paid for playing rugby.

However, in the Borders region, where Rugby Union was the most popular sport and the main source of employment was agricultural, incomes were low and the opportunity of being paid to perform was too good for many Union players to ignore. Thus, the main flow of players to Rugby League came from the Hawick-Kelso region.

At a time when there was no Scotland Rugby League team to represent, Scots either played for their adopted country - England, Other Nationalities or, if they were top-class talents, Great Britain.

Scot Roy Kinnear played for the Lions at both codes, and Alan Tait later becoming a second Scot to achieve this distinction, following his return to Union from Rugby League.

Considering the lack of prominent Scots in the history of Rugby League, it is surprising how many SRU internationals and other players came south in search of a living from rugby. Here are the leading players and those who played a lesser role in that historic story. Much of the original research for this chapter was in a feature by Trevor Delaney in *Code XIII*; yet despite this, there are almost certainly some other Scottish players we have not included.

Dave Valentine

David Donald 'Paddy' Valentine, who was born in Hawick on 12 September 1926, won just two Rugby Union caps for Scotland before switching codes to play for Huddersfield in 1947, thanks to persistence of fellow Scot Bill Cunningham, Huddersfield's chairman at the time.

He was an instant success in a fantastic star-studded Fartown side and was selected for the full Great Britain team in only his second season of Rugby League. He made his international debut in the defeat of Australia at Headingley on 9 October 1948, and went on to gain a total of 15 caps for the Lions at loose-forward.

According to Ray French, the "black-haired, craggy" Valentine "revealed all the qualities we associate with Scottish Rugby Union back-row forward play - pace, a safe pair of hands, a nimble and far-seeing rugby brain and that rugged approach to tackling which is encouraged in the Border Country."

Few would argue with French's assertion that Valentine "led by example, always in the thick of midfield pack skirmishes but he was a thinker on the game who liked to indulge in open play with the backs".

Having stood in on the wing for the injured Drew Turnball of Leeds - a fellow Scot - on the tour of Australasia in 1954, Valentine's greatest hour came a few months later, when he was appointed captain of the Lions in the first ever World Cup of either of the rugby codes.

Much-ridiculed by the press at the time, the four-team World Cup was treated in a parochial fashion by the RFL, who regarded it as less important than the recent Ashes series. Rather than sending their strongest possible team to France, they sent a scratch squad. After the ugly recriminations from the violent trip down-under earlier in the year, several players were blacklisted by the RFL. Many of the rest boycotted the event in protest at their team-mates' treatment (although having to take even more time off work can not have been too attractive either), including Barrow legend and previous skipper Willie Horne, which allowed Valentine the opportunity to make history.

When several more star players pulled out injured - including Billy Boston - in the days before the trip, only three Lions survived from those that mauled their way across Australasia weeks previously.

"The three bruised-knuckle stalwarts, Phil Jackson, Gerry Helme and Valentine took the boat train from Victoria in late October 1954 with 15 wide-eyed tyros", according to Frank Keating in *The Guardian*'s preview of the 2000 World Cup, dressed in their own sports jackets - the RFL having failed to order the badgered blazers in time for delivery. They changed trains at Paris and headed for Lyon, where the early action would take place.

The players were ludicrously under prepared. As player-trainer-coach-captain, Valentine had time to take just two coaching sessions in the evenings before the squad got on the coach from Leeds to London, and when they got to France, their first session was missed when the bus driver could not find the ground. They even resorted to training with a rolled-up coat because they had no rugby balls.

However, they still managed get revenge against the Australians for their Ashes series defeat that summer with a superb and stunning 28-13 win over the Kangaroos, and a 13-13 draw with France in front of over 37,000 home fans in Toulouse - a French RL record - meant a win over New Zealand was crucial for Great Britain. Thanks in no small part to five tries, including one from fellow Scot David Rose, the Lions roared to a 26-6 victory in Bordeaux's Velodrome. This left the final table with Great Britain and France on 5 points each. On 13 November, in front of 30,368 supporters in Paris, Great Britain won 16-12. David Rose scored a try as Valentine became the only Scotsman ever to lift a world cup in any sport.

A year later, his international career was over. Having played in all but one of the post-war Other Nationalities sides - 16 consecutive international appearances - he ended that chapter of his life in style: captaining Other Nationalities for the first time as they beat England 33-16 at Wigan. After finally becoming Huddersfield skipper for the first time on Christmas Day 1954, Dave's career lay in tatters when he broke his ankle three times, retiring from club rugby in November 1957.

He made an attempted comeback in 1960 for the Yorkshire Cup Final, which Huddersfield lost to Wakefield and he retired a second time after a defeat at Hull KR in April 1961. His last appearance was at the Dublin Festival of May 1962 for Huddersfield against Widnes.

Valentine went on to be hugely successful in a short spell as coach of Huddersfield. He took the Fartowners to the championship and a Wembley final appearance in 1962. He secretly coached Huddersfield RU in the mid-1970s. In those days before Union allowed professionalism, former League players were not allowed to be involved in Union clubs even as a coaches.

After his death at the early age of 49 on 14 August 1976, Valentine was almost forgotten. But with the 2000 World Cup being staged partly in Scotland, his story was publicised once more and the accolades followed. He was posthumously honoured by the British Rugby League Lions Association in 1999 when his son Ian accepted a commemorative medal; the man of the match award in the Super League Academy Grand

Final is awarded the Dave Valentine Memorial Trophy (won in 2001 by Leeds's Danny McGuire); and Scotland Students at the 2001 Europa Cup wore a new specially-designed SRL tartan - the fifth colour being Hawick green, in recognition of Valentine's hometown club.

David Rose

A team-mate of Valentine's at Huddersfield, Rose was a winger signed from Jed-Forest after being capped seven times by Scotland RU.

Shortly after joining Leeds, he was called up late to the depleted 1954 World Cup squad after the controversial players' revolt, referred to in the Dave Valentine section of this chapter. He was visiting home in Jedburgh when he got the call - Billy Boston had been injured playing in a club game just a few days before the squad was due to depart. But Rose came in to replace the Wigan star in superb fashion, scoring tries in all four games to claim his place in folklore. His try in the final playoff - along with those of Gordon Brown - won the cup for Britain.

Indeed, if Valentine were not Scottish or had not captained the Lions in France, there can be little doubt that Rose would be considered the Scottish Rugby League legend. He was rightly honoured, along with Valentine, by the British Rugby League Lions Association in 1999.

He was still a regular spectator at Jedburgh Rugby Union Club into the late 1990s.

Roy M. Kinnear

Wigan caused a furore when they paid several thousand pounds to snatch Kinnear, one of the stars of British Rugby Union, from Heriot's Former Pupils on 29 January 1927. It was a massive deal, taking the Scotland international centre away from a sport where he was at the heart of the British Lions to play professionally 'down south'.

Kinnear scored a try on his debut, against Pemberton Rovers in the Challenge Cup, and went on to notch 81 tries altogether in 184 appearances for the Cherry-and-Whites. His finest moment came in the 1929 Challenge Cup Final - the first at Wembley - when he scored a try against Dewsbury as Wigan won 13-2 in front of 41,500 supporters.

Later that year, Kinnear became Scotland's first double Great Britain international when he played his sole League Lions test, against Australia at Craven Park, Hull. He was blamed after an 8-31 defeat and was never picked again, although he did go on to play three internationals for Other Nationalities.

He died tragically early, collapsing in possession of the ball during a Union match at Uxbridge on 22 September 1944, where he was a PT instructor to the RAF. His last legacy to the world was his son, television star comedian Roy Kinnear.

George Wilson

Nicknamed 'Happy', Wilson was signed as an expensive addition to the Huddersfield side in 1948-9. The 24-year-old arrived from Kelso for a reported £1,000 fee, but easily repaid that sum, switching codes with sensational try-scoring ease. The winger was prolific, flying down the line as befitted a professional paratrooper. He also later worked as a butcher.

Wilson was capped in his first season by Other Nationalities at full-back and then made his debut for Great Britain two years later after moving to Workington Town in 1950. And what a debut. 'Happy' scored a hat-trick of tries against the Kiwis and not surprisingly kept his place for all three tests. He went on to win a Challenge Cup Final medal at the end of the season in the win over Featherstone Rovers. He played 148 games for Workington, scoring 129 tries.

George Fairbairn

George was born in Peebles in 1954 and started his rugby-playing career with nearby Kelso.

Having narrowly missed selection for the Scotland Rugby Union team, George decided to make a living from his talents and headed south. Despite being a full-back at Kelso, George made his debut for Wigan on the wing on 17 November 1974, scoring Wigan's only try in a dismal 14-5 defeat at Dewsbury's Crown Flatt.

Despite playing for a poor side - and being Scottish - he showed enough promise to get an England call-up within six months of playing the 13-a-side game. With no Scotland or Other Nationalities side to play for at the time, Fairbairn made the first of 15 England appearances in the 1975 World Cup defeat by Wales in Brisbane, kicking two goals.

His two tries and four goals in the 17-17 draw with the Kiwis at Auckland's Carlaw Park gave George star billing and his two goals in the 10-10 draw with Australia in Sydney salvaged pride for coach Alex Murphy's side, who had earlier surprisingly lost to Wales.

When the tournament returned to the northern hemisphere, Fairbairn kicked England to victories over Wales, France, New Zealand and Australia as England finished just a point behind the champion Kangaroos in the final table.

He made his Great Britain debut against France in the 1977 World Cup in Auckland, going on to play 16 more times for the Lions. His last appearance was in the Ashes humiliation by the 1982 Kangaroos.

Fairbairn's attempts to almost single-handedly keep a woeful Wigan side in the First Division in the 1979-80 season was described by Mel Woodward in *XIII Winters* as a "weekly re-enactment of Custer's Last Stand". He really was a true Braveheart - it is a pity that he did not get the opportunity to represent his own country in the game he loved.

He stayed at Central Park and became player-coach as they bounced straight back into the top flight, winning the annual Man of Steel award for his efforts. But after over 200 appearances for Wigan, in June 1981 he joined Hull KR for a then world record transfer fee of £72,500.

At Rovers he scored a club record-breaking 166 points in 1981-82, helped them to the First Division Championship in 1984 and 1985 and the 1986 Challenge Cup Final when they were narrowly beaten by Castleford (revenge by the Tigers for the Premiership Final two years earlier when Fairbairn's try and two goals saw Rovers scrape to victory.)

After scoring 2,880 points from 92 tries, 1272 goals and 32 drop goals, George retired from playing and went into coaching, leading Hull Kingston Rovers from May 1991 to May 1994 and then Huddersfield until October 1995 when he was thrilled to take charge of the newly-launched Scotland team at the Emerging Nations World Cup. He has remained involved with Scotland in a coaching or managing capacity ever since.

John Wilson

Like fellow Kelsonian Dave Valentine, Wilson was another of the most important men in the history of British Rugby League. But rather than his exploits on the pitch, it was Wilson's role as one of League's top administrators that made him famous. He moved to Hull in 1901, played for Hull KR and joined the club's board five years later.

He had a very varied career in sport, representing Great Britain at cycling at the 1912 Stockholm Olympics (one of his sons, Andy, died in 1925 at the height of an outstanding trial cycling career) before becoming a member of the Rugby League Council in 1918. He was business manager of the Northern Union (Great Britain) team which toured Australia and New Zealand in 1920, but the squad was hit so hard by injuries that Wilson had to play as a forward in three matches.

Wilson became the Northern Union's first paid official when he was appointed secretary that year. He went on to lead the sport for over a quarter of a century, presiding over many important developments, including the name change from Northern Union to Rugby Football League, although this was initiated by the Australians.

He was heavily involved in the decision to take the Challenge Cup Final to Wembley in 1929, and was a leading figure in the establishment of the game in France in the 1930s.

Wilson's reign lasted until the end of the Second World War in 1946, and sadly his wife died shortly after his retirement. Following this, he became a director at Headingley - the Leeds Cricket, Football and Athletic Co. Ltd - a position he held until his death at his home in Street Lane, Leeds on 20 November 1957, six days after his 81st birthday.

Tributes poured in. The *Yorkshire Post* obituary quoted Harry Hornby, former Chairman of the RFL, saying: "Every man looked to him as the kindest man in Rugby League football." Swinton secretary B. Mannon added: "I do not think there is anyone in Rugby League circles in this country, France, Australia or New Zealand who could but speak of him in the highest possible tones", while Walter Popplewell of Bramley said: "We used to call him 'Gentleman Jim'. His actions were always that way. His reputation was worldwide. He was looked up to everywhere."

Other Scots in British professional Rugby League, 1895 to 1995

1895 to 1918

From the earliest days of the Northern Union, Scots came south to play for clubs in Yorkshire and Lancashire. In particular Bradford, Broughton Rangers, Oldham and Halifax all found talented players from Scotland.

W. H. 'Scottie' Donaldson

One of several Scots who came south to play for Heckmondwike and Manningham in 1893 without the clubs having permission from the Scottish RU. When he attempted to return to Hawick two years later after only a few games of Northern Union, he was banned. Instead, Scottie returned to Yorkshire, helping Manningham to win the very first NU Championship in 1895-96.

George Frater

Frater joined Oldham at the start of the 1896-7 season from Melrose RUFC. A hard working forward, he made 262 appearances for Oldham, scoring six tries and 28 goals. He also played for Lancashire, and captained Other Nationalities against England in 1904. With James Moffatt and Jim Telfer, he was one of three Scots in Oldham's victorious 1899 Challenge Cup Final team.

James Moffatt

A hard-working forward from Melrose, he signed for Oldham in 1896-97, and scored a try in the 1899 Challenge Cup Final triumph over Hunslet. He played 96 matches for the club until the 1900-01 season. He joined Leeds in 1902, and played 63 matches for them. He was selected for a challenge match team 'The Rest' against champions Runcorn in 1900, and was also capped by Other Nationalities

Jim (E. W.) Telfer

Telfer was the third of the three Scots who played for Oldham in the 1899 Challenge Cup final, having first played for the Roughyeds in 1897-98. He made 117 appearances in five seasons, scoring six tries and one goal.

Alex Laidlaw

Alex Laidlaw was the first Scottish Union international to join a Northern Union club when he left Hawick for Bradford in the 1898-99 season. He also played for the Yorkshire County side, and kicked a goal for Bradford in their 1906 Challenge Cup Final victory over Salford. He also won Other Nationalities honours.

George Melvin

The first of three Scots at Halifax at this time, Melvin played just three games in 1899-1900 season. He was signed from Ebbw Vale RU, the result of a Halifax scouting mission for Welsh Union talent.

Andrew Hogg

Hogg was a former Hawick Union wing-threequarter, who joined Broughton Rangers around the turn of the century. He won many honours, being capped for Other Nationalities in 1906, the Northern Union and England against New Zealand in 1908, and for England against Wales in 1909 at Tonypandy, when his adopted country lost 35-18. He also played for Lancashire against New Zealand in 1908. He was top try scorer in the NU in 1903-4 with 34 tries, and Broughton's top try scorer in 1905-6 with 31, making him second highest in the NU. He scored a try for Broughton in their 25-0 Challenge Cup Final victory over Salford in 1902, and won a Lancashire Cup winners medal with Broughton in 1906-7.

Bob Wilson

Another prolific try scorer, Wilson formed an all-Scottish centre partnership with Andrew Hogg at Broughton Rangers. He was selected for Lancashire in the County Championship, and scored 28 tries for Broughton in 1905-6, making him third-highest try-scorer in the NU.

Adam Jardine

A forward who was signed by Oldham at the start of the 1903-4 season, Jardine made 67 appearances for the club, scoring three tries. His younger brother Billy also played for the club, but their careers did not overlap.

W. Scott

A Hawick threequarter who joined Hogg and Wilson at Broughton in the early 1900s. He played for Broughton in the 1911 Challenge Cup final.

Jimmy Dechan

Dechan, the 'Scottish battering ram with limbs of oak' joined Laidlaw at Bradford's then Park Avenue home after signing for a hefty £50. Described in 1905 as "perhaps the finest wing threequarter in the

Northern Union". He was Bradford's leading try scorer in 1904-05, 1905-06 and 1906-07, and his 28 tries in 1904-05 included six in one match against Widnes. He won a Challenge Cup winners medal with Bradford in 1906.

W. Sinton
Bradford's leading try-scorer in 1901-02 with 20 tries, 1902-03 with 14 and 1903-04 with 21, Sinton returned to Scotland in 1904 but came back to help Bradford win the 1906 Challenge Cup. He also played for the Yorkshire County side.

Robert Marshall
Marshall was a left-winger from Galashiels who played 10 times for Halifax in 1904-05.

W. Drummond
Drummond joined Halifax in 1904 from Jed-Forest and played 35 games at three-quarter before going on to Batley in 1906 and later Keighley.

Anthony Little
Hawick's SRU international forward, Anthony Little, signed for Wigan in July 1905 in a deal supposedly done by candle light in his attic. He played 22 games for Wigan and played for Other Nationalities.

C. L. Gillie
Gillie scored 40 tries and kicked 16 goals in 119 appearances for Leeds after signing from Melrose in 1908-09. He later played for Hull KR.

Ephriam Curzon
Curzon was a forward who signed for Salford at the start of the 1908-09 season. According to the RFL's records he was Scottish and joined from Kirkcaldy RU club. However, press reports at the time said he was recruited from local Rugby League. He made 102 appearances for Salford in three seasons, scoring eight tries. He also played for Lancashire, and was a 1910 tourist to Australia, winning two test caps.

Billy Jardine
The younger brother of Adam Jardine, Billy joined Oldham in July 1908 from Jed-Forest RUFC, and played 164 games, scoring 26 tries and 60

goals. His playing career finished in the 1914-15 season. He came back from the First World War in poor health, and died in 1916, shortly after there had been a collection for him at a friendly match against Hull. He was one of seven Oldham players lost due to the war.

Thomas Helm
Helm almost became the first Scot to play for the Northern Union. A forward, he was selected in 1910 to tour down under after signing for Oldham from Hawick, but was injured en route and did not play. He played 43 games for Oldham, scoring six tries, in the 1909-10 and 1910-11 seasons.

James Aitchison
A forward from Galashiels RU who played once for Wigan in 1908-09.

James Brown
Brown was a forward who played 81 times for Halifax between 1913-16 after moving south from Melrose for £90.

Harry Paterson
Paterson was a winger who scored 16 tries in just 27 appearances for Halifax after his £50 transfer from Galashiels.

John Ewart
Former Selkirk winger Ewart made just five appearances for Halifax in the 1914-15 season.

1919 to 1945
Groups of exile players have often been attracted to certain clubs, and Halifax in the 1920s had more Scottish recruits than any other club at that time. Oldham and Huddersfield also recruited Scottish players.

George Douglas
A Scotland international forward who joined Batley from Jed-Forest RUFC in 1921-22, Douglas helped them win the Championship for the first and only time in their history two years later, playing 25 games and scoring 2 tries in Batley's greatest ever season.

Peter Reid
Reid joined Huddersfield from Selkirk RUFC at the start of the 1921-22 season..

William Stewart
A reserve for Scotland RU against Wales, threequarter Stewart quit Union to join Keighley in 1921. The club broke gate receipt records when he made his second-team debut against Normanton.

Roy Thompson
Thompson was a Hawick threequarter who left Union after playing in two unsuccessful trials for Scotland and joined Barrow in March 1922.

Jimmie Douglas
A second-rower from Jed-Forest RUFC who went to Halifax with Swan, Beattie and Murdison in 1923, Douglas scored 13 tries in 83 appearances for the Thrum Hallers. He went on to join Leeds in 1928, and played for them in the 1932 Challenge Cup Final. He made 152 appearances for Leeds, scoring 27 tries, and later became secretary-manager of Salford in 1949. He helped recruit Tom McKinney for Salford from Jed-Forest. McKinney had been born in Ballymena, and was one of the few players from Northern Ireland to play professional Rugby League.

Andrew Murdison
Murdison was one of four Scots to join Halifax from Galashiels in 1923-24. He was a flying winger and came close to selection for Lions' 1928 tour. He scored 92 tries and kicking 135 goals in 173 games for Halifax. He also won international honours for Other Nationalities.

George Swan
Swan became a stalwart at Halifax after joining from Galashiels in 1923, racking up 204 appearances in which he scored 17 tries. He was capped by Other Nationalities against England in 1926.

Jock Beattie
A forward who scored 36 tries and three goals in 100 appearances for Halifax, Beattie had joined the Thrum Hall side from Galashiels in 1923.

Billy Renilson
The uncle of Charlie Renilson, Billy joined Halifax in 1925-26 and played 40 times in three seasons, touching down twice.

Jimmy Gill
Gill signed for Halifax from Galashiels in 1929 when he was just 22. The threequarter played 109 times, scoring 34 tries in the next five years.

James Jupp
A stand-off or centre signed by Oldham from Jedburgh RUFC in January 1936. He played six games for the Roughyeds in the 1935-6 season.

William Welsh
After winning the last of his 21 Scotland Rugby Union caps as they won the 1933 Five Nations without defeat, Hawick's British Lion star Welsh quit Rugby Union for London Highfield RLFC, the team Brigadier-General A. C. Critchley had taken lock, stock and barrel from Wigan to play at White City.

He must have wondered if he'd made the right decision when he did not appear for London in their early games, including the defeat by Australia, but he eventually became a regular and played in the victory over Jean Galia's groundbreaking France team.

Welsh went out with a bang. In their final game in west London, Highfield, who were still based in Lancashire and just travelled down for their midweek floodlit home matches, Welsh "played probably his finest game since becoming a professional", according to one report. He scored a record-breaking four tries in a 59-11 romp over Bramley, having scored just six in his previous 20 appearances. Despite a winning record - won 20, lost 18 - as London, Highfield returned north at the end of the 1933-34 season and became Liverpool Stanley. Welsh went on to play for York and toured France in 1937 with a Rugby League XIII.

Alex Fiddes
Alexander Erskine Fiddes, a Scottish Union international trialist, followed a well-worn route from Hawick to Huddersfield in 1933. He made his debut against the touring Australians and went on to become a Fartown legend, and played a key role in the club's successes in the 1930s. Fiddes captained Huddersfield in the 1935 Challenge Cup final

defeat to Castleford but lifted the cup 10 years later when they beat Bradford Northern in a two-legged wartime final. In fact, if it were not for the war's intervention, Fiddes may well have been another Scotsman to play for the Lions: after captaining Huddersfield to a Yorkshire Cup triumph in 1938, his form would have warranted a place on the cancelled 1940 tour. His benefit match against Salford in 1946 earned him £500 after 13 years playing service, followed by a spell as team manager. He later coached Batley.

Bill Fairbairn
Fairbairn played 16 games for Oldham in the 1935-6 and 1936-7 seasons, scoring six tries.

Gordon Cottington
A former SRU international from Kelso RUFC, winning five RU caps, hooker Cottington also played Union for Headingley before changing codes by signing for Castleford in 1936-37. He played 102 games for Castleford, scoring two tries.

Gordon Gray
Gala's Scotland international hooker, Gray changed codes by signing for Huddersfield in 1937-38.

1946 to 1995
Huddersfield signed various talented Scots in this period, including Dave Valentine and Jock Anderson. Leeds also recruited players from Scottish Rugby Union at this time. In the 1960s, Workington and Whitehaven had some Scottish players, and in the 1990s, Carlisle fielded numerous Scots.

Robert Johnstone
A forward from Selkirk RU, played 4 games for Wigan in 1944-45.

Bob Robson
Robson was a second-row forward who scored 12 tries in his debut season, 1945-46, for Huddersfield and played for an English RL XIII against France in Paris. He won three Other Nationalities caps. He moved to Salford in January 1951, and played 58 games for them, scoring five tries and 16 goals.

Jock Anderson

The 'Flying Scot' left Hawick for Huddersfield straight after scoring two tries for Scotland against New Zealand at Murrayfield in 1946 for a reputed £850 signing-on fee. The right-wing or threequarter went on to play in the Championship Final that season when the Fartowners lost to Wigan in front of 67,136 at Maine Road. After deserting the club for a while to train for the famous Powderhall sprint athletics title, which he won in 1947, Jock returned and played in the 1949 Championship Final when Huddersfield beat Warrington 13-12 in front of more than 75,000, again at Maine Road.

Archie Ferguson

Another Scot who came south to join Huddersfield, Ferguson played in Huddersfield's victorious 1949 Championship final team. Only three players in that Huddersfield team were English, and rarely in Rugby League, Scotland, Ireland and Wales were all represented in the same team. Followed G. Tate to Hull KR in 1950, but he lasted only a few weeks at Craven Park before being transfer-listed.

Andrew (Drew) Turnbull

Turnbull arrived at Leeds with Thomas Wright from Hawick in a double deal, aged just 17, and scored on his debut against Bramley in August 1948. His first two seasons were disrupted by National Service but he reportedly returned even quicker with "rapid acceleration and a wonderful body swerve and sidestep that bamboozled covering defenders". The young winger earned a Great Britain call-up for the third test in 1951 against New Zealand. In the Headingley mud, Turnball scored two match-winning tries. That was his only test appearance - he went on the tour of Australia three years later, but only played two games, scoring twice, because of injury.

His career was blighted by ill-fortune, leaving him with no major honours despite being a try-scoring sensation at Headingley for eight seasons. He scored seven Challenge Cup tries in 1951-52, eight a season later, and was a beaten semi-finalist in 1954, but never reached the final. A season after he left Headingley for Halifax, Leeds won the cup.

The pinnacle of Turnbull's magnificent club career came in 1954-55 when he scored an astonishing 42 tries for Leeds in just 26 first-team appearances, including three hat-tricks, four tries once and five tries in a match twice. He went extremely close to the feat of scoring a try a game in his Leeds career: 228 touchdowns in 230 appearances.

Thomas Wright

The ninth SRU international to turn professional, centre Wright, along with Turnbull, signed for Leeds from Hawick in the summer of 1948. Injury prevented him fulfilling talent in League. He played 17 games for Leeds, scoring nine tries.

Jimmy Chalmers

Chalmers joined Oldham in the 1948-49 season. He played 14 games that season at stand-off, scoring one try. He appeared in a further three games the following season.

G. Tate

Tate was a half-back who left Kelso to join Hull KR in January 1950.

Hugh Duffy

Duffy was a Shotts-born forward who left Jed-Forest to turn professional with Salford immediately after winning his first Scotland Union cap, against France in 1955. He had actually already made his League debut on Christmas Day 1954 against Wigan under the imaginative pseudonym 'McDonald'. Duffy went on to become an all-time Salford great, although honours in the game almost entirely eluded him.

He was a non-playing reserve for Great Britain in 1959, although he did play twice for the Rugby League XIII in 1961, against the touring Kiwis at Manchester's White City and against France at the Parc de Princes. He also appeared for Salford against New Zealand in 1955, which was, coincidentally, Salford's television debut and against Australia four years later, when the Kangaroos sneaked a 22-20 victory.

Duffy joined Halifax in 1962-63 for £600 plus Ernie Critchley moving to Salford in part-exchange. His last major match for the Thrum-Hallers was a substitute appearance in the 1966 Championship Final defeat by St Helens at Swinton.

Charlie Renilson
The nephew of Billy Renilson, Charlie left Jed-Forest for Halifax in 1957 and had a decade of huge success in League. A loose-forward in the Valentine mould, Renilson scored 70 tries in 302 games for Halifax, playing in a final every year from 1963 to 1966, including the 1965 Championship Final triumph over St Helens and the defeat by Saints a year later, both at Swinton.

Renilson stepped up to the Great Britain side, making eight appearances from 1965 to 1968, including all three matches in the 1968 World Cup down under. He returned to Australia to play out his career with Newtown and Eastern Suburbs.

Rob Valentine
Robert Angus Valentine, younger brother of the legendary Dave, signed for Huddersfield from Hawick in November 1963. A great tackler in the back field, he played just once for Great Britain, winning his cap against the Australians in 1967. He went on to join Wakefield Trinity just after their great domination ended before winning Other Nationalities selection in the County Championship while with Keighley.

Stan Cowan
Cowan was a winger who scored 66 tries in 163 appearances for Hull, including the 1959 and 1960 Challenge Cup Finals defeats by Wigan and Wakefield respectively, although he scored a try in the latter.

Brian Shillinglaw
A highly-entertaining and talented scrum-half who played for Whitehaven, the former Scotland Union international was transfer-listed in December 1962 when he refused to return to the club from Scotland. He had signed for the Cumbrian side in 1962 from Galashiels. Harry Edgar recalls in his history of Whitehaven RLFC that "he really enjoyed playing Rugby League far more than his original game because it allowed him to use the full range of his skills". However, he wanted to play at a higher level, and joined Wigan for £5,000 in May 1963. He retired after breaking his leg in 1964.

Ron Cowan

A shock signing for Leeds in 1962, Cowan had starred for Selkirk and Scotland and had toured South Africa with the Union British Lions. A winger or centre, he twice topped Leeds's try-scoring chart with his most famous try coming in the Championship Final defeat to St Helens in 1970 before Odsal was submerged in a monsoon. A year earlier he won the Championship, his only major League honour. Later, he played with elder brother Stan at Hull before founding Carlisle RLFC. He played 227 games (plus 6 as sub) for Leeds, scoring 119 tries.

Alex Cassie

One of only three non-locals in the Whitehaven side of 1963-64, lovingly described by Harry Edgar in the book *XIII Winters*. Cassie signed in July 1962 from Melrose, and took time to learn the new code but, according to Harry Edgar, he "became one of Whitehaven's most popular players". He made 288 appearances for the club, scoring 796 points.

Alistair Ford

Ford was a winger who scored after a few minutes of his debut for Huddersfield against Bramley in October 1962, having signed from Kelso.

Bill Hollands

Hollands followed fellow winger Ford to Huddersfield in November 1962, signing from Union club Gala.

Oliver Lawson

A full-back from Selkirk, Lawson joined Keighley in September 1963.

Drew Broatch

A centre, the nephew of Alec Fiddes, who was recruited by Leeds in 1963 from Hawick aged 23, Broatch brought a fine reputation from Union, having played for South of Scotland and the Barbarians. He was successful with Leeds and Bradford Northern, but often missed the big occasions. He played 151 games (plus two as sub) for Leeds, scoring 32 tries. He coached Hunslet from 1979 to 1981.

Greg Ballantyne
Ballantyne was a professional sprinter who left Hawick to sign for Hull KR in August 1967. He returned to Scotland to play for Rovers against Salford in end-of-season promotional match at Jedburgh in 1968.

Glenn Turnball
Turnball signed for Workington from Hawick in the 1963-64 season, and became established at scrum-half. He played 84 games (plus 20 as sub) between 1963 and 1969, scoring 20 tries and kicking 76 goals.

Harry Whitaker
Whitaker joined Turnball at Workington in 1968, where they recreated their half-back partnership at Hawick in the 1968-69 season. He played 83 games (plus 3 as sub) for the Cumbrians, scoring 24 tries and kicking 54 goals over four seasons.

Alan Tait (senior)
Another Scot at Workington in the late sixties, Tait scored 40 tries and three goals in 135 appearances (plus 7 as sub) after joining from Kelso in 1967. He then signed for neighbours Whitehaven in the 1973-74 season, making one appearance for Other Nationalities in the County Championship in 1975-76, his last season at Whitehaven. He is the father of the dual-code British Lion of the same name.

John Hegarty
Yet another Hawick player who changed codes, Hegarty signed for Wakefield Trinity in August 1970. He moved on to Dewsbury in 1974 for £2,750, but his career there was hit by injuries.

Phil Manning
This Essex-born winger signed for Carlisle in August 1990 from Ayr RU, aged 28. He stayed with the club until the merger with Barrow at the end of the 1997 season, moving to play in the Scottish RL Conference.

Colin Paxton
Paxton was recruited by Carlisle from Hawick Harlequins in January 1992 when already aged 30 and played 37 games (plus 1 as sub), scoring 7 tries.

Derek Armstrong

Armstrong signed for Carlisle from Hawick RU in April 1992, aged 25, and was one of eight Scots (residents or exiles) at Carlisle in the 1994-95 season. He made 55 appearances (plus 46 as sub), scoring 15 tries in six seasons at the club.

Grant Harris

Harris followed Armstrong to Carlisle from Hawick in September 1992 at the age of 24, the seventh Scot at the club that season. It did them little good though - they won just seven league and cup games all year. He played for two seasons, making 15 appearances (plus three as sub).

Jack McLeary

A stand-off or centre who was born in Kirkaldy in 1964, McLeary joined Batley in the 1982-3 season and stayed at the club for 6 seasons.

William McPherson

McPherson joined Barrow in September 1994 from Kelso RU, but only made two appearances as a substitute.

Graham Smith

Smith had won Scotland RU under-21 honours, but switched codes in March 1996, joining Wakefield Trinity from Orrell RFC.

Gregory Hayter

Hayter signed for Workington Town in July 1998, having previously played Union at Dundee High School.

Top: Drew Turnbull playing for
Leeds against Warrington in
1953 in the Challenge Cup

Bottom: George 'Happy' Wilson

(Photos: Courtesy Robert Gate)

165

Scottish Great Britain heroes:
Top: David Rose
Bottom: Charlie Renilson
(Photos: Courtesy Robert Gate)

Part 5: Rugby League in Scotland

Development Officer Mark Senter with the Scotland Rugby League van
(Photo: Gavin Willacy)

14. Professional club matches in Scotland

There had been several professional club matches played in Scotland before Super League took a couple of games 'On The Road' to Tynecastle in the late 1990s. On 29 May 1968, Salford played Hull KR at Jedburgh, the first League match in Scotland for more than half a century. This exhibition match took place at Bridgend Park, home of Ancrum football club, and Hull KR included Scottish sprinter Greg Ballentyne in their line-up.

There was little movement between the countries or codes in the 1970s and 1980s, but as Union slowly moved towards open professionalism, more opportunities arose for demonstrations of what League had to offer to the Scottish public. Workington played Hull KR in a pre-season friendly at Galashiels in August 1994 and then, on 22 August 1997, Carlisle took their Premiership match against Lancashire Lynx across the border to Hawick. The crowd of 424 was no bigger than the Border Raiders would have got in Carlisle.

Around this time, numerous possibilities arouse for a Scottish team in Super League. A Glasgow consortium prepared an application for an expansion franchise, to be called Scottish Bravehearts, which would play at Partick Thistle FC. Then RFL chief Maurice Lindsay claimed an Edinburgh consortium wanted to take Paris St Germain's place in Super League III. And finally there

Publicity for Edinburgh's 'On the Road' match
(Courtesy Super League)

169

was even talk of the troubled Hunter Mariners moving from Australia to Glasgow lock, stock and barrel when Super League merged with the ARL, leaving them in limbo. Mariners chief executive Bob Ferris admitted the club had visited Scotland in 1996 to conduct a feasibility study. But it was a false dawn and there was no 'Firhill for Thrills' as the popular saying goes. Instead, a year later Glasgow withdrew its Super League franchise bid, to little surprise. Hunter and Paris folded and expansion went to Gateshead instead. They were soon on show in Scotland anyway.

On the Road

London Broncos 22 Bradford Bulls 8 at Tynecastle, Edinburgh 18 July 1998

Super League's 'On the Road' programme saw every team play a game at a new venue around Britain. With Super League considering franchise applications from Edinburgh, Glasgow, Gateshead, Swansea, Cardiff and Northampton, it was a chance to test the water in these locations.

The London Broncos came from England's capital to Scotland's, supposedly to face a hiding against the champions Bradford. Instead, watched by 6,863 fans at Hearts football ground, the underdogs pulled off a great win.

A star-studded international array of talent put on a fascinating tie, with London's tries coming from Kiwis Grant Young and John Timu, Shaun Edwards and Sussex-born Great Britain squad member Tulsen Tollett. Bradford's only scores came from tries by Australian Graeme Bradley and Yorkshireman Jon Scales. It was fitting that London forward Terry Matterson should kick three goals for the Broncos. The Australian veteran, who made his reputation with the Brisbane Broncos, was later named in the Scotland Tri-Nations squad. However, just as he remained the best uncapped Australian forward of the modern era, he failed to make an international appearance for Scotland either. Terry qualified for Scotland through Scottish ancestors.

Incidentally, the crowd of nearly 7,000 was the biggest crowd away from Murrayfield to watch a game of rugby in Scotland that year. Scottish Rugby League had been represented when Edinburgh Eagles played Kinloss Hunters in a curtain raiser.

170

League 'On the Road': Broncos versus Bulls in Edinburgh
(Photo: Courtesy Mike Haddon)

Bradford Bulls: Spruce, Scales, Bradley, Vaikona, Paul, Calland, Deacon, McDermott, Lowes, Donougher, Forshaw, Dwyer, McNamara. Subs: Graham, Medley, Fielden, Hodgson.
London Broncos: Toshack, Smyth, Timu, Ryan, Cotton, Tollett, Edwards, Young, Beazley, Carroll, Retchless, Gill, Matterson. Subs: Spencer, Air, Salter, Dunford.
Scorers:
Bradford: Tries: Bradley, Scales.
London: Tries: Young, Edwards, Tollett, Timu; Goals: Matterson (3).
Referee: Steve Presley.

Gateshead Thunder 20 Wigan Warriors 16 at Tynecastle, Edinburgh
1 August 1999

Super League returned to Tynecastle for another summer outing but this time with new boys Gateshead Thunder taking on defending champions Wigan. Gateshead's Australian star Willie Peters and Wigan flier Jason Robinson promoted the game by dressing in team shirts and kilts outside Edinburgh Castle, but the majority of the 4,978 crowd were still northern English who had made a weekend trip to Edinburgh.

However, they were treated to a stunning spectacle as the Thunder, coached by soon-to-be Scotland boss Shaun McRae, pulled off a shock 20-16 win thanks to a brace of tries by Scotland international Matt Daylight. The hundreds of delirious Thunder fans could not believe what they were seeing. McRae reacted by saying that "something special" was

171

happening in Gateshead. It certainly was but not for much longer because the club had to merge with Hull Sharks at the end of the season for financial reasons. McRae and manager Shane Richardson headed down the east coast with most of the Thunder team. The next time they were back in Edinburgh was on Scotland duty.

Gateshead Thunder: Sammut, Carney, Grogan, Simon, Daylight, Robinson, Peters, Lee, Jenkins, Felsch, Wilson, Grimaldi, Bird. Subs: Maiden, Maher, Walters, Carvell
Wigan Warriors: Radlinski, Robinson, Connolly, Moore, P. Johnson, T. Smith, Clinch, Cowie, M. Smith, O'Connor, Betts, Cassidy, Farrell. Subs: Florimo, Chester, Gilmour, Goldspink
Scorers:
Gateshead: Tries: Daylight (2), Carney, Wilson; Goal: Sammut, Drop Goals: Wilson, Peters.
Wigan: Tries: Betts (2), Farrell; Goals: Farrell (2).
Referee: Stuart Cummings

15. The 2000 Challenge Cup Final

When the news came that Wembley Stadium was due to be demolished at the end of 1999, the Rugby Football League had to make plans to stage the showpiece Challenge Cup Final elsewhere. There was talk of Twickenham, Old Trafford, Dublin or the new Millennium Stadium in Cardiff, but for the first match away from London they settled on Edinburgh and the Scottish Rugby Union's Murrayfield HQ.

The choice was controversial – the final had never been staged outside England before – but the distance and expense involved for travelling fans from the north of England was little different to the London journey and the chance to have a weekend away at another capital city proved irresistible. When Leeds and Bradford won through to the final, a month of feverish phone calls saw 67,000 fans book up match tickets, seats on trains and hotel rooms, ensuring much of west Yorkshire would descend on Edinburgh.

Before the game

For the first time since Wembley 1968, when heavy storms left the pitch flooded and meant that the final is remembered as the 'watersplash final', the Challenge Cup Final was nearly postponed. Torrential rain in midweek left much of Edinburgh flooded, not least Murrayfield. On Thursday morning the stadium was under three feet of water. "It was like a swimming pool," admitted RFL acting chief executive Dave Callaghan. "Straightaway we said we were going to do our damnedest to get this game on."

And they did, thanks to the tireless efforts of hundreds of volunteers who pumped water from the field, including the Royal Navy Rugby League team, the water subsided overnight for the game to go ahead. The front page publicity the situation attracted did the game no harm either.

The pre-match entertainment was provided by former Spandau Ballet star Tony Hadley, who belted out 'Gold' to the rapidly-filling stands, while Glasgow Schools Under-11s became the first Scottish team to play in the traditional Little League curtain-raiser, against Scarborough Schools. Having had to run the last part of the journey to Murrayfield after being stuck in appalling traffic jams with the team then scrambling into their new kit, coach Alex Bibby was proud of Glasgow's performance in defeat.

The match

After experiencing three straight final defeats, Bradford finally won an all-or-nothing encounter. Having lost the 1996 and 1997 Challenge Cup Finals and the 1999 Grand Final - all to St Helens - Matthew Elliott's men were never in danger of making it four heartaches in a row.

The Paul brothers reigned supreme, Henry winning the Lance Todd Trophy for man-of-the-match, following sibling Robbie's achievement four years earlier. His tactical kicking was immense, giving Leeds winger Leroy Rivett a miserable afternoon in the rain, for Rivett the opposite extreme as his four-try romp in the Wembley sunshine 12 months earlier. Irish-Australian Michael Withers towered over Rivett to claim several Henry 'bombs', scoring twice in the same corner in the first 16 minutes.

Leeds coach Dean Lance's decision to bring back Rivett in place of teenager Chev Walker badly backfired. He was low on confidence and out of practice at the start and a gibbering wreck by the time Withers added his two tries to Henry Paul's second minute penalty to give Bradford a 10-0 lead. Leeds, who had endured their worst start to a league campaign for more than 40 years, never fully recovered.

Nathan McAvoy, with a superb solo kick-and-chase effort, and Stuart Fielden added further tries with Leeds barely getting a sniff of the Bradford try line. The Bulls were coasting at 20-4 and with 32 minutes still left to play the prospect loomed of the Rhinos having their own record win - set a year earlier against London - shattered already.

But Leeds restored their battered pride with a gutsy fightback that cut the deficit to just four points and tested the big-match nerves of the fallible Bulls. Iestyn Harris moved to stand-off in an attempt to wrest the initiative and Leeds pulled a try back on 54 minutes when second-rower Andy Hay reached out of a two-man tackle after Francis Cummins had regathered a kick from Ryan Sheridan.

Henry Paul and Harris then traded penalties before the Rhinos set up a dramatic finale when substitute full-back Marcus St Hilaire followed up Harris' grubber kick to touch down. Video referee Gerry Kershaw finally awarded the try after countless replays and Harris added his fifth goal from as many attempts. Eighty minutes had passed but when the crowd were informed that there was another nine minutes of actual game time to go, it looked like Leeds could complete an incredible comeback.

But after six minutes of Leeds' pressure, Blackmore's pass was intercepted by Vaikona, who then had the ball torn from him in a tackle, gifting Bradford a penalty - and the match. The hooter sparked wild celebrations as they won the Challenge Cup for the first time since 1949.

After the game

Although Harris claimed Leeds "were the better side out there" and coach Dean Lance considered Adrian Morley "the most outstanding player on the field", there could be no disputing Bradford's superiority. Indeed, the Bulls would have been out of sight but for a rare off day with the boot by Henry Paul, who missed with four of his eight kicks at goal. Younger brother Robbie, the Bradford skipper, had vowed to become a Cup winner after discarding his two losers' medals and the success was particularly sweet for veteran forward Bernard Dwyer who, in his final season picked up his first win after four defeats at Wembley.

Despite both sets of fans making up much of the 67,000 crowd, with hundreds of Yorkshiremen in Kilts and afro wigs, the police announced that there had no arrests. "The whole event went magnificently," said Callaghan. "It makes you proud to be involved in the sport."

Bradford Bulls 24 Leeds Rhinos 18
Saturday 29 April 2000, Attendance: 67,214
Bradford Bulls: Spruce, McAvoy, Naylor, Withers, Vaikona, H. Paul, R. Paul (c), Anderson, Lowes, Brian McDermott, Peacock, Forshaw, B. Mackay. Subs: Pryce, Fielden, Dwyer, Boyle.
Leeds Rhinos: Harris (c), Rivett, Blackmore, Senior, Cummins, Powell, Sheridan, Fleary, Lawford, Barrie McDermott, Morley, Anthony Farrell, Hay. Subs: St Hilaire, Mathiou, Barnhill, Jackson.
Scorers:
Bradford Bulls: Tries: Withers 2, McAvoy, Fielden; Goals: H. Paul 4
Leeds Rhinos: Tries: Hay, St Hilaire; Goals: Harris 5
Referee: Steve Presley

Murrayfield 2000 (Photo: David Williams)

16. The 2002 Challenge Cup Final

Five months after the Challenge Cup began in Edinburgh, when Edinburgh Eagles hosted Leigh East, the trail ended back in Scotland's capital city. And it certainly seemed at home there.

The night before

On the eve of the match, Scotland's champions, Edinburgh Eagles, took on the Rugby League Conference winners Teesside Steelers in the inaugural 'Champion of Champions' Challenge Match at Broughton RUFC, the Eagles' home ground. The Steelers' 30-20 win was fine entertainment on a pleasant evening for fans who'd arrived in the capital well ahead of the Challenge Cup Final.

The Steelers led 24-12 at half-time but the home side improved after the break and would have won if it wasn't for missing all five conversions in a swirling wind. The Eagles' try-scorers were captain Steve Bisset, Andy Kane, who scored two, and winger Ross Neil with the final two, the first of which was a wonderful team effort involving Kiwi Louie Matiluno and Clint Brown.

Eagles media officer Mark Brown rightly described the event as: "a marvellous concept… a perfect stage to show what we have to offer at amateur level." The entertaining game made the back page splash in Saturday's *Edinburgh Evening Mail*, with a full colour picture of Eagles' prop Tommy McGhee. The Scotland amateur international, who also stars in Union for Boroughmuir RFC, spent the next night serving League fans in Bennetts' Bar, owned by former Scotland international Andy Knight.

The Scottish media certainly indulged in the big occasion. The Challenge Cup Final made the front, back and middle pages of every paper, with the unanimous verdict that the 60,000 plus fans who descended on the city were roundly welcome.

Match day

The sun shone on a chilly day, putting fans in fine spirits as they wandered down Haymarket towards Murrayfield. St Helens supporters outnumbered Wigan two to one, although there were shirts representing every Super League club, most of the NFP and NRL, plus countless BARLA clubs and international teams such as Ireland, Italy and the USA. But few Scotland RL shirts were to be seen.

Wigan, incredibly, had sent back 5,000 unsold tickets, accounting for the shortfall in the capacity. Their pessimistic supporters could see nothing but a Saints' win and could not face another humiliation like the one they suffered at the hands of Bradford at Old Trafford six months earlier. But those stay-aways must have been awfully sorry they missed arguably the Warriors' finest hour in the Super League era.

The Kellogg's Challenge Steve Mullaney Testimonial Match was played out by two of the SRL's development teams: Edinburgh's Wardie Primary School, coached by Ross Neil, who'd starred for Edinburgh Eagles the previous evening next door to the school, and St Elizabeth Seton from Cranhill in east Glasgow.

Then pop trio Atomic Kitten performed a couple of numbers to what was a worryingly empty stadium. But by the time the teams came out to a sensational firework and tickertape welcome, accompanied by a pitch-side cannon, the atmosphere was, as former Scottish League star Alan Tait later said, "unlike anything Murrayfield's ever seen before."

Wigan got the main attraction off to a flier. Full-back Kris Radlinski, who had spent four days that week on a drip in hospital and had fluid drained from an infected ankle 90 minutes before kick-off, slipped a wonderful pass between his tackler's legs to allow Gary Connolly to put Brett Dallas in at the corner for a thrilling opening try. Andy Farrell kicked the difficult conversion.

Seconds later, Adrian Lam timed his run from the backfield to perfection to take David Furner's short pass and waltz in for a second try. Farrell's kick made it 12-0 with just 16 minutes on the clock.

Saints looked stunned but finally settled down when Sean Long's towering kick successfully exposed Jamie Ainscough in Wigan's left-hand corner and Darren Albert rose magnificently to catch the ball and touch down. Long missed the kick from an acute angle.

That did not seem to matter when Martin Gleeson, a revelation at centre, showed delightful footwork to score Saints' second try in the same corner, but again Long missed the kick to leave the game tightly

178

poised at 12-8 at the break. After the touring Locomotiv Moscow and Kazan Arrows teams had been introduced to the crowd at half-time, the final resumed with most fans believing the next team to score would win.

That it was Wigan was testament to the patience of Stuart Raper's side, who defended doggedly, none more so than Radlinski. He was hardly able to run before the break but made several try-saving tackles, including sending a flailing leg under the ball as Keiron Cunningham appeared to touch down after a typical bulldozing run just before the half-time hooter. The video referee ruled it out.

Saints certainly had enough possession to win the game but their error count was ludicrous as they dropped the ball time and time again. When Julian O'Neill broke through on a diagonal, jinking run, enabling Gary Connolly to score - both players showing their true class on the big occasion - Wigan seemed to have the game in the bag, especially when Farrell converted yet again from out wide.

His accuracy with the boot was the opposite of Long, who missed an absolute sitter after Paul Sculthorpe had scored a simple try from close-range. At 18-12, the only difference was the conversions, but Wigan's feel-good factor was enhanced when Adrian Lam slotted over a drop goal and Saints knew it was all over. Farrell's last-minute penalty merely rubbed their noses in it.

Despite being underdogs, Wigan had put in a superb team display to smother Saints' attacking options, limit their superstars to only a handful of openings, and take their scoring chances with relish to win a great game, 21-12.

After the match

The reaction of the Wigan players showed just how much it meant to them to finally take a trophy back to the JJB Stadium, leaping around in front of the delirious, but relatively small band of Wigan fans. Radlinski, tears running down his face, showed his Lance Todd Trophy to the media scrum after his man-of-the-match performance achieved on one good leg and an aching body.

On the trail back to town for another night of celebration of a tremendous Rugby League occasion were a dozen Captain Thunders from Gateshead and a posse of Ali G look alikes. It was that kind of trip.

With the event worth at least £7m to the local economy, it would be a surprise if this wasn't the last of many major Rugby League finals to be played in Scotland's capital.

St Helens 12 Wigan Warriors 21
Saturday 27 April 2002, Attendance: 62,147

St Helens: Wellens, Albert, Gleeson, Newlove, Stewart, Martyn, Long, Britt, Cunningham, Shiels, Joynt (c), Jonkers, Sculthorpe. Subs: Hoppe, Stankevitch, Higham, Ward.

Wigan Warriors: Radlinski, Dallas, Connolly, Johnson, Ainscough, O'Neill, Lam, O'Connor, Newton, C. Smith, Cassidy, Furner, Farrell (c). Subs: Carney, Hodgson, M. Smith, Bibey.

Scorers:

St Helens: Tries: Albert, Gleeson, Sculthorpe.

Wigan Warriors: Tries: Dallas, Lam, Connolly; Goals: Farrell 4; Drop-Goal: Lam.

Referee: Stuart Cummings

17. The Domestic Game

Despite rugby players emigrating from Scotland to play professionally in England since the 19th century, apart from occasional visits by the professional game, the first Scots to play organised Rugby League in Scotland were the schoolboys who took part in the Dave Valentine Challenge Trophy, a competition launched in Lanarkshire in the late 1980s by Lancastrian teacher Harry Callaghan.

Although a Scot - Alan Gibb - was then chairman of British Amateur Rugby League Association (BARLA), there seemed to be little interest from the heartlands in helping to establish the game north of the border. It was only after Mal Reid started the Scottish Students team at Aberdeen University that two other Englishmen, Mal Dunning and Graham Watson (once a teenage player with Bradford Northern), along with Mick Trei, organised the first men's Rugby League in Scotland in the early 1990s.

Dunning launched a 10-a-side event at Whitecraigs which was such a success that, when followed by the inaugural Scotland XIII match against the North-East at Meadowbank in 1994, League enthusiasts in Scotland gathered together to put a plan into action.

Making it official

Seventeen people were at the inaugural meeting of the Scottish Rugby League Development Association at The Pitz, Portobello on 6 September 1994: John Risman (appointed chairman), Graham Watson (secretary), Hector McNeil (treasurer), Mal Dunning, Paul and Jacqueline Scanlon-Wells, Vic Semple, Alan Bothwell, Kenny Johnston, Norman Sutherland, Bill and Scott Lothian, Frank McGroarty, Martin Corrigan, Cameron Prendergast, Chris Cunningham and Simon Newbould.

Risman reported on the recent Scotland development game at Meadowbank, a game which should have been a celebration but instead became notable for the furore caused by the Scottish Rugby Union (see below). Undeterred, Risman declared that the way ahead for Scotland RL was to provide more coaching courses "to give future players a taste of Rugby League and to educate those who may wish to play".

Sutherland, whose company had backed the North-East game and the staging of Hull KR's clash with Workington at Galashiels, proposed summer rugby. With most adult players being students, many leave Scotland in the summer, so this proposal was not implemented until 1997. However, it was unanimously accepted that the Scottish Students, represented by player Hector McNeil (who became chairman of North London Skolars), and the amateur organisations should run in parallel.

Now all Scotland needed was a Rugby League club.

The pioneers: Forth & Clyde Nomads

Founded by Roland Just, the Forth and Clyde Nomads were aptly-named: they played in England's North-East League because there was no-one else to play in Scotland. A couple of other clubs did appear fleetingly around 1995-96, one in Aberdeen and one in Stirling, based on the domestic players in the Scotland squad, but neither lasted.

"John Risman asked me, Billy Gamba and Iain Stanger if we could get a Rugby League team together in Aberdeen," recalled former Scottish Student Neil Hendry, who played against the North-East at Meadowbank, but missed the full internationals in 1995 because of injury. "We had a couple of friendlies at Countess Wells. We all enjoyed it, but we were up against it: it was difficult getting guys interested in playing on Sunday because they were playing Union on Saturday."

Only the Nomads survived a whole season. Based at Bo'ness, near Linlithgow, they played against Gateshead Panthers, Durham Tigers, Benfield Lions and Teesside Steelers (future Rugby League Conference finalists). "It was a bit of a problem raising a team for away games on a Sunday morning." admits Kevin Rudd, who heard about the Nomads from Graham Watson after his engineering job saw him move to Dunbar on the east coast in 1996. "We'd have to leave Glasgow at seven or eight in the morning and we ended up taking anyone we could get out of bed. It was a real struggle. Apart from the travelling, we were relying on Union clubs, having to hire their facilities for training and matches. We played at Hamilton Park - every home game cost money, and so did all the trips south."

Although there were a few experienced English 'leagies' like Rudd, Eastmoor's Mick Trei, and Wigan St Patrick's Peter Burrows, the

Nomads were epitomised by characters such as Jamie Baxter, an ex-boxer, 'The Flying Florist' went on to play second-row for Glasgow Bulls and Scotland amateurs; founder Roland Just, who also played for Whitecraigs Warriors and Glasgow Bulls and still referees in Scotland; Persil (a forward who never got his shirt dirty.); Gonzo; and Big Chris, the 18-stone vegetarian sports instructor.

Despite their problems, the Nomads completed all their away matches but were disappointed when only half their scheduled English visitors made it to Hamilton. However, the North East League committee awarded the Nomads their Team of the Year prize for their efforts.

And they lifted the first senior honour in the Scottish game, beating Stirling University 30-24 on their own patch to win the Scottish Challenge Cup on 12 May 1996 (Craig Armstrong 2, Robert Taylor, Peter Burrows, Neil Young and Chris Cadman got the Nomads' tries). But, other than that, universities and forces' teams were the only competition the Nomads got in their own country and it proved too much. The club folded, just before Scotland got its first league at last.

A new era - the 1997 Scottish Rugby League Conference season

If the Nomads had managed to survive a few months longer, they may have become a force in the newly formed Scottish Conference League, launched by the renamed Scotland Rugby League. The SRL was being run by an executive of Nomads duo Mick Trei (chairman) and Roland Just (PRO), Brian Meichan (vice-chairman), Graham Watson (secretary), Mal Dunning (treasurer) and Development Officer Graeme Thompson working out of Glasgow City Council's Community Recreation Division.

After Scottish Students won the six-team OBC Challenge Cup at Grangemouth in June, the inaugural Scottish Conference kicked off with just five teams: Central Centurions, Inverness, Linlithgow Lions (based in West Lothian), Lomond Valley Raiders (Dunbartonshire) and Whitecraigs Warriors (south-east of Glasgow). The majority relied on Union players who wanted to play rugby in sunshine rather than snow.

Lomond, in their varsity colours of light and dark blue, were only formed by Graham Watson in March 1997 and yet, in mid-August, they were Scottish champions after going unbeaten through their fixtures. Watson also became SRL chairman with Lomond's Scottish Amateur international Clive 'Perry' Mason taking over as treasurer, before he later became chairman. Peter Burrows took over as secretary; Mark Dingwall, a Rangers fanzine editor who had caught the League bug, became PRO; Rory Scott was Referees' Society chairman; and Glasgow North player Ian Johnston, who became Development Officer from 1998 to 2000, came in to work in junior development.

The 1998 season

Paul Scanlon-Wells's Border Eagles were crowned champions, not surprising considering the presence of ex Great Britain forward Hugh Waddell and former professional Jason Thurlow, although Thurlow missed the inaugural SRL Grand Final against Edinburgh Eagles.

In his 40th year, Waddell put on a masterclass in the Grand Final at a wet Hillhead Sports Club in Glasgow, scoring two tries, one fittingly in the last seconds. Two more from Darren Jessop and five goals from former Carlisle professional Pete Manning, who won man-of-the-match for his superb display at full-back, saw the Borders comfortably home 40-14 in front of nearly 300 fans. Kevin Rudd and Dave Williamson touching down for the Eagles and Chris Blackhall kicked three goals.

Hillhead - or Hughenden, as it is known locally - was the home of Glasgow North, founded by Graeme Thompson, in the Union stronghold of west Glasgow. They played at the delightfully quaint home ground of Hillhead-Jordanhill RFC and the city's professional Union side, after renaming themselves the Bulls, courtesy of Bradford's Bulls' Connection programme.

The Eagles were coached by their founder, Mark Senter, a Zambian-born soldier from Hampshire, who had converted to League while stationed with the South Yorkshire/Doncaster Gunners. "The officers were all Rugby Union so we staged a rebellion with the Queens Lancashire Regiment next door and the Cumbrians in the Queens Dragoon Guards on the other side."

A knee injury meant Senter was billeted in Glen Corse near Edinburgh rather than Bosnia and when he came out of the Army in 1997, he put his love of League to good use. Incidentally, a midweek league for the services was up and running in 1998, with the Naval Bases at Rosyth and Faslane plus Tayside Chiefs police side all involved.

The decision by the RFL to extend the 1999 Challenge Cup and involve the champions of France, the armed forces, the universities, plus amateurs from Ireland and Scotland, seemed a wonderful reward for the Scottish Conference winners and an incentive for the development of the game in general. However, Scottish clubs were never going to give a true account of themselves when first round matches took place in early December, four months since most players had last played Rugby League. Some teams had to play Challenge Cup ties the day after being in 15-a-side action.

That preparation explains some heavy defeats, although the draw has often been vicious to the Scots. However, on most occasions, they have recovered from being blown away in the first half to put in highly respectable second half displays once their 13-a-side skills clicked back into action.

History was made on Sunday 6 December 1998 as Border Eagles took on Cumbria's Wath Brow Hornets, although the game was delayed a week by a frozen pitch at Hillhead. Borders were still caught cold though, getting a real hammering in the first half before recovering in fine fashion after the break to keep the score to a very respectable 34-10 defeat against that season's BARLA National Cup finalists. Man-of-the-match though was the Eagles' Chris Sullivan. Victory for the Scots would actually have given them a 'winnable' tie against London Skolars.

The 1999 season

A new-look Edinburgh Eagles, who had moved from Currie to Costorphine RFC on the western edge of the city, topped the 1999 Conference and duly went on to complete a predictable victory over Portobello Playboys in the Grand Final at Hillhead, making up for the previous season's disappointment. Another recognition of Scottish RL's progress was the Border Raiders versus Linlithgow Lions play-off quarter-final which was held as curtain-raiser to the Barrow versus Widnes NFP match.

In the Grand Final, Edinburgh scored two tries in the opening 10 minutes through half-back Neil Matthews and winger Steve Bissett and although the men from Calvary Park hit back through Mike Montgomery and Chris Thomas, Edinburgh raced away and were 30-8 up at the break and never looked like losing. Despite a comeback by Dave Hardy's Portobello, who were without inspirational Scottish Students' stand-off Andrew Borthwick, who had helped Montpelier win the French third division the previous term, Edinburgh won 48-20.

The Scottish champions were again given a really tough draw in the first round of the Challenge Cup, with a visit from arguably the top amateur team in England. Woolston Rovers, from Warrington, had been champions three times and runners-up twice in the seven years of the National Conference, although they had had a bad start to the season.

Edinburgh were missing scrum-half Kevin Rudd, who was working in Malaysia, but they did bring in three Scottish Students internationals from Glasgow Bulls on loan: Andrew Borthwick, Ross van der Hoek and Chris Houston, plus Gala's Kiwi prop Aaron Satchwell, a local bouncer who had played at NPC level in New Zealand, and former Lancashire Lynx star P. J. Solomon. The Eagles' performance was arguably the best from any Scottish team in the history of the game. While they did not win, they gave Woolston the fright of their lives before going down to a 12-17 defeat at Corstorphine. That represented a magnificent comeback as Edinburgh trailed 16-0 at the break, defeated again by their poor start.

The 2000 season

Scotland Rugby League were finally granted 'recognition status' by SportScotland in October 1999 and went into the new season with added purpose. Edinburgh Eagles, who had moved to Broughton RFC in Wardie, won nine of their 10 league games, racking up an incredible points difference of plus 330, to reach another Grand Final. Their only defeat came in the last fixture when they were surprisingly beaten 24-0 by second-place Borders, who had former Carlisle man Tony Scott and Darren Clarke, once of Barrow, in their ranks.

Ground alterations at Hillhead also forced Glasgow Bulls to move, up the A81 to the ancient West of Scotland RFC in Milngavie. That seemed to affect them as they won 5 and lost 5 during the league season, but came good in the play-offs, beating Rhu Raiders (formerly Lomond) and Borders to reach the Grand Final again.

Despite going behind to a first-minute try by Edinburgh's Kiwi scrum-half Shannon Warren, the Bulls bounced back to win in style -

and avenge the previous year's defeat - in front of 300 fans at the Eagles' home ground. In the Glasgow side, coached by Scottish Students' vice-captain Andy Borthwick, were Scotland Students star Barry Edgar, Canada scrum-half Ross van der Hoek and 16-year-old winger Sam Onions, who soon won student representative honours.

But without their coach, an ill-prepared Bulls side were hammered 72-0 by Wigan Rose Bridge in the Challenge Cup, despite having Tommy McGhee, Clint Brown and Shannon Warren on loan from Edinburgh Eagles. However, former Brisbane Wests' loose-forward Howard Cameron was voted man-of-the-match. The Australian had been capped by Scotland amateurs under the residency rule and was chiropractor to the senior Scotland squad at the 2000 World Cup.

The 2001 season

Six teams started the 2001 Conference - although there were Police, Navy, Marines, RAF and Prison Services teams playing in the mid week Scottish Services League - but some rural clubs failed to fulfil their fixtures because of the foot-and-mouth outbreak closing grounds, stranding players and wrecking agricultural livelihoods.

Even without that distraction, the title was always going to be fought out between Edinburgh and Glasgow, whose only defeats of the league season were imposed on each other. Having beaten Rhu Raiders in the semi-final, Edinburgh took the title with a first-half scoring blitz, taking a 24-0 lead with two tries each from prop Clint Brown - soon to join Workington - and winger Andy Dalglish, who ran the length of the pitch for both. In the last half hour, the Bulls fought back with three tries, but went down 30-16 as Edinburgh gained revenge for the previous season.

They even went to the first round draw of the Kellogg's Nutri-Grain Rugby League Challenge Cup in confident mood. After all, with the final due in Murrayfield, what better way to start the tournament than with a Scottish win? Bradford Bulls' star Tevita Vaikona warned the Eagles contingent that they would be all right as long as they avoided Leigh East. So who did they draw? Leigh East, of course.

The National Conference side showed their class immediately, scoring after just 50 seconds and rattling up 40 points before the half-time break. However, in the second half, the Eagles went toe-to-toe for

187

half an hour, scoring tries through loose-forward Chris O'Neill and Andy Dalgliesh, who produced another magnificent touchline dash from well inside his own half, before going down 68-10.

"I was very proud of the lads," said Edinburgh coach Simon Harrison. "They all played for their Rugby Union teams yesterday and to come out today and turn on a performance like they did in the second half, when they got their League heads on again, was fantastic. We made really good plays against a very strong team and we went down fighting with our heads held high." Leigh coach David Kay, whose side thrashed the RAF 48-10 in the next round, concurred: "Edinburgh have some tremendous players, they tackled like demons all day and they didn't let themselves down by any means."

2002 and beyond

There were major changes planned for the Conference in 2002. Rhu imploded on the eve of their BARLA National Cup tie at Millom in January, but moved from Helensburgh to Loch Lomond RFC and reformed as Dumbarton Dragons. Under Keith Smart, Linlithgow moved to Dalgety Bay and became Fife.

Glasgow, Edinburgh, Portobello and Dumbarton will make up a new First Division with Lanarkshire, Fife, Borders and Clyde Bucks. Clive Mason had had a trying year with newcomers Clyde, who played at Bishopston and relied on Union players for their squad. Subsequently, he and wife Karen resigned as chairman and secretary respectively of Scotland RL in 2002.

The next big step for the SRL is to launch a new Glasgow club, representing the SRL Conference, and operating in the Cumberland League in 2002-03. The aim is to reach a standard that will enable Glasgow to bid for a place in the RFL's proposed National League Division Three. "We want to have a Glasgow side based on the Brisbane Broncos system, where they have loads of feeder clubs providing them with a base of players," says Senter, who has an agreement with Glasgow City Council to use Nethercraigs Stadium when it is revamped. "We would have a lot of the Scotland Amateurs players and bring through the Under-19s and Students, providing the best of them with a semi-professional club on their doorstep."

18. 'Give us a game' - Scotland amateur internationals

When Graeme Thompson (the tournament's director, coincidentally) announced that the first Four Nations Championship would take place in the summer of 2002, it was a godsend for International Rugby League fans and all those working in development areas. They had been asking the RFL to launch a League version of Union's Five (now Six) Nations for years, now they had something similar, albeit for amateurs only. Scotland will play Ireland, Wales and England (the last represented by the Summer RL Conference). While this will unfortunately leave Scotland's professionals in limbo, this British Championship finally gives the SRL a major marketing tool to use north of the border.

"As we wait to see what's going to happen with the 2005 World Cup, we are beginning to introduce home-grown players," Thompson told *League Express*. "There was a credibility problem in the last World Cup and we are doing something about it now. We are adding value to what is already going on domestically. It gives officials in the participating nations something else to sell the game with."

Scotland have had an amateur side since 1997, when it became clear the RFL-run Scotland senior side was destined to be filled with professional players from the English and, eventually, Australian competitions. In the previous three years, ever since John Risman's Scotland XIII played the North-East at Meadowbank, Scotland RL had included students and amateurs in their ranks. Now they were being forced out by better players, but who, in some cases, were not particularly Scottish.

The SRL decided to continue to provide a representative team for those left behind. The Scottish Development XIII's first game was a pulsating win over Cumberland League side St Nicholas Arms in a curtain-raiser to the Carlisle Border Raiders versus Leigh Centurions match on 15 June 1997, Royal Marine Al Hendry scoring a hat-trick of tries and David Calderwood winning man-of-the-match. They then made the first of what became an annual weekend trip to Bradford Bulls to play Conference side Birmingham Bulls before going on to attend a Super League game and, with the help of player-coach Dale Lyon of

Central Centurions, played a number of friendlies in England to improve their skills and keep Union players involved in League during the summer.

First amateur international

Scotland's first amateur international, on 25 October 1997 against Ireland at Blackrock College near Dublin, was a cracker. After Steve Anderson made history with Scotland's first try and team-mate Clive Mason followed him to square the game at 12-12 at half-time, a try by the excellent Jason Syme gave Scotland, captained by Colin Wilson, a great chance of victory. Andy Gowrie had kicked three goals, but it was not enough, much to the dismay of Scotland's travelling band of fans: Anderson's brother and wife, another player's friend, a father, a bloke on his holidays and *Daily Herald* reporter Brian Meek. In the very last minute, Matt Freeman touched down for Ireland to add to tries from man-of-the-match Conor O'Sullivan, who scored twice early on, Mick Browne and Sean Cleary. Gareth Doherty kicked two conversions and a drop goal to give Ireland a 25-18 win.

But it was £50 well spent by each of the Scots who had had to pay to play for their country. The honour was worth every penny.

Television coverage

The success of that game led the SRL to invite Ireland to Kilmarnock the following year where they played the first home amateur international, at Bellsland Park on 30 May 1998. BBC Scotland's television cameras were in a crowd of 250 to see Scotland clamber back from a 0-10 half-time deficit to lead 16-11 with a few seconds left... only to end up losing by 21-16.

Future Wigan star Brian Carney was one of Ireland's first half try-scorers, but after Scotland boss Tony Howard - who played for British Police in the Scottish Courage Cup - had sorted his side out at the break, Tony Newell touched down after 44 minutes,

SCOTLAND RUGBY LEAGUE

AMATEUR INTERNATIONAL

SCOTLAND
vs
IRELAND

Bellsland Park, Kilmarnock

Saturday 30th May 1998, kick-off 3pm

Programme £1

unfortunately breaking a shoulder while doing so. Rob Gill finished off a great run by scoring and Whitecraigs Warriors' Alex Donaghy - a groundsman at Glasgow Rangers FC's Ibrox - kicked two goals to put Scotland ahead.

Gary Bamford's try appeared to have won it for the home side but they threw away possession in the last minute allowing Ireland's Innes Gray to score. Mick Molloy converted to give Ireland the lead and Gareth Doherty scored five minutes into injury time to end Scotland's dream of a first win.

In 1999, the Celtic Nations' Cup was launched. Scotland threw away their chance to win the inaugural event with a disastrous defensive lapse 90 seconds from the end of their clash with Wales at Portobello on 19 September. They allowed Darrall Thomas through to square the game at 20-20, giving Wales the draw they needed to clinch the title on points difference. Both sides had beaten Ireland.

By the time Scotland played Ireland on 9 September 2001, two years later, amateur international matches were established in the SRL calendar, with captain Simon Corrigan becoming Scotland's most capped amateur international player on his seventh appearance. He celebrated with a try in his team's 28-12 defeat at West of Scotland RUFC, Gregor Mathieson getting Scotland's other four-pointer.

Another defeat - by the heart-breaking result of 36-30 - followed a week later against Wales in a game staged at Hull's historic Boulevard. Former London Broncos Academy player Sean Farrell, a gym instructor from Hampshire who qualified for Scotland under the three-year residency rule, scored a hat-trick and was voted man-of-the-match. The rather more Scottish Hamish McKinnon also touched down.

The introduction of a Four Nations' competition should ensure a rosy future for British amateur international Rugby League. The strength of Scottish Students suggests that, in future, any student players who do not turn professional should progress into the Scotland amateur side rather than being lost to League when they move on to playing open-age rugby. The make-up of the Scotland Rugby League XIII which lost to the touring Sydney amateur club Renown United at Scotstoun in November 2001 - a mixture of amateur and student internationals, with many eligible for both - could become a familiar one.

The Scotland amateur squads

1997 versus Ireland
Andy Gowrie, Brian McMurtie, Simon Corrigan, Dale Lyon, Brian Boundy, Derek Anderson, Phil Horne, Colin Wilson (c), Perry Mason, Al Hendry, Johnathan King, Steve Anderson, Jason Syme, Alex Donnaghy, David Newel-Cook, Matt McCann, Richie Birnie.

1998 versus Ireland
Graeme Thompson, Phil Horne (both Glasgow North), Gary Bamford, Rob Gill, Warren Dean, Jonathon King (all Kinloss Hunters), Simon Corrigan, Tony Newell (both Lomond), Dale Lyon, Alan Manson, Mark Crossley, Tony Howard (all Central), Alex Donaghy, Stephen Anderson, Alastair Collie (all Whitecraigs), Colin Wilson (Linlithgow Lions), Jackie Munro (Edinburgh). (No 1999 squad available)

2000 versus Wales
Shaun Boyle, Chris O'Neill, Daniel Oosthuizen, Andy Dalgliesh, Steve Bisset, John MacDonald, Grant Proctor (all Edinburgh Eagles), Keith Smart, Alistair Swanson, David Wood (all Linlithgow Lions), Mike Wilson, Simon Corrigan, Hamish McKinnon (all Rhu Raiders), David Jamison, Howard Cameron, Ross van der Hoek, Dave McPhail (all Glasgow Bulls), Darren Clark, Darren Jessop (both Border Raiders). (No match report available)

2001 versus Ireland and Wales
Simon Corrigan, Stephen Dennison, Mark Sloan, Gregor Mathieson, David McGrath, David Ridings, Hamish McKinnon, Drew McGinty (all Rhu Raiders), Craig Armstrong, Graham Walker, Ian Young (all Clyde), Mikel Richter, John Malakoty, Craig Barrie, M. Lloyd (all Glasgow Bulls), Andy Dalglish, Teak Thompson, Shaun Boyle, G. S. Pahal (all Edinburgh Eagles), Sean Farrell, Liam Bryson (both Lanarkshire Storm), Jordan Ingham.

Scotland Women's XIII

The SRL's Rugby League Festival in February 1998 saw the first women's international between English and Scottish Select XIIIs. Coach Dave Newall-Cook and manager Rory Scott had a squad of mainly district Union players who played a series of friendlies over the summer in Glasgow and Edinburgh before entering the WARLA Challenge Cup in the winter. Despite their lack of League experience, the Scots romped to a 42-6 triumph.

Scotland Select (versus English Select): Anna Cochrane, Rachel Lewis, Kathleen Scougall (all Aberdeen Quines), Krysty Steele, Suzanne Ritchie (both Preston Lodge), Caroline Pye (Glasgow University), Karen Campbell, Lindsay Ann Docker (both Haddington), Mhairi Hay, Audrey Laird (both Kirkcaldy), Caroline Lawrie, Bronwen Scott (c) (both West of Scotland), Joan Hutchinson (Glasgow Southern), Frances Mullins (Hillhead/Jordanhill), Hayley Bird (Edinburgh Accies), Laura Snook (Keele University). N.B. All clubs are Rugby Union.

19. Junior Rugby League in Scotland

In 2001, it became theoretically possible for Scottish school children to play Rugby League from the age of nine to 19. A series of initiatives, stimulated and put into practice by both the SRL's development officer Mark Senter in Glasgow and Scottish Students across the nation, meant that thousands of young Scots were playing in primary schools, secondary schools, colleges and universities. The best were representing Glasgow Under-11s, or Scotland at Under-15, Under-19 and Student level. This was huge progress.

Starting at the base of the pyramid, Scotland's Development Officers have been coaching in primary schools since Graeme Thompson took the job in 1996. His initial target area was Glasgow, and that remains the focal point, particularly the deprived areas around the southern belt, despite some work in Edinburgh and East Dunbartonshire when Ian Johnston was incumbent.

With up to a thousand children involved in the coaching scheme every year, the number of Scottish kids who continue playing the game should increase every year. Although Senter has only one full-time coach working for him, his seven part-time coaches, which include Glasgow Bulls player Ian Glenn and Scottish Students international Barry Edgar, can be found in Glasgow's schools every day of the week. "Our policy is to saturate an area, get the game established, coach some coaches and then move on," explains Senter.

His assistant, Alex Bibby (who was acting development officer during the 2000 World Cup) is a prime example of the sort of person Scotland Rugby League rely upon. He saw what Thompson was doing at his son's primary school and volunteered his services. He was soon escorting young Ben and the rest of the Glasgow Schools Under-11s to Old Trafford to play in the nine-a-side Puma Little League curtain raiser before the 1997 Test match against Australia. Bibby now also takes Glasgow Schools to the annual Warrington Peace Festival, coaches in up to 10 schools in any period, spending six one-hour-a-week skills sessions with 9 to 11-year-olds.

"We had 40 kids turn up to our first session at St Angele's in Darnley," recalls the former Rugby Union player. "We were overwhelmed. But we learned to cope. Having six blind kids at one session was a challenge though - they loved the tackle bags."

Having established the game at primary level, Senter's team moved into secondary schools. One Scottish secondary school, Bannockburn High, has been playing Rugby League for five years, thanks to teacher Les Obre, a Dunbartonshire lad who fell in love with the game after watching it on television in the 1970s.

In 1998 a Glasgow Junior League for Under-12s involved Bellahouston Bulls, based near Ibrox Stadium, who benefited from Bradford Bulls' development scheme; and Queen's Park Warriors, both of whom supplied players for Old Trafford in 1997; and Pollok Pirates. There are now also after-school clubs in Castlemilk and Darnley.

Queen's Park could be the physical centre of Scotland Rugby League if Senter has his way. Glasgow City Council have given the SRL sole use of the six red-blaze pitches and changing rooms at the pleasant Victorian park which lies on the other side of Mount Florida from Hampden Park, close to Pollok and Castlemilk: the heart of Senter's work. If they can get sufficient funding and assistance, those dreary dressing rooms will become the SRL's headquarters and clubhouse, with Rugby League played every weekend around it.

"Castlemilk is one of the most deprived areas of the city but it has been our most successful development area," says Senter, who works closely with Glasgow City Council's Community Action Teams to provide sport as a means of social inclusion for young people. With up to 16 different racial groups, including Iranian asylum seekers, trying to settle among a very territorial native population, one of Rugby League's aims is to improve cultural awareness. For example, the SRL send under-11 teams of all races to the annual Scottish Asian Games at Kelvin Hall.

One of Castlemilk's success stories is a 16-year-old pupil at the local high school. A year after taking up Rugby League, he was representing his country. "This player had problems - he was uncontrollable," explains Senter. "But Rugby League has helped him enormously. We've given him individual ball skills tuition to add to his natural running ability and now he's in the national Under-19 squad. If he continues to improve at this rate, we'll have a proper player on our hands."

Seeing the yawning gap between his exciting development work in Glasgow's schools and the adult game, Senter realised talented players need stepping stones or else they will be lost to the code. In 2001 he launched Scotland representative sides at Under-15 and Under-18 level.

Although the Under-15s were annihilated 84-0 on their international debut against Wales at Woolston in Warrington on 7 October 2001, it was a start. With a lot of effort and a bit of luck, some of those players will be playing for the Under-19s by 2005, the Students a year later and eventually a home-grown senior Scotland side.

Workington Town's Karl Higgins missed a few of these stepping stones but still scored Scotland Under-18s' first international try when still only 16-years-old, in the 48-4 defeat to the touring French semi-professionals at Peebles RFC on Sunday 3 March 2002. Scotland's coaching staff were satisfied at the battling performance in appalling conditions from their new side, who trailed just 14-4 at half-time. The French started and finished strongly with man-of-the-match Cedric Duzant scoring four tries.

With players based from Aberdeen to Cornwall, the Scotland youth team were divided into the same 'residents' and 'exiles' camps as the Students, with both elements coming together for their first Home Nations Under-19 tournament in Cheshire in April 2002. After a predictable defeat to England at Alsager College, Scotland were thrilled to chalk up their first win, 26-14 against Wales, to finish second.

Scotland were inspired by captain Mark Webster and the creativity of halfback pairing Gareth Skillan and man-of-the-match Chris Fletcher, as they fought back from an eight point deficit to score five tries. Fletcher, the Great Britain Under-19s captain, also impressed against France with a skilful and hard-working display, and was soon making his debut for Gateshead Thunder, coached by his father, Paul.

There can be little argument that Scottish Students and Under-19s are vital to the future of Rugby League in Scotland. The students have improved on the field to justify the levels of time, effort and expense invested in them, and are now producing players capable of playing at a high senior level. With lottery money hopefully arriving to fund coaching schemes, the future looks bright.

Администрация   **Management Team**

Нил Вуд	Niel Wood
Ник Эванс	Nick Evans
Стефан Хоупвелл	Stefan Hopewell
Гарри Оурам	Gary Owram

Шотландия   *Scotland Team*

Йен Гилмор	п/защ.	Ian Gilmour	stand off	02.03.80
Роб Кларк	защ.	Rob Clarke	centre	26.06.81
Логан Колбек	защ.	Logan Colbeck	wing	23.08.79
Джеймс МакКей	2 линия	James Mackay	second row	21.07.78
Клинт Браун	2 линия	Clint Brown	second row	27.09.75
Джон МакДональд	2 линия	John McDonald	second row	22.01.75
Барри Эдгар (кап.)	защ.	Barry Edgar (capt.)	fullback	23.04.79
Симон Хогг	нап.	Simon Hogg	hooker	06.06.79
Нил Макдональд	п/защ.	Niall Macdonald	scrum half	20.05.80
Сэм Онионс	защ.	Sam Onions	centre	06.10.83
Адам Шоклей	защ.	Adam Shockley	centre	22.04.78
Эл Стюарт	нап.	Al Stewart	hooker.	28.12.74
Джеймс Нобл	нап.	James Noble	prop	17.10.75
Марк Вебстер	защ.	Mark Webster	wing	28.10.82
Том Уайлд	нап.	Tom Wild	prop	24.01.80
Том Филлипс	2 линия	Tom Phillips	second row	22.06.79
Джек Хависон	нап.	Jack Howieson	prop	28.07.01
Нил Фостер	защ.	Niel Foster	wing	13.08.80
Эндрю Бортвик	нап.	Andrew Borthwick	loose forw.	27.08.77
Райан Кэмпбелл	защ.	Ryan Campbell	centre	23.09.81
Кевин Радд	тренер	Kevin Rudd	coach	09.10.71
Джон Рисман	мен.	John Risman	manager	09.10.44
Вик Семпл	врач	Vic Semple	1st aid	22.11.44
Рой Викерс		Roy Vickers	piper	26.09.46
Кейт Кохран		Kate Cochrane	media off.	24.05.80
Фил Слэни	пом.тр.	Phil Slaney	assist.	29.12.56

Student Europa Cup 2001: The Scotland squad as listed in the programme.

Below: Clint Brown collects the Best Defensive Player Award. (Photo: Kevin Rudd)

196

20. The future for Scottish Rugby League

There is now a consensus among people involved as to how to provide a sound future for Rugby League in Scotland: to broaden the base and provide distinct steps to the top. The dream of having a Scottish Super League franchise which has a trickle-down effect has been banished by all but the occasional romantic writing to the letters page of the Rugby League press. Most Super League clubs lose money and only a couple regularly attract five-figure gates. Among all the sports clubs in Scotland, only Rangers, Celtic, the Scotland Rugby Union team and the NFL-funded American Football Scottish Claymores do that regularly, so what chance Rugby League?

The future for Scottish Rugby League must involve a slow growth rate, with the base of players increasing at all age groups; the establishment of more clubs; an increased representative programme; and a continuation of welcoming big games to Caledonia. In a fans survey in *Rugby League World* magazine in 2000, Murrayfield was the first choice to stage the Challenge Cup while Wembley is out of use - proving Scotland has a role as host to major Rugby League events.

Scotland's hopes of competing in one of those events are two-fold and long-term. On the club front, the SRL's ambition is to have a representative side playing in the National League and eventually increasing its abilities on and off the field until it is ready to become a semi-professional club. The next step - Super League - is another huge leap. To get to National League level, the existing Conference clubs need to have secure bases, second teams, academies and a concentration of League players, not part-time Unionists. For that, they need a lot of people's time, effort and money.

The chief executive of SportScotland is Auckland Warriors founding officer Ian Robson and yet still Scottish Rugby League gets hardly a drop of the £32m distributed every year, as it is not among SportScotland's 60 partner sports.

"We've had a little to do with the Scottish Rugby League," admitted Robson, who also worked at Super League for two years. "But it's a case of the sport making a case for funding. Rugby league has a tiny number of participants in Scotland compared, for example, to swimming, which has one million a month. It is so hard to convert people. It is going to take a long haul and they are starting from a very small base. But we will work with anyone, regardless of size, as long as it is growing. The RFL are responsible for the strategy of the sport in Scotland but I don't know if they can fund that development at the moment."

Scotland need funding if they are to become self-governing. As retiring chairman Clive Mason said: "The SRL will, in the near future, be looking to break away from the apron strings of the RFL which has been its lifeline for so long."

At this time (April 2002), Scotland have not played a home international since the 2000 World Cup and they have none in the diary. Plans for a European Championship in 2003 are unconfirmed and hopes that the touring Kiwis would play in Scotland in 2002 have diminished.

The SRL need high-profile international competition to get the media and therefore the Scottish public, behind them. And that means matches against England. The amateur Four Nations tournament is a start, but an annual match against an understrength England team while Great Britain are in Test action would be a huge fillip.

There are three ways of increasing Scotland's shallow pool of talent.
a) persuade Union players to convert to League;
b) recruit further Scottish-qualified Aussies, Kiwis and Sassanachs to pull on the navy jersey;
c) develop sufficient numbers of young players in Scotland via the schools and students from which a handful of professional players will eventually emerge each year.

The first choice is a non-starter. The SRL have neither the money nor the desire to convert professional Union players, and even if they did, as Martin Johnson said recently: "I'm not sure I'd fancy Rugby League - there's no hiding place in that game". Thankfully, the SRU have yet to recruit many Scottish-qualified League stars either.

The second option is the easy way out and will provide no long term solution. And the indigenous Scots are not interested in a 'Jockeroos' team. The media's reaction to the World Cup team was lukewarm, if not icy, compared to the warmth they showed towards the early Scotland sides. The reason? The 1995-96 teams had players with Scottish accents.

Indeed, when Scotland's squad failed to match the community work done by opponents Samoa in Glasgow during the 2000 World Cup, development officer Mark Senter was relieved: "It was probably a good thing as the kids wouldn't have understood all those Aussies" he said. "They'd have wondered who those blokes were pretending to be Scots." Instead, the Samoans went down a storm in Pollok's primary schools. Burnbrae Primary School has photos of Samoa on their wall rather than Scotland. Scotland needs Scots in the team to make an impact.

So the answer has to be c). Several thousand Scots have played Rugby League over the last decade. Now it's a matter of getting more interested and keeping them interested. That will come by the increased schools development work and by providing more open-age amateur clubs. Without them, we will have a situation like in the USA where, once out of university, keen football players who do not make it professionally have nowhere to play and are lost to the sport.

"If the game is to flourish in Scotland we must produce Scottish players," admitted Scotland coach Shaun McRae after the World Cup. "The only way we can do that is with more resources and finance to develop the amateur game."

There is little point in fielding a Scotland side filled with second-grade players from the Northern Ford Premiership who happen to have Scottish grandparents, let alone playing internationals on wet Tuesday nights in November at Firhill and hoping to market it as international rugby. "We need to go to the RFL and ask whether they have any long-term ambition for Scotland because we all showed at the World Cup that we can be competitive," added McRae. "If not, let's let it go and leave them to play football and Rugby Union."

The future for Scottish Rugby League lies with inclusiveness, a cosmopolitan, non-sectarian, sporting community that sees experienced Rugby League folk from England, Australia and New Zealand sharing their knowledge with the committed residents. It is happening at every level below the professionals: schools, students, amateurs.

The SRL even have their own tartan to wear with pride at the obligatory kilted official ceremonies, combining red, to signify the Lion Rampant; purple, for the Scottish thistle; navy blue and white to reflect the Saltire; and Hawick green, a tribute to Dave Valentine. Scotland can be proud of what they have achieved in Rugby League so far - Valentine would be stunned. Whether Scottish Rugby League becomes a footnote to the nation's sporting history only time can tell. Let's hope not.

Appendix 1: International Results

Unofficial Senior International
Friendly 13 August 1995
versus Ireland at Royal Showgrounds, Dublin: lost 22-26

1995 Halifax Emerging Nations World Cup: Group One
Monday 16 October 1995
versus Russia at Post Office Road, Featherstone: won 34-9
Wednesday 18 October 1995
versus USA at Sixfields, Northampton: won 38-16
Friday 20 October 1995
versus Cook Islands at Wheldon Road, Castleford: lost 10-21

Full Internationals
Friendly: Tuesday 6 August 1996 versus Ireland at Firhill, Partick: won 26-6
Friendly - Wednesday 9 July 1997 versus France at Firhill, Partick: lost 20-22

Clash of the Nations
Friday 11 November 1998
versus France at Stade Jean Laffon, Perpignan: lost 22-26
Friday 18 November 1998 versus Ireland at Firhill, Partick: lost 10-17

Lincoln Financial Group Triangular Challenge
Friday 22 October 1999 versus Wales at Firhill, Glasgow: won 36-16
Sunday 31 October 1999 versus Ireland at Tolka Park, Dublin: lost 10-31

Lincoln Financial Group World Cup
Sunday 29 October 2000
versus Aoetearoa Maori at Firhill, Glasgow: lost 16-17
Wednesday 1 November 2000
versus Ireland at Tolka Park, Dublin: lost 6-18
Sunday 5 November 2000 versus Samoa at Tynecastle, Edinburgh: lost 12-20

Friendly: Tuesday 3 July 2001 versus France at Lezignan, 3 July: won 40-24

Super League World Nines
Thursday 22 February 1996: Pool A
Scotland 12 USA 6; Scotland 4 Western Samoa 8; Scotland 6 Australia 26
Saturday 24 February 1996
Plate Semi-finals: Scotland 4 Fiji 14
Plate Play-off: Scotland 34 Italy 0

Appendix 2 : International appearances

Scotland international appearances and scorers

(includes unofficial international against Ireland and Emerging Nations World Cup in 1995 but not World Nines. Up to end of 2001. Substitute appearances in brackets)

Paul Anderson: 1 (+1)
Danny Arnold: 7; 7t
Geoff Bell: 3; 1t
Glen Bell: 1
Joe Berry :2 (+3)
Alasdair Blee :4 (+1); 2t
Mark Burns: 4
Graham Cameron: 1 (+1)
Logan Campbell: 2; 1 t
Paul Carr : 1
Gary Christie: 1; 1 t
John Coumbe-Lilley: 1
James Cowan: 1
Andy Craig: 2
Scott Cram: 6
Matt Crowther: 7 (+1), 3t, 21g.
Sean Cusack : 4; 1t
Mat Daylight: 3
Mike Dixon: 1 (+2)
Struan Douglas: 0 (+2)
John Duffy : 3 (+1); 1t, 4g
Andrew Duncan: 0 (+1)
Richard Fletcher: 1
Jason Flowers: 2 (+1)
Billy Gamba: 5
Lee Gilmour: 3
Scott Gilmour: 0 (+1)

Nathan Graham: 4 (+2)
Daniel Heckenberg: 3
Gareth Hewitt: 0 (+1)
Iain Higgins: 1 (+1)
Richard Horne: 3
James Howe : 3; 2t
Mark Keenan: 1
Martin Ketteridge: 3 (+1); 1t, 5g
Alex Killen: 0 (+2)
Andy Knight: 1
Simon Knox: 1 (+1)
Andrew Lambert: 0 (+2); 2t
Dale Laughton: 4
Scott Logan: 3
Neil Lowe: 1 (+2); 1t
Graham Mackay: 1; 1g
David Maiden: 3 (+3); 2t
Gavin Manclark: 2 (+1);2t
Nick Mardon : 2; 1t
Charlie McAlister: 3; 4g
Stuart McCarthy: 3 (+1); 1t
Ryan McDonald: 0 (+1)
Wayne McDonald: 3 (+3)
Danny McKelvie : 0 (+1)
Jim McLaren: 1

Lee Milner: 1
Gareth Morton: 0 (+1)
Gary Murdock: 1 (+1)
Jon Neill: 2
Chris Orr : 2
Lee Penny: 3; 1t
Andrew Purcell: 2
Scott Rhodes: 3 (+1); 1t
Jason Roach: 4; 2t
Michael Rush: 2
Danny Russell: 9; 3t
Darren Shaw : 8 (+4)
Graeme Shaw : 0 (+2)
Darrall Shelford: 5; 5t
Mark Smith : 3; 1t
Pehi James Solomon: 3
Iain Stanger: 0 (+2)
Jason Syme: 0 (+1)
Alan Tait: 4; 5t
Steve Tait: 2 (+1)
Graeme Thompson: 4 (+1); 1t, 7g
Phil Veivers: 1
Adrian Vowles: 4; 1t
Hugh Waddell: 4; 1t
Michael Wainwright: 4; 1t
Colin Wilson: 0 (+2)

International Records

Most senior caps (total including 1995 appearances)
Danny Russell: 9; Darren Shaw: 8 (plus 4 sub); Matt Crowther: 8.

Most tries
Danny Arnold 7; Alan Tait 5; Darrall Shelford 4

Most points
Matt Crowther: 42 - 21 goals Graeme Thompson: 18 - 7 goals and one try

One cap
Not including 2001 debutants, 18 players have played only one senior official international for Scotland. Gary Murdock played one full international as a substitute, but also started against Ireland in 1995 and went to the World Nines. Seven players made their one and only appearance against France in 1997. John Coumbe-Lilley and Andy Knight were the only players to appear against Ireland in 1995 but never play again. Four players have made just one appearance off the bench. Three players' only SRL appearances were at the World Nines in 1996: George Graham, Billy McGinty and Chris Simmers.

Great Britain
George Fairbairn 17 caps
Lee Gilmour 1 cap (plus 1 sub)
Richard Horne (2 as sub)
Roy Kinnear 1 cap
Dale Laughton 4 caps (plus 1 sub)
Billy McGinty 4 caps
Charlie Renilson 7 caps (plus 1 sub)

David Rose 4 caps
Alan Tait 10 caps (plus 4 sub)
Drew Turnbull 1 cap
Dave Valentine 15 caps
Robert Valentine 1 cap
Hugh Waddell 5 caps
George Wilson 3 caps

England
George Fairbairn 15 caps

Hugh Waddell 1 cap

Other Nationalities
J. Beattie 1
J. Douglas 1
G. Frater 1
J. Gill 1
A. Hogg 1

R. Kinnear 3
A. Laidlaw 1
J. Moffatt 1
A. Murdison 1
B. Robson 3

W. Scott 1
D. Valentine 16
G. Wilson 1

Other Nationalities (County Championship)
J. Hegarty 1; A. Tait (snr) (1 as sub); R. Valentine (1 as sub).

Appendix 3: The Scottish Rugby League Conference

The Scottish Rugby League Conference honours board

1997 Champions Lomond Valley Raiders

1998 Border Raiders bt Edinburgh Eagles

1999 Edinburgh Eagles bt Portobello Playboys

2000 Glasgow Bulls bt Edinburgh Eagles

2001 Edinburgh Eagles bt Glasgow Bulls

The SRL Champions

1996 Forth & Clyde Nomads won Scottish Challenge Cup vs Stirling University on 12 May
Kevin Rudd, Mick Trei, Peter Burrows, Ian Anderson, Steve Anderson, Jamie Baxter, Roland Just, Simon Newbould, Neil Young, Neil Clifford, Alistair Collie, Martin Corrigan, Andy Bowes, Tom Shepard, Michael McKinlay, Neil Froggatt, Craig Armstrong, Willie Drever, John Thompson.

1997 Lomond Valley Raiders won League Championship

1998 Border Eagles beat Edinburgh Eagles 40-14 in Grand Final on 23 August at Hillhead
Squad: Peter Manning, Michael Welsh, Darren Jessop, Cameron Pollock, Phil Manning, Andrew Johnstone, Stevie Jardine, Gordon Sykes, Kenny Stobie, Hugh Waddell (c), Robert Graham, Russell Tod, Darren Clark, Neil Halliday, Murray Forbes, Robert Currie, Ally Graham.

1999 Edinburgh Eagles beat Portobello Playboys 48-20 in Grand Final on 8 August at Hillhead
Squad: Euan Craig, Andy Dalglish, Mark Nesbitt, Steve Bissett, Daniel van Oesthuizen, Neil Matthews, Brent Clement, Martin Murray, Kevin Rudd (c), Tommy McGhee, Clint Brown, Chris O'Neill, Simon May, Kelly James, Elliott Lorimer, Gary Boyd, Will Chambers, Will Drever, Andy Kane, Dave Stephen.

2000 Glasgow Bulls beat Edinburgh Eagles 47-22 in Grand Final on 6 August at Costorphine
Squad: Paul Bassinder, Ally McVicar, David McPhail, Barry Edgar, Iain Glen, Ross van der Hoek, Mickey Lloyd, John Thompson, Darren Whittam, Nigel Holdsworth, Jamie Baxter, David Jamieson, Howard Cameron, Alisdair Macaulay, Gordon Dunford, Lindsay MacDonald, Sam Onions, Brian Taylor, Chris Deacon, Kevin Vaiulumuli, Roland Just.

2001 Edinburgh Eagles beat Glasgow Bulls 30-16 in Grand Final on 15 August at Milhgavie
Squad: Ross Neill; Melvin Hart, Ryan Webb, Tommy McGhee, Andy Dalgleish; Steve Bisset, John MacDonald; Teek Thomson; James Knight, Craig Rush, Sean Boyle, Chris Makowski; Chris O'Neill, Craig Gilbert, Ian Robertson, Dan Norbury.

Competing Clubs 1997-2001

Arbroath Marines: 1997

Border Raiders: 1998-2001

Central Centurions: 1997-98

Clyde Buccaneers: 2001

Edinburgh Eagles: 1998-2001

Glasgow Bulls+: 1997-2001

Kinloss Hunters: 1998

Lanarkshire Storm: 2001

Linlithgow Lions: 1998-2001

Portobello: 1999-2001

Rhu Raiders*: 1997-2001

Whitecraigs Warriors: 1997-98

*initially as Lomond Valley Raiders.

+ initially as Glasgow North

The Scottish Rugby League Tens

1997 Central Centurions

1998 West Yorkshire Police

1999 West Yorkshire Police

2000 West Yorkshire Police

Appendix 4: Scotland Students

1989 Student World Cup
Group Games
versus Ireland at Heworth, York: lost 12-16
versus Australia at Post Office Road, Featherstone: lost 22-36
versus England at Knowsley Road, at St Helens: lost 4-54
7th/8th Place Play-off: versus Holland at Heworth, York: won 20-10

1992 Pepsi Student World Cup
Group Games
Saturday 15 August versus Papua New Guinea at Carrington Park, Bathurst: won 42-14
Tuesday 18 August versus Australia at No 1 Oval, Sydney University: lost 10-38
Thursday 20 August versus Kingdom of Tonga at University of West Sydney, Milperra: lost 12-56
Quarter-final: Saturday 22 August versus New Zealand: lost 18-24
Plate final: Scotland 31 England 20. Scotland finished fifth.

Scotland squad: Martin Joss (Staffordshire University), Nick Mardon, Glen Howitt, Mike Kerr (all Edinburgh), Alastair Stevenson (Cambridge IoT), Tim Sanderson, Mark Nicholson, Mark Couttle, Charlie Claydon (all Loughborough), Steve Tait (Leeds Poly), Craig Errington (Salford), Graham Harvey, Mike Little (both Bedford), James Wallace (Manchester Poly), Richard Sheldon, Iain Stanger (both Heriot-Watt), Shaun Delany (St Andrews), Bob Baxendale (c), Billy Gamba, Paul Gowdy (all Dundee), Craig Westcott (Exeter), Graeme Lees (Aberdeen).

1996 Student World Cup

Group Games
Saturday 17 August versus Japan at Wilderspool, Warrington: won 90-4
Scorers: Tries: Ballantine 7 (Student World Cup record), Blee 3, McCarthy 2, Coumbe-Lilley, Norris, Thompson, Gilmour, Miller, Rudd; Goals: Rush 7, Thompson 2.
Tuesday 20 August versus England at Gateshead: won 10-4
Scorers: Tries: Blee, McCarthy; Goal: James Howe.
Saturday 24 August versus France at Wheldon Road, Castleford: lost 2-36
Scorer: Goal: Thompson.

Bowl Semi-Final
Tuesday 27 August versus South Africa at York: lost 16-42.
Scorers: Tries: Rush, Blee, Burns; Goals: Rush 2.
7th/8th Place Play-off: Friday 30 August versus Russia at Dewsbury: lost 20-26
Scorers: Tries: Ballantine, Blee, McCarthy, Craig Carter; Goals: Rush 2.

Scotland squad: Mark Burns (c), Steve Bailey (all Lancaster University), John Ballantine, Mike Rush, Paul McMillan (all Edge Hill), Alisdair Blee (Loughborough), John Coumbe-Lilley (Crewe & Alsager), Scott Gilmour, Jason Syme (Abertay, Dundee), James Howe, Kevin Rudd (Edinburgh), Chris Houston, Roddy Lawson, Chris Norris (Glasgow), David Marshall (Stirling), Stuart McCarthy (Anglia), David Miller (Salford), Ian Rafferty, Lee Turnball, Craig Carter (all Nottingham Trent), Richard Ribeiro (Leicester), Graeme Thompson (Moray House Edinburgh). Carter and Norris replaced Damian McColgan (Crewe & Alsager) and Patrick Watt (Glasgow).

1999 *The Independent* Student Rugby League World Cup

Glasgow Group
Sunday 3 October versus South Africa at Hillhead, Glasgow: drew 26-26
Scorers: Tries: Lambert, Edgar (2), McVicar, van der Hoek; Goals: Fisher 3.
Saturday 9 October versus England at Hillhead, Glasgow: lost 4-20
Scorers: Try: Lambert.

Final Glasgow Group

England	P2	W2	D0	L0	F54	A22	Pts4
South Africa	P2	W0	D1	L1	F44	A60	Pts1
Scotland	P2	W0	D1	L1	F30	A46	Pts1

Plate Semi-final
Wednesday 13 October versus Japan at Post Office Rd, Featherstone: won 70-0
Scorers: Tries: Armour 3, Connell 2, Fisher 2, Steel, van der Hoek, Bellamy, Kennedy, Kennedy, Brown, Houston; Goals: Fisher 7.

Plate Final
Saturday 16 October versus Canada at Wheldon Road, Castleford: won 26-16
Scorers: Tries: Lambert 3, Rudd, Edgar; Goals: Fisher 3.

Scotland squad: Alistair McVicar, James Mackay (both Loughborough), Barry Edgar (Glasgow), Andrew Lambert (West Cumbria), Craig Kennedy (Paisley), Ross van der Hoek (Caledonian-Glasgow), Ash Carroll © (Uni Central England), Kevin Rudd, Clint Brown (both Edinburgh), Frazer Kennedy (Sunderland), Andrew Borthwick (Strathclyde), Tommy McGhee (Jewell & Esk Valley), Ash Bellamy (Liverpool John Moores), Richard Wilken (Aberdeen), Stuart Connell, Ross Connell (both Crewe & Alsager), Rory Steel (Liverpool Hope), Matthew Tunstall, Chris Brown, Ross Armour, Chris Houston.

2001 Europa Cup

Group Games
Thursday 6 September versus Russia at Stadium Locomotiv, Kazan: won 38-16.
Scorers: Clarke, Campbell, Edgar (2), Colbeck (2) tries. Goals: Edgar 7.
Saturday 8 September versus New South Wales at Stadium Locomotiv, Kazan: lost 18-42
Scorers: Tries: MacDonald 3, Colbeck; Goal: Edgar.
Monday 10 September versus Wales at Stadium Rubin, Kazan: lost 8-19.
Scorers: Try: Foster; Goals: Edgar 2.

Group Table

Wales	P3	W1	D1	L1	F39	A28	Pts4
Scotland	P3	W1	D0	L1	F46	L35	Pts3
Russia	P3	W0	D1	L1	F36	A58	Pts1

Semi-final: 12 September versus England at Stadium Locomotiv, Kazan: lost 12-13
Scorers: Brown, McDonald tries. Goals: Edgar (2).

Squad: Barry Edgar (c) (Uni of Glasgow); Logan Colbeck, Ian Gilmour, Rob Clarke, James MacKay (Loughborough); James Noble, Al Stewart (both Crewe and Alsager); Niall McDonald, Sam Onions (Edinburgh Uni); Jack Howieson, Neil Foster (Sheffield Hallam); Tom Phillips

(Chester Coll), Clint Brown (Telford Coll), Adam Shockley (St Martins, Lancaster), Mark Webster (St Helens Coll), Simon Hogg (SAC Edinburgh), John McDonald (NDLC), Tom Wild (Nottingham Trent), Ryan Campbell (West Cumbria Coll), Andrew Borthwick (Uni of Strathclyde), Kaveh Bahadori (Stafford Uni).

9 December 2001 versus Queensland Students at Cambuslang RFC: lost 13-32

Scotland: Brantingham, Foster, Clarke, Campbell, Webster, I Gilmour, Knight, Howieson, Borthwick; Caroll (c), Onions, MacDonald; MacKay. Subs used: Bahadori, MacInally, McGhee, Williams.

Scorers: Tries: Campbell, Clarke; Goal: Campbell 2; Drop-Goal: Gilmour.

Scotland Students in Great Britain & Ireland Students XIII

Neil Hendry versus Russia, 1994.

Glen Howitt, Richard Ribeiro, Iain Stanger, John Coumbe-Lilley, Graeme Thompson, Mike Kerr versus Morocco, 1994.

Chris Houston versus France, 1997.

Craig Fisher, Jack Howieson, Ian Gilmour versus New Zealand and Australia, 2000.

Scotland Students in GB Students Development squad/ Emerging GB

Borthwick, Hayter, Mark Nesbitt & Ash Carroll: German tour, 1998.

Ash Carroll (c) and James Mackay: USA tour 2001.

Neil Foster, Rob Clarke, Tom Wilde & Gujinder Pahal: Dec 2001, versus Queensland Students

Under-18/19s

Sunday 3 March 2002 versus France at Peebles: lost 4-48; Thursday 4 April 2002 versus England at Alsager College: lost 12-66; Saturday 6 April 2002 versus Wales: won 26-14

Squad: Carl Higgins (Workington Town), Mark O'Hara (Blackpool Stanley), Mark Webster (Thatto Heath), Charles Gallagher (Castlemilk High School, Glasgow), Alan Smellee, David Anderson, Ian Rogers, David Grieve, Rob Linton, Donald Anderson, John Drury (all Peebles RFC), Mark Scott (Glasgow Bulls), James McGhee (Elland), Edward Stewart (Livingston RU), Sam Onions (Glasgow Bulls), Chris Fletcher (Gateshead Thunder), Keir Bell (London Broncos), Mike Wallace, James Callion.

Bibliography

Leeds Rugby League Football Club 100 Greats by Phil Caplan & Peter Smith, pub Tempus.

The International Grounds of Rugby League by Trevor Delaney, pub Delaney, 1995.

Chocolate, Blue and Gold - 50 years of Whitehaven Rugby League Football Club by Harry Edgar, pub Edgar Publishing / Open Rugby Nostalgia

100 Great Rugby League Players by Ray French

The Struggle for The Ashes II by Robert Gate, pub by Robert Gate

Getting Physical by Scott Gibbs, pub Ebury Press.

Thrum Hall Greats by Andrew Hardcastle pub A. Hardcastle

The Rugby League Challenge Cup - An Illustrated History by Les Hoole pub Breedon Books

The Rugby League World Cup pub by League Publications Ltd

A People's Game - The Official History of Rugby League 1895-1995 by Geoffrey Moorhouse pub Hodder and Stoughton

Salford Rugby League Club 100 Greats by Graham Morris, pub Tempus.

The Forbidden Game by Mike Rylance, published by League Publications Ltd.

Rugby Rebel - The Alan Tait Story by Alan Tait with Bill Lothian pub Mainstream 1998

Oldham RLFC - The complete history 1876-1997 by Michael Turner pub M.A.Turner

Magazines

Our Game Issue 2 published by London League Publications,
Code 13 – Journal of Rugby League Heritage, Issue 10, published by Trevor Delaney

Rugby League books from London League Publications Ltd

The Great Bev - The Rugby League career of Brian Bevan
By Robert Gate

Brian Bevan is one of the few players in the game's history who is a genuine legend. The top try scorer in British Rugby League's history, he scored 796 tries from 1945 when he joined Warrington until he retired in 1964. His speed, swerve and anticipation made him the greatest winger the game has ever seen. This is the first book on Bevan's career, written by the game's leading historian. Lavishly illustrated with a full statistical record.

To be published in August 2002 at £14.95
Special pre-publication offer £14.00 post free

I, George Nepia - The autobiography of a Rugby legend
By George Nepia and Terry McLean

George Nepia is arguably New Zealand's greatest ever Rugby Union player. This new edition of his autobiography, first published in 1963, also has new and reprinted material that gives a full picture of Nepia's life and Rugby career. It has new chapters by Terry McLean, Huw Richards, Peter Lush, Robert Gate and Dave Farrar. Fully illustrated. Of interest to followers of both Rugby codes.

To be published in September 2002 at £13.95
Special pre-publication offer £13.00 post free

The Rugby League Grounds Guide by Peter Lush and Dave Farrar

Published in 2001, covers all the British professional clubs, plus basic details of leading amateur, French and Australian clubs. Essential for all travelling League fans.

Published at £7.95, special offer to readers of this book: £7.00 post free

From Fulham to Wembley - 20 years of Rugby League in London
Edited by Dave Farrar and Peter Lush.
Published in 2000 to celebrate the 20th anniversary of the London Broncos.
Published at £8.75, special offer to readers of this book: £8.00 post free

The Fulham Dream - Rugby League tackles London by Harold Genders
Published in 2000 - covers the birth of Fulham RLFC and their triumphant first season
Published at £6.95, special offer to readers of this book: £6.00 post free

The London Double: Order both *From Fulham to Wembley* and *The Fulham Dream* for **£12.00**

Tries in the Valleys - A history of Rugby League in Wales.
Edited by Peter Lush & Dave Farrar. Foreword by Jonathan Davies
Published in 1998 at £14.95. Special offer: £8.00 post free

Order from: London League Publications, PO Box 10441, London E14 0SB.
(Cheques payable to London League Publications Ltd - no credit cards)